D1605403

Public Policy
and Policy Analysis
in India

Public Policy
and Policy Analysis
in India

Editors

R S GANAPATHY
S R GANESH
RUSHIKESH M MARU
SAMUEL PAUL
RAM MOHAN RAO

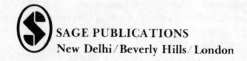

SAGE PUBLICATIONS
New Delhi/Beverly Hills/London

First published in 1985 by

Sage Publications India Pvt Ltd
C 236 Defence Colony
New Delhi 110 024

Sage Publications Inc	**Sage Publications Ltd**
275 South Beverly Drive	28 Banner Street
Beverly Hills, CA 90212	London EC1Y 8QE

Published by Tejeshwar Singh for Sage Publications India Pvt Ltd, phototypeset by The Facilis and printed at Pearl Offset Press.

Library of Congress Cataloging-in-Publication Data

Main entry under title :
Public policy and policy analysis in India.

   Selected papers presented at a national workshop on public policy analysis in India at the Indian Institute of Management, Ahmedabad, held in April 1982.

     Includes bibliographies and index.

     1. Policy science — Congresses. 2. India — Politics and government — 1947 -   — Congresses.
I. Ganapathy, R. S. II. Indian Institute of Management, Ahmedabad.
H97.P78   1985   361.6'1'0954   85-14385
ISBN 0-8039-9496-6 (U.S.)

Contents

Preface

Over the years the Public Systems Group at the Indian Institute of Management has been involved in a number of studies on policy implementation and evaluation. These studies have covered a wide variety of sectors such as rural development, health and population, energy, transportation, education and urban development. The last decade of research at IIMA has been largely concerned with management aspects of development programmes. This focus on operational problems of public programmes led to the increasing realisation that our research must encompass the analysis of policy options and assumptions as there is a close link between the public policy process, policy choice and implementation. However, before broadening the scope of the Institute's research agenda we decided to review the existing state of art in public policy analysis in India. A national workshop was organised in April 1982 which brought together thirty academicians, journalists, legal experts, administrators and politicians from all over the country. As public policy as a specialised academic discipline has been well developed in the West, specially in the US and the UK, it was decided to invite a few specialists from these countries also to learn from their experiences.

The workshop was structured around the following themes :

1. Conceptual *approaches* and *methodologies* for policy analysis.
2. The *processes* of *policy-making* and *implementation* in India.
3. The role of specialised academic institutions and other formal organisational mechanisms such as committees and commissions in public policy analysis.
4. Learning from the western experiences of developing policy analysis as a professional field.

These themes were explored over a three-day period through discussions of state of art review papers and case studies of policy formulation and implementation. This book brings together a selection of papers and cases presented at the workshop. They are organised around the following five sections :

1. Approaches to policy analysis.
2. Sector reviews of policy formulation methodologies.
3. Case studies on policy-making and implementation.
4. A historical perspective on the development of the policy field in India and the role of institutions in policy analysis.
5. A review of international experience with special reference to the UK, US, and other developing countries.

Approaches to Policy Analysis

Thomas Schelling, one of the leaders of the public policy movement in the US, initiates the dialogue in the first chapter by critically examining the 'rational choice' approach to policy analysis. He doubts whether such an approach has proved capable of resolving many of the great policy disputes of our time. Drawing on the US experience, specially relating to studies of poverty and racial integration, Schelling concludes that most policy research has had no major impact on such critical issues; it has been effective only in minor and routine policy matters. He, therefore, advocates that policy analysis must be viewed within a paradigm of conflict rather than rational choice. Analysing the *interests* and *participants* may be as important as analysing issues : 'Creative use of darkness may be as much needed as the judicious use of light.' Thus, the policy analyst should view his role not as an 'impartial helper' but as 'a participant in the dispute,' and play a legitimate role in support of advocacy. R.S. Ganapathy further develops this non-conventional critique of the 'mainstream' policy analysis in the second chapter by examining the nature of methodologies for policy analysis, and their relationship with social science theory and implementation. Like Schelling he also views major social problems as basically conflictual in nature which require an advocacy role for the policy analyst. Ganapathy outlines a 'critical policy analysis' approach as an alternative to the rational choice approach. Accordingly, a 'critical policy analysis' is undertaken through the exploration of multiple perspectives and a critical examination of their underlying assumptions, world-views and values. Applying this new concept to the analysis of poverty in India, Ganapathy argues that the 'mainstream policy analysis' reflects only one perspective (that of government agencies) and ignores that of the poor people.

It is indeed refreshing to see both Schelling and Ganapathy, an American and an Indian scholar, in broad agreement in their respective critiques of the 'mainstream' rational choice approach to policy analysis. This theme emerged many times during the workshop as the Indian participants underscored the need to look at structural causes of social problems, and not merely limit policy analysis to measurable economic and technological criteria. Also, the emphasis on the process of consensus building and negotiation between different perspectives in policy analysis set the stage for examining policy-making and the implementation process in various sectors. Sections 2 and 3 present studies of policy formulation and implementation.

Sector Reviews

The first set of sector reviews in section two deals with policy analysis in rural development, energy, health, and population. Dantwala and Barmeda provide a historical view of the evaluation of rural development policies since independence. They show how the policies of rural development have evolved over the years through various concepts of community development, area development, target group oriented projects, employment generation, welfare orientation, and finally integrated multisectoral development. There is a definite, even though slow and incremental, process of learning from an analysis of policy implementation. Of course, the two major weaknesses that persisted relate to lack of coordination between various government departments and neglect of the poorest strata of the rural population. Both these continuing weaknesses in policy implementation also reflect an inadequacy of policy analysis to take into account the major structural causes of underdevelopment.

Giridhar, Satia and Subramanian review policy studies in the areas of morality, fertility and migration. They highlight major conceptual frameworks and methodological approaches used by policy studies and their influence on policy development. The evolution of health and fertility control policies also show slow but steady learning from pilot projects and the evaluation of programme implementation. A variety of methodological approaches have been adopted by policy analysts. These range from more formal approaches — such as, macro-economic growth models, cost-benefit analysis, survey research, simulation models for generating demographic scenarios and action research — to less structured field observations and consensus building through committees. Major changes in policy directions have emerged from a dialogue between different actors through a committee process. International professional opinion, specially through the WHO, has played an important role in pushing innovative ideas within the government. Interestingly enough, the fact that many of these new ideas were well demonstrated by private voluntary organisations in India provided further legitimacy to innovative policy and programme initiatives.

Unlike the health and fertility control policies, there is no identifiable single agency responsible for the formulation and implementation of migration policies. This has inhibited the development of a comprehensive migration policy. The migration policy illustrates problems of developing a comprehensive policy analysis in areas which cut across several sectors of the economy. In Chapter 4, Shankar shows how this problem was tackled in the energy sector by developing a national policy thrust through the Planning Commission and an inter-ministerial coordinating organisation. However, integration at the policy level did not solve the problem of implementation which remained fragmented through different agencies.

All three sector reviews show learning from past experiences of policy implementation and in each case a move towards a more comprehensive policy analysis. However, the energy sector stands out in sharp contrast to rural development and the health-population sectors in terms of greater influence of formal policy analysis on policy choices. Shankar shows how the Energy Survey Committee (1965), the Fuel Policy Committee (1974) and the Working Group on Energy Policy (1979), made increasingly greater impact on official government policy choices. Each of these committees also improved on the methods of analysis adopted by their predecessors. They used a variety of forecasting methods, mathematical models to decide the location and capacity of refineries, and the scenario approach to project demand. The composition of each committee and the nature of its sponsor were critical determinants of the scope and nature of policy analysis conducted by each committee.

In terms of methodologies of analysis, quantitative forecasting and mathematical models played a prominent role in the energy and, to a lesser extent, the population policy fields; institutional analysis seems to be critical to health and rural development policies. Irrespective of the methods of analysis, all sectors illustrate the use of the committee process to develop policy consensus in a democratic society. In each case, policy analysis played a supportive role to a process of political decision-making. The extent of weightage given to rational criteria of an economic and technological nature depended on the definition of the policy problems, perceptions of the various actors involved in the process, and the extent of direct influence on the common man.

Case Studies

The less measurable but at times more important factors in policy process — such as, ideology, political environment, orientations of various actors, historical legacy, and interest group pressures — are well brought out in Section 3 through case studies of adult education, health manpower policy, science and technology plan, and women's development.

Rao analyses the implementation of the adult education drive from the perspectives of specialists, bureaucrats and politicians. He shows how a change in government and a consequent change in the ideology of the governing political elite gave a tremendous push to the policy of implementing the adult literacy programme through decentralised and voluntary structures. It also influenced the approach to policy analysis which was one of learning through innovation and experimentation. Instead of developing comprehensive policy analysis at the beginning, the whole programme was designed to generate experiments and the social learning process.

A study of health manpower policy during the years 1949-75 vividly highlights the role of political factors in policy-making. Maru's account of policy evolution focuses on a shift from a 'professional' to a 'populist' orientation in health manpower policy. Such a shift was dictated by a change in attitudes and orientations and the relative influence of key actors as well as environmental influences such as resource constraints, popular pressure for redistribution of resources, ideological milieu and external influences. Maru also introduces a concept of policy arena such as the Prime Minister's office, Parliament, bureaucracy, and the Planning Commission. He argues that the nature of policy outcomes was influenced by the dominant policy arena within which a particular decision was made.

Ahmed compares the processes of decision-making regarding a plan for science and technology at two different points of time. The first S&T plan was developed through a process of broad-based participation involving many groups of scientists, administrators, and users. However, the second S&T plan was formulated by a small group of establishment scientists and administrators. These two distinctly different approaches were the result of differences in orientation of the top political and administrative elites. While the broad-based approach helped to develop a comprehensive inter-sectoral plan and generate the involvement of implementors, it created problems of integrating the S&T plan with the overall national resource planning process. The second approach of limited participation may have helped greater consistency between the S&T plan and national planning but is also likely to create a greater hiatus between planners and implementors.

Vina Mazumdar's analysis of the influence of the women studies programme of the ICSSR succinctly illustrates the strengths and limits of an advocacy role played by an outside policy analysis group. In terms of changes within the government policy, the group's work seems to have had a limited impact. Although the government did not accept the major recommendations arising out of the various research studies, it did eventually accept women's concerns as legitimate factors in development policy. Similarly, in relation to the social science research community, the research group helped in examining women-related biases in social science methodologies and theories.

Evolution of the Policy Field in India

This section includes three papers, each one reviewing the role of policy analysis in India from the perspective of the analyst. Guhan takes a broad look at the role of policy analysis in policy-making and summarises his conclusion in one poignant statement : 'India is rich in both policy and in analytical perspective; it is rather poor in policy analysis.' His hypothesis for this gap between analysis and policy is that most policy analysis does not go beyond what is said and what is done and try to analyse the continuous doctrinal struggle that lies behind them. He brings back the ideas presented by Schelling and Ganapathy in the first two chapters and emphasises the need to be openly partisan in policy analysis. According to Guhan, 'Who gains and who loses has to be the central question of policy analysis'.

Ganesh and Paul look at policy analysis from the perspective of autonomous institutions engaged in policy research. Although there is an increasing realisation of the link between policy research and policy formulation, there is still a feeling that there is a lack of systematic and continuous impact on policy-makers through institutional efforts. Another important observation emerging from the policy researchers' perspective is that sound methodologies are important for policy impact. They feel that good social science research does bring greater credibility to the researcher. Ganesh and Paul feel that the linkages with the administrative elite through training needs to be strengthened.

The sector papers and case studies in Sections 2 and 3 highlighted the saliency of the committee process of decision-making. It is, therefore, important to review trends in the use of committees and commissions for policy analysis. Ram Mohan Rao reviews these trends for the years 1974-81 and finds that committees and commissions have played a significant role in policy-making. However, he also points out the limitations of the committee system :

1. The policy outcome depends on the composition of the committee.
2. Recommendations tend to be vague due to the need to achieve compromise.
3. Committees may collect a great deal of data, but their uses tend to be limited.
4. The recommendations of earlier committees tend to be given disproportionate weightage in policy-making, thereby reducing the possibilities of innovations.

The International Experience

Public policy as a separate discipline originated in the West. Donoughue and Klitgaard review experiences in the UK, the USA, and other developing countries.

Donoughue describes his own experience with the Central Policy Review Staff (CPRS) which played an important role in providing advice to the British cabinet during the mid-1970s. But, since 1979, under Prime Minister Thatcher, the CPRS is considerably truncated. Donoughue's account of the CPRS underscores the important role of the political structure and nature of bureaucracy in supporting policy analysis. The British bureaucracy is not very responsive to professional policy analysis. Therefore, even the universities and research institutions have not developed professionally trained policy analysts. Most courses within universities are descriptive; they do not prepare students for prescriptive policy analysis.

Unlike in the UK, political and administrative structures in America are open to the recruitment of public policy analysts in government agencies. Klitgaard traces the development of public policy disciplines in the US to the failure of two wars involving America during the 1960s — the war in Vietnam and the war on poverty. By the late 1960s a degree of disillusionment had set in due to the failure of policy analysis to tackle some of the major social problems. Klitgaard attributes this failure to a gap between bureaucrats and politicians on the one hand and social scientists on the other. While the former failed to comprehend the complexities of analytic techniques, the latter were unfamiliar with the politics of policy-making. This led to a restructuring of public policy programmes to ensure a blend of policy and management analysis skills, insights into political processes of decision-making, and an understanding of the larger ethical issues.

Reviewing recent trends in the Phillipines, Indonesia, India, Thailand, Nicaragua, etc., Klitgaard concludes that the initial stirrings of the public policy field in developing countries also emphasise an interdisciplinary approach combining quantitative skills, political analysis, and social ethics. These programmes face problems similar to those experienced in the US, specially those of integrating various disciplines and forging successful linkages between teaching and practice. Given these similarities in approach and problems, international collaboration in comparative public policy research may be mutually helpful to both America and the developing countries. Such comparative research need not aim at a grandiose theory of policy-making. Instead, the objective should be to develop middle level generalisations through studies of intersectoral problems and cases of successful policy implementation across different contexts.

Drawing mainly on a review of the policy analysis experience in India, but supplemented by theoretical and practical issues arising from the western experience, the workshop generated many insights into this emerging academic field. Most participants broadly agreed with the need to develop an interdisciplinary approach combining policy and management analysis with political and ethical appraisal. But, it was also pointed out that policy analysis in developing countries cannot afford to ignore the major social-structural causes of poverty and underdevelopment. This task is qualitatively different from what most conventional schools of policy analysis have attempted. Thus, the participants echoed Ganapathy's advocacy of 'critical policy analysis' with multiple perspectives and Guhan's plea for taking policy analysis 'in the nature of exposure and exposition rather than evaluations leading to blue-prints'. Learning from the failures of policy analysis in the western countries, Indian academics should probably avoid the temptation of confining policy analysis to specialised public policy schools; instead, we should develop policy analysis as an integral part of basic social science and management disciplines. In management schools, policy analysis should build on the strength of a strong understanding of the problems of implementation at the micro-level.

The main task facing the policy analyst is of developing an indigenous craft of public policy analysis which is at once useful in solving practical problems and sensitive to social-structural issues. Of course, no policy analysis research can be rendered 'useful' unless policy-makers recognise analysis as an important aid to decision-making. A climate of mutual trust and understanding between policy-makers and policy analysts can be forged through integrated programmes involving research, training and consultation. We hope that the following papers will provide an opportunity to examine some of the key assumptions which are critical in developing such a relevant agenda for public policy research and education.

Many people have helped to make this volume possible. A generous grant from the Ford Foundation made it possible to bring participants from various corners of India and also from the USA and the UK. Prof. V.S. Vyas, the then Director of IIMA, provided encouragement to launch out into the new field of public policy analysis. We express our thanks also to all our colleagues in the Public System Group and the participants who provided the intellectual content to the structure of the workshop.

Ahmedabad
June 1985

Rushikesh M. Maru
Chairman
Public Systems Group

I

Approaches to
Policy Analysis

T.C. SCHELLING

1 Policy Analysis as a Science of Choice

The discipline that has contributed most to policy analysis in the United States — and I would dare to guess most everywhere — is economics. Economics is concerned, among other things, with choosing among alternative actions to achieve optimally some mix of objectives to satisfy a coherent set of values. Economics has been developed to handle probabilities as well as certainties and objectives located at different points in time, and even to economise informational resources in the process of economising itself. And economists have equipped themselves with analytical aids like queuing theory, dynamic programming, Markov processes and large-model simulation, while becoming directly involved over the past three decades in solving problems and giving advice in business, in government, and in matters of public concern.

The RAND Corporation was initially a cluster of physical scientists and mathematicians with a few economists and political scientists, and RAND became known for some of its early work in earth satellites and man-machine simulations; but what made RAND famous and brought RAND into the Kennedy Administration's Defense Department was the work in choice among strategies and weapon systems, and that work was under the intellectual leadership of economists. PPBS (Programming, Planning, Budgeting, Systems) were economic analyses that, having appeared to bring some order into defense policy-making, were introduced throughout the executive branch under President Johnson as a universal framework for policy choice. Even in the White House, national security advisors publicised the notion that their function was to identify 'options' for the President.

Schools of policy analysis, in contrast to what used to be called 'public administration,' have been in the ascendant for a decade in America; more than a dozen can be identified among the sponsors of the new Association for Public Policy and Management. While these schools are noteworthy for the mixture of disciplines and professions they incorporate, the dominant discipline — not without some resistance and protest that testify to its dominance — has been economics, broadly defined to include decision theory and the analytics of management, which fit better into economics than into any other discipline.

The most important innovation of recent years in the Congress of the United States was the Congressional Budget Office. It consists mainly of economists and undertakes policy analysis with a strong economics component. True, budgets are about spending, and spending appears to be economics : but budgeting is mainly decision-making and policy-making, and the kinds of choices include foreign policy, education, medical care, law enforcement, and natural resources, and the mere fact that money is going to be spent does not convert all of these into economics. Economists seem to dominate because theirs is the profession concerned with rational choice. And policy often appears to be choosing.

An economist myself, I might at this point be expected to advance even further imperialist claims for the discipline that drives policy analysis in public affairs and that does so through its command of the science of choice. But instead I want to express some dissatisfaction and to raise questions whether policy analysis as *policy choice* has proved capable of resolving many, or even any, of the great policy disputes of our time — at least in the United States over the past couple of decades.

Some evidence that policy analysis is not the ultimate key to political choice is painfully current in the Reagan Administration's declared effort to undo most of what policy analysis helped to get done during the twenty years since President Eisenhower left office. Policy analysis appears to be playing little role in the major decisions of the new administration. The process that policy analysts thought they were contributing to during at least five successive administrations — the Nixon Administration, though not generally thought of as smoothly continuous in the line from Kennedy and Johnson to Ford and Carter, did promote policies based on analysis — has now been declared the evil, not the cure. I say this not to imply that policy analysis has at last been dethroned, nor to endorse the view that good analysis 'in the small' can cumulatively add up to a monstrous aggregation of government initiatives that threaten to break the back that has to carry them. I say it only to remind ourselves that the effectiveness in practice of policy analysis depends at least on the hospitality of the environment within which decisions are taken, and to suggest that when unusually important changes in direction must be navigated, intuition may have to take over, and analysis have to wait, until the situation is normal again and the problems are those routine ones that analysis is so good at handling.

I do not believe, but if I did believe, that the great affliction in America was the assumption of too much federal responsibility by five preceding administrations, and the most urgent need was to unload massive amounts of responsibility that had been centrally assumed, I cannot be sure that the time available and the scope of the job would allow policy analysis, the science of the policy choice, to be of much help.

A question that obtrudes is whether policy analysis leading to efficient policy choice is better for small decisions than for big ones and no good at all for the grand ones; and even the little decisions lead to results that are correct only locally and in the short run, not globally nor in the long run.

But the question I most want to raise does not depend on the somewhat anti-theoretical or anti-analytical or even anti-intellectual atmosphere that we have been breathing in America for the past few years. I can raise the same generic question about the role of the science of choice by examining just what policy analysis contributed, even during the years in which it was in good repute, to the largest problems that exercised decision-makers.

A central issue in American policy for the past two decades has been racial integration. Policy analysis has been able to concern itself with some of the smaller (but still large) policy issues, like 'Headstart' programmes to overcome pre-school disadvantage, the assessment and remedy of badly distributed health care facilities, and job training programmes. There are not many policy-analytical successes. But more important, on the major issue of busing school-children in metropolitan areas, policy analysis had little influence.

Policy analysis, especially as the science of choice among well-defined alternatives in furtherance of complex but compatible goals, has neither great successes nor great failures to its credit. Policy analysis there has been; but good or bad — and much of it may have been quite good — it has not had a major impact on policy.

Why is that? I can think of at least three reasons. One is that much policy has been made by the courts, and the judicial process is peculiarly unable to formulate and to debate issues in straightforward policy terms, and has a restricted choice of instruments through which to enforce its decisions. Good policy analyses have been brought to bear on judicial decisions, and their contribution has probably been positive; but they have to work through a forensic process for which policy analysis is not especially well suited.

Second, there is a holistic quality to racial integration that is different from the aggregation of its separate parts. Analysis may successfully come to grips with particular issues relating to jobs, schools, residences, crime, voting and electoral politics, but be out of its element in attempting to synthesise a revolutionary change in social relations.

And third is what I think is usually decisive. When values conflict, analysis cannot resolve them. Analysis may be good at helping an individual choose in the light of his own values. Analysis may be good at helping like-minded individuals with compatible values choose the best means of achieving commonly held objectives. But when the goal is in dispute, there may be little that analysis can do.

True, if compromise is desperately needed there is an 'integrative' function for analysis : sorting out those compromises that minimise the sacrifices that need to be made by both sides. But there are disputes in which the partisans would rather risk all to win all than to compromise, because the compromises are merely intermediate and not superior points; there are disputes in which some crucial participants prefer non-reconciliation to any compromise that might resolve the issue; and there are even disputes that are most readily compromised if a little deception, even self-deception, can be enjoyed. Analysis that spotlights the points in dispute can even inhibit the process by which old positions are abandoned, reversals are rationalised, and wishes can color results.

Let me turn to some other controversial issues that seem hardly to have yielded to policy analysis. Abortion was a quiescent issue politically until a decade ago. For reasons that I do not think anyone has yet adequately explained, abortion suddenly leaped into public consciousness, a few states drastically changed their laws, and the courts quite suddenly reversed nearly a century of tradition. What would have happened had only the legal status of abortion been reversed I find hard to predict retrospectively, but what did happen was that the issue of public financing of abortion arose in the context of publicly financed medical care; and on that issue the traditional opposition to abortion, which had been caught unorganised and surprised by the court decisions, rallied to counter-attack. Where this will all come out, it is too early for me to tell. But I would observe that policy analysis could probably demonstrate that the issue of federally financed abortions had been grossly exaggerated by both sides in the debate, I do not know of any good publicised analysis that actually showed that publicly financed abortion had comparatively little to do with the ease and frequency with which abortions would be obtained, although there is recent evidence to the effect that public financing has a significant but not substantial effect. My impression is that the controversy is now a partisan dispute much more concerned with issues of right and wrong than with either assuring that abortions are in fact obtainable or assuring that abortions are in fact not obtained.

Gun control sounds like an issue that ought to be susceptible to analysis. I know people who do good analysis on what might be accomplished by different kinds of restrictions on the possession, use, carrying, selling, importing, or manufacturing of firearms, ammunition, and other weapons. There is no sign that good analysis or bad analysis has any influence on attitudes toward guns and gun control, on specific legislative proposals, on the terms in which public debate occurs, or on changing the minds of any of the significant leading individuals or organisations.

The same can probably be said about marijuana. The campaigns against marijuana of a decade ago have lost a large part of their motivation, and farming communities in northern California are beginning to assert their agricultural right to participate in the marijuana market. Fatigue rather than analysis has gradually led to a conclusion, right or wrong (and I think right), that waging a vigorous war against marijuana is too costly in terms of both resources and consequences. But the current situation may be far from the most satisfactory. Analysis should be able to help identify at least directions in which the legal status of marijuana might be changed. Little analysis is done, and the little that is done has virtually no influence.

There may even be an interesting incompatibility here of beliefs on two issues that are quite distant from each other — guns and marijuana. People permissive toward marijuana tend to be restrictive toward guns, and vice versa. One of the arguments made most strongly by those who would be permissive toward marijuana is that restrictions are unenforceable and, because they are unenforceable, should be removed. One of the arguments made most strongly by people who favour possession of guns is that restrictions would be unenforceable, and being unenforceable would be bad. Analysis that might lead to a powerful argument in favour of a person's views on one of these emotionally loaded issues may be an embarrassment if the argument applies but changes sides on another of one's favourite issues.

I could go on to nuclear power and nuclear waste and point out that there have indeed been analyses, and analyses and analyses, and they seem impotent to affect the policy impasse in this emotionally charged field. Here we may get another clue to the unpopularity of analysis. It is a fair observation for the United States that the policy relation of nuclear electric power to nuclear weapons is historical and symbolic but otherwise negligible. Those who despise nuclear power insist on coupling it with nuclear weapons (or perhaps it is that those who despise nuclear weapons take advantage of the public fear of nuclear power). The coupling is deliberate; and analysis that might lead to a decoupling of those two issues is either incapable of penetrating or, having penetrated, is deliberately rejected for tactical reasons. But the same association is made on the other side, though a little less glaringly : nuclear weapons and nuclear power, sometimes generalised to military strength and economic growth, are coupled by many of the opponents-of-the-opponents of nuclear power. It is hard to find a policy field in which more good analysis (leave aside bad analysis) has been done in the past seven or eight years than in energy alternatives; and it is hard to find an important field in which public stances and political decisions have been less affected by the careful analysis of policy choice.

One of the outstanding growths in social policy over the past dozen years has been in the field of *protective regulation*. Many parts of the American economy have been regulated since the late

nineteenth century with a view to economic performance : competition and monopoly, public utility rates, sharing the electromagnetic
spectrum, securities and commoditi.s markets, etc. Since the late
1960s there has been a crescendo of regulation of environmental
safety and amenity, occupational safety and health, consumer product
safety, foods and drugs, to say nothing of airport noise, endangered
species, oceans and wilderness and neighbourhood communities.
Few policy areas have attracted policy analysis, good analysis, the
way environmental protection has during the past decade. For
years, however, analysts have been frustrated by the doctrinaire
refusal of agencies like the Environmental Protection Agency, the
Occupational Safety and Health Administration, and the Consumer
Product Safety Commission, in refusing even to admit the legitimacy
of policy analysis. Even something as straightforward as the
comparison of costs and benefits has often been denied in principle
on grounds that where risk to life itself is at stake, however small,
or genetic damage, cost should be no object and no benefit too
small to be worth pursuing. Issues have been so formulated that the
beneficiaries of protection are treated as dependent or the allocation
of resources by a beneficient agency, without regard to whether the
ultimate incidence of the costs would fall on the beneficiaries
themselves, for whom it might sometimes be a bad bargain.

I entertain the possibility — only barely, I don't really believe
it — that politically it is wiser to eschew analysis on grounds that
once people learn to allocate resources rationally, they may rationally
not permit you to allocate resources — their resources — where
you would like to allocate them. But I am willing to make my point
either way. It is enough to argue that possibly analysis has simply
not been appreciated in those major regulatory agencies that I
should have thought would be wholly dependent on the science of
careful choice, or else that those agencies were run by leaders who
made the political judgment that on balance they would come
closer to reaching their own goals by keeping analysis from shedding
light on political debates that they thought they could win better in
the dark.

I could go on with other areas where analysis, especially in
policy choices, has been impotent. One that is bound to loom in the
future, and would be recognised now if there were not a collective
refusal to face it, is policy toward the dying. I have in mind policy
toward those who are terminally ill, ill and aged beyond recovery,

or chronically incompetent, immobilised, uncomfortable, and incapable of enjoying life; and about whom the question might properly be raised, should they be allowed to die, or even helped to die, if they are able to express such a preference. Also, to what extraordinary lengths should money be spent and technology applied in extending the physiological lives of people who may be beyond any enjoyment of life or even consciousness, or in such suffering that extending their lives can only be self-indulgence by those responsible for not letting them die. This crucial policy area is gradually becoming recognised, I think irreversibly, and ultimately will be far more divisive, and more consequential in its policy choices, than the current issue of abortion. This is a policy area in which analysis has done little because of psychological intimidation. I do not mean that somebody is intimidating somebody else, but that even those who might find it feasible to initiate policy analysis are intimidated by the issues. It is even difficult to voice alternatives to current policy.

In public health, there is probably nothing more important than what to do about the smoking of tobacco. There is plenty of analysis to demonstrate that smoking is hazardous to health. (There is continuing analysis into just what it is about smoking that is bad for what aspects of health.) There has been remarkably little analysis of policy alternatives, partly because so few alternatives have been identified. A general prohibition of smoking is usually considered unfeasible or improper or both; suppressing the tobacco industry might have been feasible if it hadn't been in existence for centuries but appears politically out of the question now. Modest efforts at public eduaction have had striking results, and indeed smoking in the United States is on the decline, dramatically among some population groups.

But mostly there aren't any policies to analyse. If policy analysis is the science of rational choice among alternatives, it is dependent on another more imaginative activity — the invention of alternatives worth considering. There are a few with respect to smoking, but so few that most people don't even know what they are. And even here there is sometimes a degree of embattlement on the part of those who prefer to declare hostilities against an enemy, rather than to seek some mitigating strategies.

And so it goes. There have been major issues in schooling and good policy analyses; and as long as the decisions can be taken straightforwardly in a chain of command the decisions can be informed by analysis. But the great swings in the social behaviour of pupils in public schools or students in colleges, and swings in the pendulum of educational philosophy — issues as apparently well-defined as bilingual education, core curricula and electives, the disciplinary value of mathematics and foreign languages, and the influence on the quality of education of budgets, teacher quality, classroom size, and the separation of faster from slower students — do not appear to have been much illuminated by policy analysis. Granted, some of these issues are fairly intractable; it isn't policy analysis, just analysis, that often leads to inconclusive results. Still, it often looks as though parents, educators, legislators and editorialists feel that education is too important to be left to the policy analysts. And it is hard to tell whether or not they are right.

I do not mean this discursive review of the non-accomplishments of policy analysis to end up being entirely pessimistic. The point I would make is that policy analysis may be doomed to inconsequentiality as long as it is thought of within the paradigm of rational choice. Policy analysis can help *me* to make up *my* mind about the policies *I* would like. Policy analysis may help us who are together in a team, with coincident goals but uncertain about how to reach them, to resolve our uncertainties and to combine our intellects. But large policy issues are matters less of uncertainty than of dispute or genuine conflict about which way to go. When values conflict, analysis can sometimes sharpen the conflict, and sharpening the conflict is not always conducive to its resolution. Analysis can show whether or not there are some tolerably acceptable compromises; it may also show that compromises, ostensibly tolerable, are actually inferior. And if unresolved conflict is what some of the participants in a dispute wish to perpetuate, highlighting the choices to identify compromises will not be welcome.

I conclude that policy analysis may be most effective when it is viewed within a paradigm of conflict, rather than of rational choice. And I believe the same kind of analysis that identifies and assesses alternatives with a view to rational choice may not be the kind that is most successful in resolving or winning a conflict. Analysing the *interests* and the *participants* may be as important as analysing the issue. Selecting the alternatives to be compared, and selecting the emphasis to be placed on the criteria for evaluation may be what matters; and the creative use of darkness may be as much needed as the judicious use of light.

But this brings us to the role of policy *analysts*. In the United States we like to pretend that the analyst is an impartial helper. He illuminates choices; somebody else makes them. We often pretend that the politician or decision-maker has values while the policy analyst has intellect; the policy analyst helps that other person choose in a way that maximises that person's value achievement. This is the doctrine of non-involvement, of aloofness, of helpfulness, of advisor and client.

There is an alternative way to construe the role of the policy analyst. It is somebody who in the first instance uses analysis to understand both the issues and interests, and then makes a choice for himself, in accordance with his or her values, and becomes a *participant* in the dispute. Policy analysis then becomes an instrument in a contest. It is then not neutral to the values to be achieved, not unconcerned with which interests get best served and how the resolution of the dispute discriminates as among the parties concerned.

I am not really proposing anything novel here. Even in deciding where to apply his or her talents a policy analyst makes some choice about the values and interests that are going to be served. The formalistic textbook pretense that an analyst does his work impartially and disinterestedly has probably not fooled or influenced anybody very often. I am not mainly concerned with what role policy analysts might prefer for themselves. I am only concluding that policy analysis may still be a powerful influence on the decisions that get made without ever being 'out front' as the vehicle that leads to some important policy choice.

I have gone through some history of the failure of policy analysis as though the analysis was supposed to resolve controversial issues and had not succeeded, or was supposed to invent alternatives and not merely choose among them. I have recounted half a dozen important policy arenas in which analysis appears not to have made a great contribution. But the analyses may have been making their contributions through partisans and activists in the conflict. And if not, maybe they could have done so, had there been a more acknowledged legitimacy to the role of policy analysis in picking sides and supporting strategies and arguments.

At least, policy analysis should be able to clarify the understanding of a participant in a conflict, even when that participant would prefer not to clarify the understandings of his adversaries. Perhaps policy analysis in support of advocacy is a legitimate role, whether or not it is the role to which legitimacy has traditionally been accorded.

R.S. GANAPATHY

2 On Methodologies for Policy Analysis

Introduction

Policy analysis is a comparatively recent phenomenon in public systems. Its origin was in the United States, in the sixties, and in India it is just beginning to come into vogue. In this paper, I propose to examine the methodologies for policy analysis; their nature as also their relationship with social science theory and implementation. Based on this critique, an attempt is made to develop an alternative, critical framework for policy analysis. The perspective of policy analysis as a critique of methodologies is still more recent.

The growth of policy analysis has been characterised by the application of prevalent methodologies in social science inquiry and research. This parallels the growth of methodology in natural sciences over the last three hundred years. There has been a positivist tradition that has made enormous efforts to attain the status of the natural sciences for the social sciences through rigorous, precise and analytic methodologies. The domination of the empirical method in social sciences and its application in policy analysis clearly reflect this effort.

Methodology can be defined *(a)* as the epistemological assumptions on which the search for knowledge is based, and *(b)* as the set of methods, techniques, and approaches that are used in the acquisition and analysis of data for the solution of a problem. In this paper the term methodology is used to mean both. The application of scientific findings in social science for practical ends is to put that knowledge to what is called 'instrumental' use. Policy analysis is concerned chiefly with such instrumental use of knowledge for planned social change. A striking parallel is that of engineering that has enabled man to control and exploit nature for his welfare. Each methodology while generating a distinctive set of conclusions has the predilection for a prior, often implicit, choice of theory and ideology. If the choice of methodology is uncritical it can only lead to predictable conclusions which support, maintain and reproduce the underlying ideology. The current differences and lack of communication among methodologies, their irrelevance to social practice, and their fragmentation and specialisation have been recognised as major problems.

Approaches to Policy Analysis : A Critique

Drawing from fragmentary and widely dispersed concepts, I have constructed a typology of policy analysis methodologies (Table 1) which explores their dimensions. This typology generates insights into the predictable relationship between choice and outcome of policy analysis in a wide spectrum. The classification of methodologies is intended to portray the major theoretical traditions in policy analysis. The classification is of 'pure' types juxtaposing major differences, though in reality there would be some combination of methods. Two caveats, however, must be emphasised : (a) (a) typologies and classifications reflect a view focusing on appearances; (b) tabular representations tend to suggest that the different approaches are equally important or powerful. This is not so, especially here. The mainstream positivist approach is 'hegemonic' and dominates others in the Gramscian sense of ideological control. Locigally, however, Table 1 illustrates important and predictable sets of relationships and tendencies (not in an absolute sense) among the theory and methodology of three influential positions in policy analysis. Though Table 1 is self explanatory, it would be worthwhile to analyse some of the important issues in these different approaches and clarify their implications.

The mainstream positivist approach to policy analysis subscribes to what Auguste Comte said, in the nineteenth century. 'From

TABLE 1
Models of Policy Analysis Methodologies :
A Profile of their Dimensions

Dimension	Model		
	Mainstream	*Reformist-Normative*	*Critical*
1. Ideology	Status quo : control over man and nature	Evolutionary change; participatory transformation; man-nature harmony; benevolent elite	Radical change; liberation and social justice
2. Theory	Positivism : modernisation	Social learning; decentralism	Praxis; holism
3. Goals	Explanation and prediction	Contextual interpretation of meanings; sustainable human change	Critique to expose underlying assumptions, values and interests; structural change; democratic control
4. Nature of knowledge	Value-free, objective, causal, cumulative	Value-laden, meaningful, problematic, non-cumulative	Value-laden; social as well as objective, praxiological
5. Social relationships	Objective; neutral; reified and commodified; law-like generalisations possible	Objective but through planned change, new laws can be established	Contextual and political; historically specific laws can be transcended by collective action
6. World-view	Static present; status quo is natural, confined to appearances	Static but present can be modified to another state through coping strategies	Diachronic, existential change; openness; concerned with essence behind appearances

TABLE 1 (contd.)

Dimension	Model		
	Mainstream	*Reformist-Normative*	*Critical*
7. Problem orientation	Recurrent pattern; universal laws; ahistorical, harmonious process; quantitative change	Contextually unique; localised interpretation; harmonious at macrolevel	Contextual and structural; structural contradictions; qualitative change
8. Argumentation	Causal-functional; decontextualised	Dialogue; advocacy; use of multiple contexts	Critique of methods and the present order; historical, relational and materialistic analysis
9. Methods	Empiricism; rational-comprehensive models; cost-benefit analysis; causal modelling; survey research	Advocacy planning; participatory management; appropriate technology; future research-technology assessment; environmentalism	Dialectics; multiple methods for synthesis and integration
10. Typical proponents	US public policy schools; think tanks; bureaucrats; established interest groups	US planning schools; futures-research groups; humanistic social scientists; Club of Rome; alternative technology movement	Radical Statistics Group — UK; Union of Radical Political Economics — US; Progressive Planners Network, US; Educational groups following Paolo Freire; School of Critical Theory in Europe; Indian School of Social Sciences; Lokayan

Science comes prevision, from prevision comes control.' This is an excellent summary of instrumentalism. Since his day, social science has found it useful to consider social reality as a form of objective, 'natural' reality. In its search for laws explaining social behaviour, it has claimed both ontological and epistemological primacy for the empirical method (Camhis, 1979). Reality exists, only in the forms that are accessible to the senses directly or through surrogate, especially quantitative, measures. Thus, energy 'exists' if we can measure it by reference to the sale of fuels, classes exist if they can be measured by people's wealth, location, and education. The main stream policy analysis accepts or rejects claims solely on the basis of whether or not they are consistent with the data. The laws that describe relationships among variables are universal, preferably quantitative and independent of context. The relationships are reified, i.e. the relationships among people appear as relationships among things. There is a clear distinction here between facts and values as well as between ends and means. The quest of the empirical method, whether it is applied in cost-benefit analysis, regression, or optimisation models is the 'discovery' of order in an apparently disorderly reality. The policy analyst contributes to the realisation of order through the translation of research into policy. Explanation and prediction are the primary goals of this methodology (hence the integral link to control).

The critique of the empirical methodology has been particularly strong. Its merits including analytic rigour, avoidance of subjective biases and the construction of complex explanations, are well known. Its important feature, however, is its usefulness in predicting, manipulating, and shaping events. With advances in quantitative methodology and more cumulative research, the assumption was that some day, social science would be as 'scientific' as natural sciences and policy analysis would be as effective as engineering.

The mainstream social science and policy analysis have traditionally focused on explanation and causation and are rarely concerned with understanding, meaning, and intentionality. The Keynesian economic theory, the Kinship theory in anthropology, the Exchange theory of Transformational grammar in linguistics, the Modernisation theory in political science, and the Cognitive Dissonance theory in psychology are basically causal theories.

The positivist methodology that was liberating man in an earlier era (freeing him from dogma, superstition, religious repression, and rampant subjectivism) has become progressively dominating in its consequences. It does not recognise the validity of other forms of knowledge or inquiry. Domination and control of nature have been extended, without reflection, to the domination of man. Due to the formal constitution of theories as generalisable laws, people are treated as objects, as passive bearers of servo-mechanisms. Skinner's theory of operant conditioning is the most infamous example of this trend. Society, moreover, is seen as consisting of atomised individuals or events. The survey research method assumes this, denying the holistic, systematic nature of social phenomena. The averaging procedures, like regression analysis, focus on surface phenomena often carelessly grasped and too readily sensed. Correlation is often taken as a substitute for causation in this method. The underlying structures and processes that give rise to the phenomena tend to be ignored and only environmental stimulii and behavioural responses are considered meaningful. Reality is what 'is' and not what we make it. People are considered as the carriers and not producers of meaning. They merely exhibit and 'emit' behaviour and do not act purposively. The status quo social order is considered 'natural'. The objective of policy analysis becomes one of preserving and perpetuating the status quo.

For example, in energy planning, energy use surveys often form the basis of forecasting energy needs. By focusing on the present patterns of consumptions (aggregated individual family consumptions) which is surface phenomenon, policy analysis ignores the underlying historical processes which generated these patterns and thus reifies patterns which perpetuate enormous inequities. Empiricism, then, has aided the policy analyst in constructing an abstract world, a world stripped of its social relations, social conflicts, social power, and social inequality and yet this is called 'applied social sciences'. The distribution and use of energy in the future would simply resemble the past. This is how policy analysis serves as a means of social control. As we would discuss later, only the critique of the present order has the potential to transcend this problem of repressive structures. Such a critique will expose the ideological assumptions and values behind methodology and nourish explicit consciousness about the consequences of every methodological choice.

Our capacity to deal with our societal problems has been declining due to two reasons. First, social problems are becoming more complex, more interrelated, and more intractable. Second, our system of education or acquiring knowledge is more fragmented and more specialised now, than ever before. In other words, we know more and more about less and less. This alienation of our knowledge system from the social reality (reflected fully in policy analysis) is the major cause of the present ineffectiveness and irrelevance of policy analysis.

Policy analysis, in our times, has become a major source of legitimation of the status quo interests and social order. It has become a new symbol of control as we mentioned earlier. A very apt analogy is Humpty Dumpty's pithy description of the use of words (the most potent of our symbols) in *Alice in Wonderland*.

'When I see a word', Humpty Dumpty said, in rather scornful tone, 'it means just what I choose to mean. Neither more nor less.'
'The question is, 'said Alice, 'Whether you can make words mean so many different things.'
'The question is,' said Humpty Dumpty, 'who is the master. That is all.'

Policy analysis, as we know it today, is dominated by the methods of mainstream, positivist economics and political science as well as management. It collapses processes (history) into results and quality into quantity. It is closely associated with the diffusion model which places research before action and implies that policy analysis must precede implementation. This is the reflection of the positivist mode where explanation leads to prediction which in turn leads to control. The experimental demonstration and pilot project approaches in policy analysis reflect this philosophy of research before action, theory before practice, and concern with control.

Policy analysis reflects what is happening in advanced industrialised societies — fragmentation and specialisation of activities unrelated to one another. These activities are disjointed from life itself where work and leisure have been separated. Policy analysis has become a professionalised, technical activity. In other words, it has become a commodity. With the growing computerisation of information, it has become the exclusive prerogative of trained people. It basically degrades work as the vast majority of people will have to implement or suffer the consequences of somebody else's policy, in the making of which they cannot participate. In other words, policy analysis encourages alienation in our society by centralising power and encouraging dependency. In as much as it is oriented towards programme management, its unstated objective is to manipulate and train people to behave in predictable ways. This managerial focus (the word 'manage' comes from the Italian word *managgiare* which means to handle and train horses) is primarily concerned with means (how), rather than the question of ends (why and what). The ends are seen as given and the task of policy analysis is to identify the means to achieve them. The vast majority of us, in the eyes of the policy analyst, have become and remain as horses. Let us face it : there are obvious limits to what horses can achieve in an environment of domination and control.

The methodologies of policy analysis, in the mainstream tradition, are usually concerned with the choice of techniques. We mentioned earlier about the epistemological concern with basic assumptions about reality and knowledge that are inherent in any question of methodology. Usually, the mainstream policy analysis ignores these questions.

Often, the methodological choice ignores the reality of policy-making and asserts the primacy of method over substance. This is what Alvin Gouldner once called as Methodolatory. Like in many areas of public life, where different professions have reached the optimal point of their effectiveness, policy analysis too has reached its optimal point. I would like to maintain that more policy analysis in the present context may not necessarily mean better policy-making. We know that more teachers do not create better student quality; more doctors would not necessarily result in higher life expectancy and certainly more lawyers does not mean that the people's sense of justice will improve.

Three basic arguments have been advanced as to why policy analysis is seen as ineffective:

1. It is a young science and with better training, more research, more rigorous methodologies, and data bases, its efficiency will improve. I tend to strongly disagree with this argument. As it is constituted now, the structural underpinnings of mainstream policy analysis will not make it effective even after one hundred years.
2. Policy analysts have become too powerful. They define the problems, they propose solutions, and they alone can evaluate

the effectiveness of the solutions. The citizen as the key stakeholder has become a residual category. Hence, we need to persuade the policy analysts to involve citizens in policy analysis and other policy-making processes. I disagree with this proposition as well because such a reformist measure will simply mean more humane change but within the same structural framework. A number of reformist methods as outlined in Table 1 attempt to do this. One can expect only marginal changes from such an approach.

3. Policy analysis is the cause of our problems. This iatrogenic argument implies that policy analysis commodifies and dominates new areas of social life and creates dependency. The professionalism in policy analysis (more training, degree programmes, development of analytic methods, professional associations, journals, conferences, and professional certification) is the cause of the problem.

Following the last view, the question is not how to do policy analysis better but rather what is it that can be done that is worth doing. Based on a critical awareness that traditional policy analysis is useless, exploitative, and harmful is the world view that our social problems are basically conflictual in nature. In this zero sum situation, policy analysis necessarily would have to take an advocacy role. Such a critical policy analysis is not one to establish optimality among a possible set of alternatives (i.e., policy analysis is not a rational choice problem). Rather it is an effort to create a richer synthesis by critically examining the underlying assumptions, world views, and values. It is a perspective that recognises that conflict of ideas creates greater enlightenment.

Multiple Perspectives in Policy Analysis

It is important to recognise that policy analysis can be carried out in several ways. Social problems are complex, strategic, political, and behavioural. There is usually an interlocking set of problems which defy easy analysis. These problems are, in the words of Ian Mitroff, typically 'messy' ones (Mitroff and Kilman, 1978). They can be formulated in many ways. Depending on the formulation, the solutions will also be quite different. Another characteristic of these social problems is that there is no finality to them. Like a Faustian bargain they require constant search, inquiry, and interpretation. As they are usually unique, the logic of replicability of solutions is inapplicable. To quote an example, the energy crisis can be formulated as (a) supply crisis, (b) demand management (c) technology/productivity deficiency, and (d) structural imbalance. These four formulations are very different and lead to different solutions.

The basic proposition I would like to argue here is that we need multiple perspectives in public policy research and analysis. Each of these perspectives may imply a different model of policy research and associated theory and methodology. A method has an implicit prior theory behind it, which organises data and facts. To gain meaningful insight into a social problem, we need multiple methodological perspectives, which formulate the problem differently. Graham Allison's pioneering work formulating the Cuban missile crisis (in *The Essence of Decision*) in three different ways (but within one — the mainstream — perspective) needs to be recalled here. A dialectical analysis of these perspectives will help us to become effective in dealing with a social problem. This approach is very similar to the ancient Jain doctrine of *Syadvada*. Its axiom is that every proposition is true only up to a point. For a true understanding of reality — creation of 'gestalt' — one must generate multiple propositions. Hence we cannot ascribe ontological or epistemological primacy to any perspective or mode of inquiry.

Table 2 illustrates the nature of such multiple perspectives of 'poverty' and corresponding typical solutions. These approaches will help us to locate ourselves along various dimensions and to learn of the consequences of such location for policy analysis outcome. For, the outcome of policy analysis is critically dependent on the prior perspective one adopts, as data analysis is organised by that perspective.

Again, policy analysis can take place at different levels of depth. To go back to our example, Table 3 illustrates that poverty can be analysed at four different levels of depth. Formulation of the problem, thus, will depend on the choice among these levels.

If the policy researcher chooses to focus at, say, the level of symptoms, the solutions he will come up with will be very different than, say, if he chooses to focus at the level of basic causes. In a recent evaluation of poverty research in U.S., it was found that it

TABLE 2
Many Perspectives of Poverty

Professional Background	Diagnosis	Typical Recommendations
Health	Nutritional deficiency; environmental stress	Vaccination; breast-feeding; sanitation
Agriculture	Low food supply	Food production; food aid; new agricultural technology
Architect/ Urban Planner	Poor physical environment; poor living conditions	More housing; new settlements
Demographer	High density; high growth rate of population	Population control; family planning, migration and resettlement
Environmentalist	Degradation of the environment whose sustainable capacity has been exceeded	Environmental protection; simpler life styles for everyone; appropriate technology
Marxist	Capitalism	Revolution of the proletariat
Manager/ Planner	Lack of management, coordination, and planning	Development planning councils; management training; systems improvement; master plans
Educationalist	Ignorance, wrong attitudes, and lack of skills	Education; mass communication
Neoclassical economist	Maldistribution; lack of supply to meet demand	Fiscal policy; income generation and employment programmes; economic growth

TABLE 3
Poverty : Level of Analysis

Level	Problem Formulation
Symptoms	Nutritional deficiency, poor health, no housing, no clothes
Immediate cause	Low income, low food intake, illiteracy
Underlying causes	Unequal access to and inadequate use of resources (food, education, and health)
Basic causes	Contradictions and interactions within the economic structure and between the economic and political-social superstructure. These causes explain how resources are produced and distributed in the society.

was focused mainly at the level of symptoms and had come up with different strategies of income redistribution (Rein, 1976). This evaluation also pointed out that strategies for creation of jobs or restructuring of economic activities were not even considered by this research programme, because of its orientation at the level of symptoms.

Policy Analysis in the US : A Historical View

We need to ground policy research in our economic and political reality. Yet it would be rewarding to consider, from a comparative point of view, the American experience in the context of developing a strategy for policy research in India. The American experience suggests that policy analysis often masks a certain form of political practice. The mainstream policy research in The United States, however, is portrayed as a more effective way of dealing with public policy questions — progressive, scientific and objective. To examine this claim critically, we need to understand the historical context in which the mainstream policy analysis has developed in that country.

As the Defence Secretary to John Kennedy, Robert Mcnamara introduced Programmed Planning and Budgeting Systems (PPBS) in the government in the early sixties. His tenure represents a historical phase in the development of policy research. Throughout the sixties several factors contributed towards creating a context for the growth of policy research. These were President Johnson's Great Society Programme, the expansion of the welfare (and military) state, and the widespread social protest — civil rights, women's and hippie movements, the Vietnam war. The growth of public policy schools since the sixties and the mainstream perspective it represents have to be understood in this historical context. Many researchers argue that the public policy research in the United States is the State's response to the crisis the society is facing in legitimating the status quo. In other words, policy research has been portrayed as the new scientism, a new form of domination. The mainstream policy research in the States concerns itself entirely with the question of means, efficiency, and accountability, and not with the question of ends. Ends or goals are always taken as given and often are implicit.

The general proposition to make in this connection is that policy research, like other branches of knowledge, reflects the historical and material reality in a society and will seek to justify the existing order, stratification, and class structure in a society. In urban planning, for example, the central place theory was developed during this period as a functionalist justification of disproportionate resource allocation for cities (and then later to suburbs) to the detriment of rural areas (Gregory, 1978). The mainstream policy research in the United States has always tacitly supported a worldview that the market economy is strong, continuous growth is possible, centralised planning is desirable in some areas, and people can be treated as passive recipients of service delivery (Mcknight, 1980). Now under the Reagan administration, policy analysis, as all forms of planning, has lost its importance relative to the restoration of the market processes.

Policy Analysis in India — Transfer from the USA

Public policy implementation in the mainstream perspective has always relied on policy research. The critical determinant in any policy process is its context — both historical and material. An uncritical transfer of policy analysis practices across contexts can often prove to be unproductive and harmful. The legitimacy of transferring policy research methods and practices from US or Europe, thus, needs to be examined with reference to the Indian context.

There is also the danger that policy research in academic institutions in India might become a strategy for academic channeling of social protest. We should recall how the widespread agrarian unrest gave rise to rural studies/rural development programmes in Indian universities in the last ten years. One of our normative concerns about policy research in India is to make it meaningful and responsive to the needs of the poor. The emergence of the profession of policy research as we conventionally understand it, may indeed be a threat to the needs of the poor. In the US, several instances of policy analysis have become sources of mystification, domination, and dependency.

Policy research is usually done from the perspective of government agencies. Again this need not be the norm. Considerable work in advocacy planning in the US and Europe demonstrates that policy research can be undertaken from the perspective of many different groups whether they be environmental or women's or consumers or the poor. Advocacy analysis is a relatively new area, with a high potential for effectiveness.

There is a common, often unstated, assumption that policy analysis improves policy making. In recent years this has been challenged in a radical way. The connections between theory and practice, knowledge and action are very tenuous and in the field of policy making they are even more so. There is considerable evidence that policy analysis is a fairly minor determinant of policy making. Other more important determinants are *(a)* the context; *(b)* the leadership; *(c)* politics of bureaucracy, interest groups, and legislatures; and *(d)* public images the media generates about the policy issues. The conventional diffusion model of policy research implies that the research gets translated into practice (instrumental use of knowledge). This diffusion model typically focuses on a single, rational decision maker and represents by and large the middle class interests in preserving status quo social order and in making incremental changes. Work in different contexts indicates that this model is not realistic. In the words of Paul Feyerabend, 'there are no data or facts independent of prior theory that organises them' (Feyerabend, 1975). This poses very clearly what I would describe as the theory-fact dilemma, that is to say, choice among competing theories needs to be based on empirical data. However, such data itself is dependent on a prior theoretical framework. The political use of policy research for postponing decisions and to justify decisions already made, are very well known. Again the question of interests looms large in the utilisation of policy analysis. For example, the policy research supported by the tobacco industry 'proved' that smoking does not cause cancer while research sponsored by the US Surgeon General 'proved' otherwise.

Policy research utilisation theory has been stood on its head, as it were, in the last few years. If consensus building and collective understanding of the policy problem is the most critical factor in utilisation, then we might say that measurement and objectivity in policy analysis methods is a threat to such consensus formation. Recent studies, supporting this conclusion, indicate that social learning rather than the experimentation/diffusion approach, is the appropriate model for policy research. The Japanese experience in adoption of policy innovations as contrasted with the American experience in policy diffusion certainly bears this out. To quote Gunnar Myrdal in his *Asian Drama* : 'There are no facts about unemployment that are independent of the policy considerations that inform them. This suggests that we have to begin with the policy and then go on to collect data.' This radical view of policy research utilisation tells us that the task of a policy analyst is not to explore how to translate research into policy but to uncover *(a)* the policies underlying policy research agenda and *(b)* the theory behind existing policies. The Indian policy research setting·is certainly unique and is, therefore, different from the US or Europe. The implications of this alternative utilisation model for India need to be explored in some depth.

Towards Critical Policy Analysis

In this section, I shall present a framework which is my recon-struction of policy analysis, drawing from the earlier critique of the mainstream approach. *Critique of all methodologies* (not excluding itself) is demanded in this framework. Aggressively exposing the ideologies, values, interests, and assumptions behind apparently neutral, disinterested, 'scientific' policy analysis approaches, the critique returns them to their unprivileged situation in the world. In this sense, a critical policy analysis approach is not simply an alternative to others but an effort to discover the transformation and synthesis. It does not criticise them, simply in order to abandon them. Such a framework is also explicitly normative in its commitment to social justice and liberation (Habermas,1971). This critical framework adopts multiple perspectives and a dialectical approach to policy analysis. Let me characterise the critical approach briefly.

1. A commitment to social justice and liberation.
2. Engagement in critique of all methods.
3. Construction of a policy and a plan from the critique, through synthesis and integration, not merely as an intellectual-cognitive activity but as a collective social action.
4. Methodological pluralism to generate multiple insights and dialogue among maximally divergent perspectives.

5. Development of policy analysis as a tool of intervention to promote equality in society (though we have enough evidence that social interventions including policy analysis in existing unequal social structures will always benefit the powerful).
6. Recognition that knowledge is both objective and social and hence public participation is essential in itself to generate vaild knowledge. It is not merely an instrument to achieve co-operation or commitment from the public.
7. Power and conflict are addressed directly as relevant issues in the critical policy analysis mode.
8. Holistic and systematic analysis in a structuralist framework : the search for underlying truth behind appearances in social problems.
9. Historical approach that involves contextual/material grounding and social specificity.
10. Generation of catalytic, facilitative, deprofessionalised roles to help people critically reflect on their condition and hence transform the society.
11. Demystification and repoliticisation of all policy analysis activities.

Policy Analysis in India

Policy analysis in India, while relatively uncommon in the form it is known in the United States, has been undertaken in a variety of ways. Our constitution and legislation make policy pronouncements and our five year plans involve a good deal of analysis about resource allocation and investment decisions. Several committees and government statements in the form of white papers, resolutions, etc., include a good deal of analysis of different policies. Most of the programmes that have been started are based on some kind of policy analysis (Planning Commission, 1969, 1980). The methods that are used are of various kinds : economic modelling, optimisation studies, social cost-benefit analysis, micro-economic analysis, survey research and input-output models. As one can see readily, there is a domination of economics in such policy analyses, and the Planning Commission and the Ministry of Finance are largely dominated in this area by the economists. There are economic advisers in various ministries. Important decisions on investment, pricing, etc., are based primarily on economic analysis of policy choice. There is a good deal of regulatory policy that is not based on economic analysis but on a legal one. The courts make policy without any formal analysis to aid them. Now areas like environmental impact assessment, technology assessment, and global modelling are being tried out in a few cases to aid policy-making.

The overall impact of policy analysis in India is largely marginal. Conflictual analysis or critique of various methods have rarely been attempted. In some instances analysis has sharpened conflict and has not been conducive to resolution. The major policy issues like foreign exchange allocation, subsidies, cow slaughter, or prohibition have hardly been influenced by policy analysis. In limited areas like identification of direct beneficiary groups for anti-poverty programmes, family planning programmes, and minimum needs programmes, policy analysis as choice among alternatives has been reasonably successful. In the energy sector, considerable policy analysis has been done in the form of studies and committee reports, addressing problems of pricing, inter-fuel substitution, demand management conservation, and new technology development. Yet, this analysis has hardly had any impact in the rational management of our energy resources. Another area where policy analysis has failed is the administration of monopolies and restrictive trade practices. The concentration of economic power has been increasing after the enactment of this legislation. In other areas like incomes-prices policy, worker participation, and regional development, policy analysis has not been effective. The reason for this ineffectiveness is perhaps due to several political and structural causes which generate the policy problems, and which are not addressed by the policy analysis. Policy analysis through replication of experiments and pilot projects has also not worked very well. The systemic nature of our problems defies conventional policy analysis which usually proposes discrete, direct attack on them. For example, public works programmes can no longer alleviate unemployment. The incomes and prices policy is no more effective for combating inflation.

Our knowledge and public policy reflect and manifest the underlying essence and systematic unity of our social relationships. Hence, it is important to probe behind the surface phenomena which are the concern of mainstream policy analysis. However, we may have no alternative to coventional policy analysis in the medium term. A reformistic approach to policy analysis can work well if we engage in it with a broad structural understanding and critical awareness of our social condition. An awareness of the limitations of such a response may help us to transcend our condition in the long run. Otherwise, the present pattern, which we observe in India, will continue to be managerial solutions (strengthening the policy-instrument nexus, strong administrative or political commitment not to dilute stated policy objectives in implementation, removal of inconsistencies among policies and strengthening the management through training, systems, and monitoring to make policy more effective). It is increasingly being realised that such a managerial or a programmatic approach to policy is very ineffective as it masks the political reality. The linear logic (policy → outcome) is faulty. The intervening structural processes that generate development and underdevelopment, justice and inequality will distort the anticipated causal relationship. The mainstream policy analysis usually ignores such structural, historical contexts.

Conclusion

To recapitulate, critical policy analysis is a unity of critical reflection and collective action, of praxis. It assumes that theory and knowledge are themselves part of the activity of changing the world rather than an 'objective' stage prior to its implementation. It cannot be transplanted or transferred but must be reinvented. What is outlined here is a model not of theoretical-methodological priority that must be copied elsewhere but rather one that can be recreated in other contexts. What Paolo Freire was engaged in during his work in Brazil and Guinea-Bissau is the only example I can think of that comes close to the critical policy analysis as outlined here. His work in adult education was not simply in literacy creation. He helped the people to read their own reality (and not merely the words in a book) and to write their own future. Development of their critical consciousness was the key focus. His work focused on learning from the masses who were to the taught.

The exploration of alternative perspectives in policy analysis here is intended to create critical awareness and sophistication in methodological choice. One finds methodological fetishism and isolationism pervasive in social sciences and in their application in policy analysis. If one is critically conscious, one may be able to overcome the structural limitations of methodologies and use them selectively, critically, and effectively in a normative framework. The policy analytic methods, critically used, have the potential of being socially purposeful and help achieve progressive social goals. This analysis is meant as a progressive contribution to this dialectical process.

References

Camhis, Marios (1979), *Planning Theory and Philosophy*, London, Tavistock.

Feyrabend, Paul (1975), *Against Method*, London, New Left Books.

Gregory, Derek (1978), *Ideology, Science and Human Geography*, London, Hutchinson,

Government of India (1969 & 1980), Fourth and Sixth Five-Year Plan documents, New Delhi, Planning Commission.

Habermas, Jurgen (1971), *Knowledge and Human Interests*, Boston, Beacon Press.

Mcknight, John (1980), 'Professional Problem,' *Resurgence* (UK), March-April.

Mitroff, Ian and Kilman, Ralph (1978), *Methodological Approaches to Social Science*, San Francisco, Jossey-Bass.

Rein, Martin (1976), *Social Science and Public Policy*, London, Penguin Books.

II

Policy-making
in Sectors

M. L. DANTWALA • J. N. BARMEDA

3 Rural Development

Evolution in the Concept of Rural Development

The concept of rural development as reflected in the various rural development programmes formulated since planning began has undergone change from time to time, judging by the approach adopted in their formulation. These approaches adopted may be classified as (a) community approach, (b) area approach, (c) target group approach, (d) employment approach, (e) welfare approach and finally (f) integrated development approach. Though at first sight it appears that the approaches were *ad hoc* in the sense of responding to emergent situations, the transitions can be viewed as reflecting improvement in the perception of the problem of rural development.

Community Approach

Rural development programmes in the First Plan were formulated against the background of debate and discussions held over nearly fifteen years. It was therefore possible to formulate conceptually a somewhat comprehensive programme for rural development in the form of the Community Development Programme which was launched on 2 October 1952. It was a broad-based programme covering all aspects of village life including agriculture, irrigation, animal husbandry, health, education, rural industries, housing, transport and communications and social welfare of women and children and supplementary employment. The components of the programme underwent change of emphasis from time to time. The main emphasis in the programme was on the development of self-reliance in the individual and initiative in the community for achieving the desired goals. The First Plan stated that 'Community development is the method and rural extension is the agency through which the Five Year Plan seeks to initiate a process of transformation of the social and economic life of the villages.'

A community project consisted of three Development Blocks, each block consisting of about 100 villages and a population of about 60,000 to 70,000. Each block had a minimum administrative set-up consisting of a block development officer, extension officers for agriculture, animal husbandry and cooperation, two social education organizers, an overseer with public health bias and ten village level workers and ancillary staff.

The community development programme was rightly concerned with the total development of the community as a whole. Much, however, depended on two major factors — finances earmarked for the purpose and coordination between developmental agencies. In both these respects the programme faced many difficulties. The programme attempted to cover a wide range of activities with very limited resources with the result that the resources were dispersed over too wide an area to make an impact. As a consequence several programmes, particularly agricultural development, made a weak impact. The programme did not bring about significant increase in crop production. But a greater obstacle in implementation of the programme was lack of coordination at the district, block and village levels. The Third Evaluation Report has pointed out that the dual control of specialists concerned with different subjects at the block level by the Block Development Officer and by the technical officers at the district level, did not work satisfactorily. This lack of coordination among different developmental agencies is a common weakness running through development programmes to this day.

Whatever the limitation of the programme, it must be recognised that it did help in setting up a network of basic extension and other development services in the rural areas. It created an awareness among the people about the potential for development through adoption of modern and improved methods of cultivation, paving the way for a smoother adoption of the new technology of high-yielding varieties when it became available.

Partly the weak impact of the community development programme on crop production but mainly the pressure generated by food scarcity necessitating continued imports of foodgrains on a large scale, drew the attention of the authorities to the pressing need for increasing foodgrain production. As a result the emphasis shifted from community development to growth in agriculture. The approach to rural development was focused on area development towards the end of the Second Plan, with the formulation of the Intensive Agricultural District Programme on the lines of the recommendations of the Agricultural Production Team (1959) of the Ford Foundation.

Area Approach Programmes

The Intensive Agricultural District Programme (IADP) was launched in 1960-61, initially in three districts and extended thereafter to cover one district in every state. The main objective of the programme was to demonstrate the potentialities of higher food production through a package of practices in areas which were specially endowed with assured water supply, that is those having maximum irrigation facilities and minimum of natural hazards, infrastructural facilities, good soil, etc. The main features of the programme in such selected areas were : *(a)* adoption of measures for quick increase in agricultural production; *(b)* emphasis on profitability at farm level; and *(c)* adoption of package of improved practices evolved for individual crops, including use of improved seeds, fertilizers, pesticides, improved implements and proper soil and water management practices. The necessary credit for inputs and marketing facilities were also to be provided.

The impact of the programme in IADP districts was quite appreciable with significant increases in crop yields achieved in the Third Plan period. The programme however received a sharp set-back due to severe droughts in 1965-66 and 1966-67. There were also several administrative and supply weaknesses which inhibited progress. Government policies, particularly regarding credit, marketing and prices, did not come up to the expectations. The 'package' concept was found useful and yielded good results. The government therefore decided to extend this programme to many more districts through a programme called *Intensive Agricultural Areas Programme* (IAAP) which was launched in 1964-65. The two drought years of 1965-66 and 1966-67 had an adverse impact on this programme as well.

The IAAP programme differed slightly from the IADP programme in that while in the latter the selection of districts was on the basis of the potential of a single crop, the former emphasised intensive agricultural development of the area as a whole. The IAAP had a wider coverage but without a corresponding increase in resources. The scale of staff and other facilities were greatly reduced. The IAAP programme covered a much larger area than IADP and accounted for over 7 per cent of the total cultivated area of the country. For the first time a sizeable proportion of cropped area in the country was brought under intensive production effort. These programmes paved the way for launching the exotic high-yielding varieties of seeds programme which became the main instrument of agricultural growth through the adoption of technological innovation in the Fourth Plan and ushering in what came to be known as the Green Revolution. Until the advent of the *High Yielding Varieties Programme* (HYVP), even this intensive effort could not impart sufficient spur to agricultural growth due to inherent limitations of existing and traditional varieties of seeds used.

The adoption of the new technology did make a significant contribution to the growth of foodgrain production. However, there were two major limitations of the programme : one, it bypassed regions which were not endowed with assured irrigation or adequate rainfall and two, by and large, the benefits of the new technology could be availed of mainly by the better-off farmers. To overcome these limitations, two countervailing programmes were launched, one for the disadvantaged regions and the other for disadvantaged sections of the farming community.

The Drought-Prone Area Programme (DPAP) was launched in the Fifth Plan as an integrated area development programme in agriculture. Since its inception in the late sixties up to March 1980, it covered 55 blocks spread over 74 districts in 13 states and programmes like soil treatment and moisture conservation, creating irrigation potential, afforestation and pasture development have made some headway. However, in the important area of developing better dry farming practices and cropping pattern, little progress has been made.

The Desert Development Programme (DDP) initiated in 1977-78, has covered arid regions in twenty districts of five states. The main emphasis in the programme is on measures to check desertification together with projects which would facilitate development of productivity and productive resources of the area and its people. Schemes of afforestation, water harvesting, animal husbandry and rural electrification have received some attention though investments in these, particularly in forestry and pasture development, are slow in picking up. What has been lacking, it is reported, is the State Government machinery which needs to be adequately equipped for these relatively new tasks.

A comprehensive programme of *The Command Area Development* was launched at the commencement of the Fifth Plan. Investment made from plan to plan has created considerable irrigation potential in the country. Its utilization however has been far from satisfactory. The under-utilization of the irrigation potential is attributed to either absence or inadequacies of programmes relating to land consolidation, scientific land shaping, construction of water courses and field channels to carry water to individual fields, field drains to carry surplus water away from the fields and a system of roads which would help farmers to carry produce to the market. For removing these deficiencies the Command Area Development Authorities were set up for certain identified projects. The progress made so far is seen in the setting up of forty-five Command Area Development Project authorities covering seventy-six such projects in sixteen states and one union territory covering an area of 15.3 million hectares.

Small Farmers Development Agency (SFDA) and *Marginal Farmers' and Landless Labourers'* (MFAL) Agency : With the initiation of these programmes, the focus of rural development programmes shifted from mere growth to programmes specifically designed for the development of small and marginal farmers and agricultural labourers, and to growth with social justice. The programmes involved helping the target group to adopt improved agricultural technology, acquire the means of increasing agricultural production such as minor irrigation and to help them to diversify their farm economy through subsidiary activities like animal husbandry, dairying, poultry, horticulture, etc. The agencies entrusted with these programmes were expected to make adequate arrangements for the supply of necessary inputs and credit at subsidised rates.

These programmes have been in operation since 1971 and up to

March 1980 covered 1,818 blocks. It is, however, reported that while the persons identified for assistance formed only a segment of the target group, the number of actual beneficiaries was only about half of those identified. The lower coverage and partial success have been attributed to the stark inadequacies of the main implementing agency. Lack of coordination among concerned government departments and inadequacies of credit are also partly responsible for slow progress. In fact, the assistance provided did not result in any specific additional asset creation, though the programme did create some employment opportunities.

A programme to benefit tribal people and tribal areas named as *Tribal Sub-Plan* was launched during the Fifth Plan. Taking into account the past experience of area development through Tribal Development Blocks, these sub-plans were evolved for areas of tribal concentration. Tribal sub-plans are in operation in 16 states and 2 Union Territories. The objectives are to narrow the gap between the levels of development of tribal areas and other areas through elimination of exploitation of tribals in land alienation, indebtedness, bonded labour, malpractices in exchange of agricultural and forest produce, etc. Development of agriculture, irrigation facilities, forest based and other industries were also programmed and oriented to provide increased incomes. One of the welcome features of the operation of the tribal sub-plan is the organization of the areas into *Integrated Tribal Development Projects* (ITDPs), each of which is geared to integrate all developmental efforts. The number of such ITDPs was 180 at the beginning of the Sixth Plan.

Employment Approach Programmes

The area approach and target-oriented programmes discussed above essentially aimed at resource development on individual or area basis. Providing employment opportunities was also one of the objectives, but it was assumed that the increasing growth rate of the economy through plan investment could take care of this problem. This was not so and the problem of unemployment, specially in rural areas, has become acute over the years. But it was not until the Fifth Plan that some concrete programmes were formulated.

In April 1971 a programme called the *Crash Scheme for Rural*

Employment (CSRE) was introduced. It was designed to provide employment to about 1,000 persons in every district during a working period of ten months in a year. The wage rate was not to exceed a specified amount. It also aimed at creation of assets of durable nature in accordance with local development plans. The operation of this programme in Rajasthan, according to an evaluation of this scheme, revealed various limitations and shortcomings. The fixing of limits on wage rate uniformly and arbitrarily for all districts did not work as these actually varied from district to district and from one season to another. Moreover, the scheme implied employment of people continuously for ten months which limited employment to a smaller number of persons. Moreover, it was in conflict with the seasonal pattern of labour activity in agriculture. There were other hurdles like lack of coordination among various departments, conflict with State Plan programme, etc. These difficulties were observed in the operation of the scheme in Maharashtra and other states.

A project called the *Pilot Intensive Rural Employment Project* (PIREP) was sanctioned in 1972-73. The main aim of the project was to obtain information regarding the employment situation in the project areas with regard to seasonal peaks and troughs including information on methodological issues involved in generating employment. It was envisaged that the scheme would create employment for about 2,800 persons in the age-group of 15 to 59 in a block through asset-producing and labour-intensive works. The PIREP was expected to provide valuable information with regard to the basis on which the rural works could be integrated with other development programmes. This helped in formulating the Food for Work programme and later the National Rural Employment Programme.

Food For Work Programme was initiated in 1977-78. It aimed at creation of some additional employment in rural areas on projects designed to create works of durable utility to the rural population. The programme was made possible due to availability of surplus foodgrains stocks as a result of higher level of foodgrains production in the second half of the seventies. In the short period that the programme had been in operation, it succeeded in creating substantial additional employment during lean season periods and particularly in the areas affected by widespread drought in 1978. This programme, however, suffered from many shortcomings at the levels of planning and supervision. The programme envisaged the preparation in each block of a shelf of projects suited to local needs and in correspondence with overall plan priorities. No serious attempt was made in this direction due to uncertainties about the continuance of the programme. In the circumstances State Governments were reluctant to build the necessary technical and administrative support to effectively carry out the programme. For want of financial backing, the tendency was to take up construction of *kaccha* roads and that too through contractors.

The Food for Work Programme has been incorporated in the Sixth Plan and is now called the *National Rural Employment Programme* (NREP). It is being implemented as a centrally sponsored programme with the Centre and States sharing the cost on an equal basis, with Centre providing its share in the form of foodgrains. Due to the depletion in buffer-stocks following the drought in 1979-80, the Centre was unable to contribute its full share in the form of foodgrains. In 1981-82 the payment of wages in the form of foodgrains was restricted to 1 kg per day per person as against the norm of 2 kg per person per day. NREP will take into account the ongoing programmes for resource development like SFDA, MFAL, DPAP, DDP, etc. It will also take care to provide, on a national basis, supplementary employment opportunities to those seeking work during lean periods. In providing employment the use of intermediaries like the contractors is being done away with. Unlike in the past, the programme aims to view employment as an indivisible component of development.

The rural development programmes discussed above were conceived on a piecemeal basis, shifting emphasis from one aspect of rural development to another as they caught the attention of the policy-makers. The programmes, individually and collectively, met with limited success in terms of coverage of the rural population and the extent of benefit provided. These programmes turned out to be inadequate as these did not view the problem of development of the rural people in its totality.

At the State level some of the states have formulated programmes for providing employment and reducing poverty. Mention may be made of the *Employment Guarantee Scheme* (EGS 1972) of Maharashtra and *Antyodaya Scheme* (AS) of Rajasthan, Uttar Pradesh (1977) and some other states. Their objectives have been unexceptionable but as in the case of several rural development programmes, their implementation has left much to be desired. In fact, the EGS which has provided employment on irrigation, road building and soil conservation projects to a very large number of people, of late is showing a few chinks. Apart from availability of technically and financially viable projects on tap, both these programmes need strict vigilance, monitoring and supervision. The objective of the Antyodaya Scheme (AS) was to help five of the poorest families in each village and help them economically according to the needs and choices of the selected families. The progress has been very slow. As the programme has run for a short time, very little information is available about its impact.

Social Welfare Approach

Minimum Needs Programme : It was introduced in 1973 during the Fifth Five Year Plan period. This programme of human resource development emphasises the urgency for providing social services in rural areas like elementary education, health, water supply, roads, electrification, housing for landless, and nutrition. The provision of these facilities, free or at subsidised rates, through public agencies would improve consumption levels of those below the poverty line and thus improve their production efficiency. Information about the progress made is not available on a firm basis. But it is reported that good progress seems to have been made in states like Punjab, Haryana, Maharashtra, Gujarat, Andhra Pradesh, Tamil Nadu and Karnataka. Madhya Pradesh, Rajasthan, Uttar Pradesh, Bihar, Orissa, West Bengal and North-east states have lagged behind considerably.

The Integrated Rural Development Programme

The experience of most of the rural development programmes discussed above has not been quite happy. None of these programmes covered the whole country. Some of them were operating simultaneously in a large number of taluks, sometimes for the same target group. Apart from the problem of overlap, the multiplicity of programmes and agencies created almost intractable problems of coordination, effective monitoring and accounting. As a consequence, in several areas these programmes were reduced to only subsidy distributing programmes without a well thought out and planned approach to the problem of the development of the rural poor and the resources of the area involved.

It is against this background that a single Integrated Rural Development Programme was formulated to cover the whole country during the Sixth Plan period. It is conceived essentially as an anti-poverty programme and is inclusive of all the on-going programmes of rural development. The programme was first introduced on an expanded scale in 1978-79, beginning with 2,300 blocks. By 31 March 1982, it covered all the 5,011 blocks in some form or another. The programme emphasised a family rather than an individual approach. Besides small and marginal farmers, the programme is more specific in regard to agricultural workers, landless labourers and rural artisans. This household programme is a fairly ambitious one, aiming to cover 3,000 families per block from the bottom deciles of the rural population below the poverty line in the five years of the Sixth Plan. There are over 5,000 blocks covering 150 million families to be reached. Apart from investment by the Central and State governments in the programme, credit is required to play a major role in its operation. The size of the problem is enormous and will greatly stretch the manpower and financial resources of banks of all types and other financial institutions. While the Sixth Plan provides for an investment of Rs. 1,750 crores for the programme, the financial institutions, it is estimated, will be required to provide credit anywhere between Rs. 4,000 crores to 4,500 crores.* The latest information shows that in the two years 1980-81 and 1981-82 the coverage of families was about 3.5 million.

In the Section which follows, we discuss some of the major issues involved in the formulation and implementation of rural development programmes.

* 'The Government has decided that the district rural development agencies constituted for implementation of the integrated rural development programme would now also be responsible for the implementation of the national rural employment programme. The district level steering committees set up under the NREP have therefore been dissolved and their functions stand transferred to the DRDAs.' *The Economic Times*, 4 January 1982.

Issues in Rural Development

Decentralised Planning

It is obvious that planning for rural development has to be
undertaken at a fairly decentralised level. Without a firm grasp of
the wide variations in natural endowments, soil and climate, social
and cultural milieu, historical legacies and group alignments, area
planning would lose much of its relevance. At the conceptual level
there is no dispute on this proposition. However, judging by the
experience of the past two decades it seems that the State governments
are none too keen to delegate the planning function to a planning
body at the lower levels. The earlier enthusiasm for the Panchayati
Raj system — with two or three tiers — has cooled down considerably.
A few States, for example Maharashtra and Gujarat, have indeed
made genuine attempts at establishing a decentralised administrative
structure, but in so far as district planning is concerned there has
been a marked erosion of the authority of the Panchayati Raj
institutions. It is difficult to be categorical about the reasons for this
retreat from the commitment to decentralised planning. The reasons
may be technical, administrative or plainly political, meaning
reluctance of the State-level leadership to share authority with a
rival focus of power at the district levels.

It is undoubtedly true that many development projects transcend
district boundaries and as such decision-making pertaining to them
has to remain with the higher level authorities. Such projects
probably consume the bulk of the financial resources of the State
Plan. But even in regard to projects and programmes which are
eminently suitable for local-level planning, it is revealing to find
that quite a few of them are 'centrally sponsored' and partly or
wholly financed by the Centre. This applies particularly to projects
meant for the benefit of the weaker sections — projects such as
SFDA, DPAP, Food for Work, and Minimum Needs like drinking
water and housing for landless workers. Of late, there has been
considerable shedding of central sponsorship, but still there is
quite a bit of it. Why does the Centre choose to sponsor or share in
the financing of projects meant for the weaker sections? Justifying
Central sponsorship of such programmes, Dr. D.T. Lakdawala, the
former Deputy Chairman of the Planning Commission, says :

There are plan priorities where the States should be interested but because of their power structure or because of limited vision or lack of resources they have to be specially spurred and induced. Many of the interesting experiments in agricultural planning like DPAP, SFDA, MFAL and CDA have come through Centrally sponsored schemes.

This is indeed a serious charge against State leadership. Yet, there are numerous examples on record which would justify Lakdawala's distrust. 'A study of the Centrally sponsored schemes would reveal that these have not been used (implemented) by some States and money alloted to them was surrendered even when no sharing was involved.' A recent newspaper report carries the headline 'States pulled up: Poor progress on Water Scheme.' The provocation is provided by a recent study which found that allocation of funds for wells is not being done on the basis of actual local requirements. For instance, in one State it was noticed that forty-one wells were dug in a district which does not have an acute water problem, while only ten wells were dug in a chronically drought-hit district. More seriously, many influential farmers manipulate allocation of wells in their favour and the poorer sections are not getting the attention they deserve.[1]

These are not stray anecdotal illustrations. They represent a pattern which is ubiquitous and poses a serious challenge to the task of decentralised rural development.

A recent editorial in *The Economic Times* ('IRDP in a Mess') puts the blame squarely on the State governments for their lethargy in implementing the Integrated Rural Development Programme. The Central Government subsidises the programme but it is executed by State governments.

The Programme seems to have been halted in its tracks by indecision in all the basic stages of its operation : identification of target groups, creation of infrastructure and finance.... Its failure has its roots in the absence of the infrastructure needed to sustain it. Precious little has been done in this sphere by State Governments.

The editorial goes to the extent of suggesting that 'Blocks where the infrastructure does not exist should have no claim to IRDP funds'.[2]

Why are the States so lethargic in implementing the programme for which adequate funds are provided and clear guidelines are issued in regard to all organisational aspects of implementation, from resource inventory to the composition of district planning bodies? The answer clearly is lack of political will, which is not just psychological, but is rooted in a cool calculation about the dispensability of the poor for the purpose of acquiring and holding political power.

Is it our contention that the political leadership at the Centre is more progressive than the political leadership at the State level, even though the two belong to the same political party? Not necessarily. It is the distance from the scene of action which permits the Central leadership to say popular things about poverty and unemployment, while the leadership which has to implement policies has to weigh the political consequences of hurting the vested interests and helping the poor. The electoral arithmetic would surely suggest the latter choice but when power equations are examined the choice takes a different turn. The dilemma is resolved by resorting to rhetoric of the policy and adjusting action with reality. As one goes below the State level to the district, block and the village, even, the rhetoric may have to be abandoned, for if taken too seriously words would rebound.

That there are genuine limitations to decentralisation in planning is not denied. But even in spheres where decentralisation is feasible and highly desirable, there is marked reluctance on the part of the State governments to share decision-making with local leadership. And it seems to us that political considerations are more dominant than the technical and the administrative in inducing such reluctance. On the other hand, given the rural power structure, the possibility of local leadership proving more reactionary than the state leadership cannot be ruled out.

Primary Objective of Rural Development

If rural development is not to remain an amorphous idea, it should be stressed that the primary objective is eradication of poverty and unemployment and further that this objective can be achieved on a self-sustaining basis only if the structure of ownership of productive assets and skills becomes more egalitarian. To impart operational significance to such an objective, the agencies formulating and implementing programmes of rural development should be told that their performance will be judged by the degree of success achieved in bringing about structural changes necessary for reduction of poverty and not by quantitative achievements under different programmes.

The emphasis on distributive justice will most probably generate an apprehension among the affluent class that such rural development will adversely affect their interests. Consequently they would try to obstruct such development. How can we escape the dilemma posed by such a situation? This is a difficult question to answer. There are of course many programmes which help the disadvantaged without hurting the interest of the rich. Rural roads, house sites for the landless, facilities for drinking water, fair price shops, primary education and health service benefit the entire community and need not give rise to a conflict situation. But then a question arises: would such primarily ameliorative measures help to build ultimately the egalitarian social and economic structure? It would to a certain extent inasmuch as such measures help to reduce the dependence of the disadvantaged group on the affluent sections and build their strength to resist exploitation. Secondly, if additional public investment is made in projects which yield larger than proportionate benefits from incremental income — for example, community irrigation wells — to the disadvantaged group, in due course asset and income distribution would become more egalitarian. It should, however, be admitted that the conflict situation cannot be avoided altogether. Measures will have to be adopted simultaneously to protect the interests of the disadvantaged group. Even such an innocuous measure like regularising and updating of land records has led to violent clashes, as Wolf Ladejinsky and others have brought out. Currently, we are witnessing the atrocities perpetrated by landlords on agricultural labourers demanding the enforcement of the legislation on minimum wages and ensuring freedom from bonded labour. Rural development cannot overlook such situations and continue with the so-called harmonious programmes.

The truth is, in a poor country (in GNP terms) like India, poverty cannot be abolished without restraints on affluence and this would necessitate curtailment of the exploitative hold of the rich and their political allies. The conflict could perhaps be made less virulent if the intellectual leadership would emphasise the fact that each type of economic system derives its sustenance from shared ethical values. An egalitarian economy can be sustained only if acquisition of wealth and political power do not receive the respectability they do.

Integration

Coming down to the mundane level, we shall discuss three issues germane to the theme of rural development. First, the concept of *integrated* rural development. Experience in India and many of the Asian countries which are experimenting with rural development suggests that integration is the most intractable problem in rural development.[3] Integrated development is often interpreted as all-round development embracing all sectors of the economy as well as development of human resources. This of course is necessary and desirable. But mere comprehensiveness does not necessarily make a development plan integrated. Integration involves consideration of horizontal and vertical linkages of individual projects with a view to making them mutually reinforcing and thereby reduce overall material as well as manpower costs and maximise overall benefits and their equitable distribution. Formulation of such a plan will need a planning body at a decentralised (say a district) level with the authority to adjust the sectoral plans of different ministries or departments. Experience shows that each ministry considers its own plan or set of projects as central to development and would in fact expect the plans of other ministries to be coordinated with its plan. After each ministry has independently formulated its own plan, coordination, at best, would be reduced to administrative consultations and bottle-neck removing operation. Integration involves adjustments during the process of formulating an area plan, that is before sectoral plans are finalised. But no ministry at the state level is prepared to delegate the authority to make adjustments in its (rural development) plan to a representative planning body at the district level assisted by a multidisciplinary team of experts. It is understood that the district planning body is not a policy-making body. That privilege belongs to the political leadership at the state level. The major concern of the district level planning body is to examine linkages of sectoral plans proposed by different ministries/departments and make them mutually reinforcing, besides conveying to the ministries their perception of the development potential and the constraints of the area and its people. In any case, the district plan as formulated by the district planning body will be submitted to the State planning body or the cabinet for its final approval. It is this reluctance on the part of State ministries and departments to share decision-making with district level planning bodies that has become a stumbling block both for the concept of decentralisation and for integration in rural development.

Agencies for Rural Development

The progress of rural development has been hindered by indecisiveness as to the appropriate agency that should be entrusted with the responsibility of formulating area development plans. At one time Zilla Parishads, as an elected representative body of the people in the district, were considered most eligible for the task. But there has been an erosion in their planning authority during the last few years.

For example, the Maharashtra State Government has constituted a District Planning and Development Council (DPDC) for each district 'with a view to providing an appropriate planning machinery at the district level for formulating co-ordinated development plans'. An interesting point about the composition of the DPDC is that a Minister in the State Government is designated as the Chairman of each DPDC, the Divisional Commissioner is the Vice-Chairman and the District Collector is the Member-Secretary. The President of the Zilla Parishad is just an ordinary member. One other Minister, plus all members of the Lok Sabha, Rajya Sabha, Vidhan Sabha and Vidhan Parishad elected from the district are members of the DPDC. It can thus be seen that the highest authority for district planning has a preponderant political element and the Zilla Parishad, which under the Panchayati Raj system was supposed to be endowed with the responsibility for district planning, has been reduced to a secondary position. Gujarat has shown more consideration for the Zilla Parishad. Though the Collector is the Chairman of District Planning Body (DPB), the President of the District Panchayat has been given the status of a co-chairman. Gujarat has also recognised the importance of professional advice. One expert from a research institute is chosen for the membership of the District Planning Body.

At this stage one may as well raise a few general questions as to the considerations which should determine the character and composition of the planning body at the district level. Obviously, such a body should have professional competence to formulate the area plan. It should be able to gauge accurately the development potential of the area in the national context, relative costs and benefits of projects, linkages, etc. At the same time, that body should be such as would command the trust and respect of the people which would help to ensure greater acceptability for the plan prepared by it. As things are, the two types of qualifications, by and large, are mutually exclusive. Very few professionals are politically popular and those who possess the knack of eliciting popular political support often lack professional competence. The way out could be to associate with the planning body a multi-disciplinary team of professionals, charged with the responsibility of formulating an 'integrated' plan within the framework of overall policy. But this still leaves open the problem of peoples' participation in the process of formulating the area plan. Will this requirement be met if the professional team holds consultations with the 'people' to ascertain their felt needs and aspirations and also to benefit from their knowledge and experience of the local situation? Apart from the fact that professionals are not particularly adept in establishing the necessary rapport with the people, such consultations may prove more embarrassing than useful. The professionals will be confronted with conflicting and quite often exaggerated demands which they may find impossible to accommodate within the plan resources and objectives. Besides, the district planning authority may have their own ideas of priorities — depending on their class affiliations — or even about the choice of projects and may not endorse the technical team's plan.

In between the professionals and the people — or strictly the politicians who claim to represent the 'people' — comes the bureaucracy or the civil service, which cannot be ignored in the formulation of the rural development plan. After all, whoever formulates the plan, it has to be implemented by the district administrative machinery, at best in collaboration with voluntary agencies (wherever they exist) in some sectors. It is therefore imperative to ensure the involvement of district officers in the preparation of the district plan. There is a point of view that the bureaucracy lacks the motivation, let apart competence, for ushering in rural development, and is therefore totally unsuited for preparing and implementing rural development plans. Whether one accepts this view or not, it would be thoroughly naive to believe that the bureaucracy can be totally excluded from the preparation of plans and much more so from their implementation. Anyway, the choice of the agency has to be made from the following : the bureaucracy, the professionals and voluntary agencies. To this we may add the cadres of political parties. It would be ideal if all these can be brought together if not in the entire process from planning to implementation, at least each one at an appropriate stage of plan formulation and implementation. Such an arrangement presupposes mutual understanding of a high order.

Frankly, the problem of combining professionalism, bureaucracy and peoples' aspirations eludes us. The people, no doubt, know better what is needed and is relevant for the development of the area and its people, but there is no point in glossing over the fact that, by and large, the people in the villages, a block or even a district have little idea about the overall resource constraints, technical feasibilities, and linkages. The administration has its own ideas and rigidities.

Besides, in a community riven by caste and class conflicts and concentration of economic and social power, the planning team and the planning authority charged with the responsibility of eliminating poverty and exploitation would find it extremely difficult to detect the genuine voice of the people. In such a situation, peoples' participation would be no better than catering to the interests of the dominant group.

The enumeration of technical, organisational, social and political hurdles should not mean writing off integrated and egalitarian rural development. Those who believe in the revolutionary overthrow of the present order as the only option should be free to adopt that line of action. But short of that, one should accept the legitimacy of the gradualist course of action, steadily extending the frontier of the possible. There are numerous 'small things' which if accomplished would build the confidence and resistance of the poor. Voluntary agencies are demonstrating this all over the country. If the genuine ones, by which we mean those committed to total change in the social order, are backed by the Government without implicit or explicit preconditions or motives of political gain in the narrow sense of party politics, substantial results can be achieved. If, however, the assumption (not altogether unwarranted) is that the Government itself or the political party in power, is not genuinely interested, whatever be the rhetoric, in the type of rural development we are talking about, the idea of Government support to voluntary agencies working for a basic change in the social order may be dismissed as naive.

Notes

1. *The Times of India*, 15 October 1981.
2. *The Economic Times*, 3 November 1981.
3. *See* M. L. Dantwala, 'Two-Way Planning : Logic and Limitations — A Critical Review of Asian Experience,' 1981 (mimeo, restricted circulation).

T. L. SHANKAR

4 Energy Policy Formulation — The Indian Experience

Suggestions were made in India to formulate a national policy on certain aspects of energy production and consumption long before 'energy policy making' became a fashionable subject for planners and governments and long before the 'energy crisis' of 1973-74. In 1955 Dr. H. J. Bhabha made an estimate, inaccurate though it was in some respects,[1] of India's total energy consumption including wood and dung, offering some possible long-term supply solutions. Earlier still, the Government of India had made some attempts to examine the consumption of non-commercial energy in the household sector with a view to increase the level of availability of fuel-wood, and to reduce the level of the use of cowdung. The Forest Policy Resolution of 1952 stressed *inter alia* the need for 'ensuring progressively increasing supplies of grazing, small wood for agricultural implements and in particular, of firewood to release cattle dung for manure to step up food production.' 'Vanamahotsava' (a celebration of forests) was launched as a scheme of national importance but was progressively devalued into ritualistic monotony until the futility of the efforts became apparent. While such ad hoc attempts were pursued on the one hand, there were a series of scientific attempts on the other to examine the overall energy situation in the context of 'the use of dung as a fuel which deprives the soil of valuable and inexpensive natural nutrients; a disproportionate felling of trees for firewood which disturbs the delicate equilibrium necessary for the preservation of natural balance.' In

1956-58, the Government commissioned an assessment of the local supplies of different domestic fuels in relation to their current demand and future needs so that the development of a rationally planned coal-based processing industry could be studied within the general framework of overall energy needs.[2] This was followed by several studies of some of the elements related to energy policy. All these studies highlighted the need for a comprehensive energy policy. The increasing oil consumption and the slackening of the demand for coal and a rapid rise in the demand for electricity contributed towards repeated attempts to examine the possibility of evolving an overall energy strategy.

The most important efforts in this direction resulted in the following three documents : *Report of the Energy Survey Committee* (ESC), 1965; *Report of the Fuel Policy Committee* (FPC), 1974; and *Report of the Working Group on Energy Policy* (WGEP), 1979.

This paper examines the details of the energy policy suggested in these reports as well as the analytic approach adopted in the formulation of this policy. It also discusses the limitations of the policy analysis and the causes for the non-adoption by the government of a comprehensive energy policy till now.

Report of the Energy Survey Committee

The Energy Survey Committee (ESC) was appointed in January 1963 by the Ministry of Irrigation and Power to provide the Government of India with the basic material for development planning in the field of energy up to 1981. The terms of reference of the Committee specified that the Committee should give consideration, among other things, to the use of energy in rural areas. The committee consisted (during the major part of its work) of eighteen members and was headed by a Secretary to the Government of India and two foreign experts — one the chairman of a large power company in the USA, and the other a university professor from the UK who was its co-chairman. The Committee also had two more foreign experts from Europe as members. The rest were Indians, drawn from the Planning Commission and government agencies connected with power, oil, coal and atomic energy. The Committee was advised by a group of three, of whom two were members of the Planning Commission and the third was the Chairman of the Atomic Energy

Commission. A Working Group consisting of two consultants of the USAID under the guidance of the British co-chairman provided the basic studies on which the conclusions and recommendations were formulated.

The ESC made a lasting contribution to the evolution of energy policy in India by its efforts to collect all available energy data, and organising the data in a form amenable to policy analyses. The vexed question of arrogating energy under the 'numeraire' was ingeniously resolved by evolving the 'coal replacement' units — each type or source of energy being measured in terms of the coal that it replaces, when both the original source and coal are used in appliances or equipment and with thermal efficiencies that are likely to be employed in practice. However, most of the policy prescriptions, other than the emphasis on the use of coal as the primary source of energy, suggested by the ESC were based on an inadequate examination of Indian conditions.

Scenarios of Growth

	Growth Rates of (per cent)		
	GDP	*Industrial*	*Agricultural*
Case I	7	10	3.1
Case II	6	8.5	2.5
Case III	5	7.0	3.9

The major concern of the ESC was to forecast energy demand up to 1981. The ESC estimated (as a broad check on the results obtained by other methods) the probable aggregate energy demand, assuming that the economy would grow at certain rates, using the observed past relationship between rate of growth, total energy consumption and national income, the relationship between commercial energy consumption outside the household sector, and the industrial production function. Accepting the 'Notes on Perspective Development 1960-61 to 1975-76' provided by the Planning Commission, the growth of GDP at 7 per cent per year in the period 1960-75 was taken as Case I scenario of growth. However two other 'cases' of lower GDP growth rates were also used for projecting energy demand.

The demand for total energy was projected on the assumption that total energy would increase in rough proportion to national income in the future as in the past. The growth in the demand for commercial energy outside the domestic sector was expected to increase in the future almost proportionately to the growth of industrial production

The sectoral demand for energy was projected separately for transport, agriculture and household consumption as well as estimated and aggregated. The sectoral demand for transport was estimated using the projection of demand drawn up by an independent study made by the World Bank Mission on the 'Transport Sector', which was assumed to be equivalent to Case I. Estimates for Case II and Case III were derived using certain assumptions of transport demand declining with GNP growth rate.

Energy consumption in the agricultural sector was assumed to grow at the same pace as it did in the past for Case I.

Household sector energy consumption was projected through a more detailed exercise using the assumption that per capita energy consumption in the household for rural and urban population would increase slowly with income and that the total increase in per capita consumption will be reflected as demand for commercial energy.

The energy demand for the industrial sector was projected by separately forecasting the demand for six major energy-using industries — namely, iron and steel, non-ferrous metals, fertilisers, heavy chemicals, cement and textiles — and treating all other industries as one group under 'other industries'. The ESC accepted most of the existing targets (for the six industries) as corresponding to Case I.

In the coal sector the ESC had made a set of recommendations — all based on the projection of growth of the steel industry made by the Steel Ministry. The Committee supported the two-product washery as the solution for obtaining coking coal of requisite quality for the steel industry; it had to deal with the disposal of enormous quantities of by-product coal from the washeries. It, therefore, affirmed that 'by-product coking coals, if suitably priced and transported in closed circuit train loads, can meet the requirements of coal for thermal electricity stations and other purposes at points far beyond most of the outlying coal fields that the Government has proposed to develop.' The Committee suggested that the wisdom of developing in the near future some of the outlying coal fields be re-examined.

In the oil sector, the ESC rightly emphasised the need to take measures which will make the use of indigenous fuels more attractive as compared to imported oil products. The Committee recommended, somewhat inexplicably, that 'the longer-term repercussions of a dieselisation policy on the balance of payments will need to be considered.' While drawing attention to the growing incongruence between the pattern of consumption of oil products and the potential out-turn of Indian refineries, the Committee recommended that 'more consideration needs to be given to the wisdom of the present taxation policies which tend to discourage the consumption of gasoline (petrol) and encourage the consumption of diesel oils' and that 'it is probably in the national interest to encourage gasoline consumption in all forms of transport.'

Carefully reviewing energy consumption and supply in the domestic (household) sector, the ESC made a farsighted recommendation that 'immediate and active measures be taken jointly by the Government of India and State Governments to formulate and implement a policy for expanding the growth of quick growing species for use as firewood'. In addition, it suggests that 'measures be taken to produce and popularise the use for domestic purposes of commercial fuels based on indigenous coal supplies'.

In the power sector, the recommendations of the ESC were primarily based on a detailed assessment of the working conditions of electricity boards. Influenced, however, by the steel production projections, the ESC considered, as an option, steam power stations based on by-product coal for most locations. Nuclear power generation was 'already competitive' in certain locations with coal power stations and the Committee felt that 'the decision to build nuclear stations should be reached on purely economic grounds'. 'Rural electrification,' on the other hand, was to be regarded more as a social service than as an economic enterprise and possibly financed in part from general revenue.

Report of the Fuel Policy Committee

The Energy Policy Committee's report was available to Government in 1965. Yet various developments in the economic field during 1965-1970 made it difficult to pursue a consistent policy in the energy sector. It was also the period when the price of oil in the international market was declining in real terms and the use of coal was being phased out in many countries of the world. There was an understandable reluctance on the part of the Indian industry to use coal, and oil imports registered a high rate of increase. The government had to think of an overall solution to these problems and a committee was set up to survey the fuel resources and to recommend and outline a fuel policy. The terms of reference of the Fuel Policy Committee were to :

1. undertake a survey of fuel resources and the regional pattern of their distribution;
2. study the present trends in exploitation and use of fuels;
3. estimate perspective of demand by sectors (in particular the transport, industry, power generation industry and domestic fuel) and by regions;
4. study the efficiency in the use of fuel and recommend :
   (a) the outline of a national fuel policy for the next fifteen years;
   (b) a pattern of consumption and measures, fiscal and otherwise, which would help the best use of available resources; and
   (c) the measures and agencies to promote the optimum efficiency in use of fuel.

The Committee consisted of eleven members, including the Chairman, who was a member of the Planning Commission, and besides had a secretary. Of the eleven members, two represented the private coal industry, two were academics and the remaining six represented agencies dealing with electricity (CWPC), petroleum (Institute of Petroleum), atomic energy (Department of Atomic Energy), Railways and ONGC and Fuel Research (CFRI). The Committee commenced its work in early 1971 and drew up an interim report (*Towards Fuel Policy for the Seventies*) which covered the period up to 1978-79 and was submitted to the Government to help in the formulation of the energy policy to be incorporated in the Fourth Five Year Plan. This was given in May 1972. But the draft final report was ready by the end 1973 but in the meanwhile there were developments in the international oil market in October and December 1973. The Committee was induced to re-examine the report in the light of the increased price of oil and the final report was completed in April 1974.

One of the interesting features of this Committee was that it consisted entirely of Indian experts and all relevant studies were carried out in the institutions within the country without any outside help. Secondly, in the official policy committee this consisted mostly of technical experts barring representatives of the coal industry. While the broad structure of the report of the Fuel Policy Committee was modelled on the *Energy Survey Committee Report,* the methodology and approach to analysis in this report were different from the ESC in several respects.

The Fuel Policy Committee accepted the perspective of economic growth as projected by the Planning Commission but attempted three energy scenarios which were claimed to be consistent with the given rate of economic growth. The three patterns of energy consumption growth detailed in the report represented different degrees of substitutions of oil by coal/electricity considered possible in the period.

Case I represented the level of energy demand derived assuming that the relative prices of fuels will continue to be the same in future as in the past and that the technology shifts would follow the same trends as in the past.

Case III gives the likely pattern of energy demand if the relative prices remain the same but all measures indicated in increasing the fuel efficiency and substitution of oil products by other fuels which are viable and desirable on techno-economic considerations are implemented to the full extent.

Case II represented an intermediate level of substitution between Case I and Case III and was considered by the Committee as the most likely configuration of demand.

The potential for fuel substitution was identified by computing the economic viability of different substitution options making certain price assumptions regarding the relevant fuels. The price of oil was assumed to be $5 per barrel and of coal the same as in 1972 for the initial studies on which the interim report of 1974 was based. In the light of the increase in oil prices during 1973, the Committee repeated the calculations assuming the price of oil to be $12 per barrel, while formulating the final report.

Case I forecast of energy demand which assumes no substitution of coal for oil was made using three methods : (a) the time trend; (b) regression models; and (c) endure or material-balance method. The forecast was made for the economy as a whole and then for different sectors. Results obtained by different methods were harmonised using the Committee's best judgement.

Certain interesting and important issues were analysed by using mathematical models, like the question of the location and capacity of refineries and the choice of fertiliser feed-stocks.

The Committee's approach has been determined largely by its perception that a meaningful energy plan should form an integral part of a national plan. The availability of energy, according to the Committee, was a necessary but not sufficient condition to sustain economic growth. Basing its views on economic studies the Committee, with its technical expertise, has painstakingly elaborated its methodology in the *Report* itself.

The Committee's major contribution has been its unequivocal declaration that coal should be considered as the primary source of energy in the country in the next few decades and that the energy policy in the country should be designed on this basic premise. The Committee urged for a synchronised investment in the transport and coal sectors, in view of the locations of coal deposits in the country. An adequate transport system is required to take the coal to the points of demand. The Committee recommended the development of all the various coal fields including those in the far south, but underlined the need for careful advance planning in respect of each one of them. This was a reversal of the recommendation of ESC. The Committee also differed from the ESC in its recommendation of the three product washeries considering the problems of utilising the by-product from two product washeries. To conserve coking coal and to provide a coal based domestic fuel, two plants to make low temperature carbonised coke were suggested. It also visualised the setting up of coal dumps in major industrial areas. In terms of the technology of coal production, it advocated an appropriate technology policy for the country as well as standardisation of equipment so as to develop self-reliance in the coal sector.

The Fuel Policy Committee recommended that there should be an oil policy designed with the specific objectives of :

1. Reducing the quantity of oil products to be imported;
2. Reducing the total foreign exchange expenditure on energy imports; and
3. Improving the security of supplies.

The FPC, like other committees, recommended the acceleration of the oil exploration programme. Based on the studies using mathematical models, the Committee made a far-reaching recommendation for the refinery sector. It was that secondary processing facilities should be established in most of the refineries as in the future there would be a surplus of fuel oil with relatively lower prices which could be used as feed-stock for secondary processing. Concluding that coal, fuel oil and naphtha should all be used as feed-stocks for fertiliser production at different locations based on the opportunity cost of these fuels at the respective location, the Committee had set out in detail the methodology to be used in determining the feed-stock choice.

In the electricity sector the *Report* strongly stressed the need for improving the plant utilisation factor and made a number of technical recommendations to achieve better utilisation of the total power system capability. The Committee estimated that the nuclear plant capacity would increase in the first ten years to 1900 MW but in the next seven years it could increase to 8620 MW. The Committee emphasised the need for increasing the availability of uranium in the country by taking up further exploration for nuclear fuels. It also highlighted the importance of developing indigenous industrial back-up for the nuclear power programme.

The household sector was studied on the lines of the ESC but more specific recommendations were made : for taking up afforestation programmes and social forestry programmes and planting of trees besides roads, canals and railways. The biogas programme was strongly supported.

The Committee felt, as far as energy pricing was concerned, that the costs of energy production should be covered by a reasonable rate of return while fixing the price of energy products. There was no case for subsidising energy for consumers other than the poor in the domestic sector. This was to reduce the use of forest fuels which have a high social cost. International parity price for crude but independent domestic price for products was recommended. For pricing electricity, the Committee recommended that the tariff should be designed to discriminate adequately the use of power between peak periods and off-peak periods. While recognising the need for supplying power to the agricultural sector at reasonable and low rates, the Committee felt that better utilisation of the connected loads in the agricultural sector like rostering of agricultural loads should be organised so as to reduce the cost of power supply to agriculturists.

The Committee recognised the need for developing institutions within the Government to deal with energy issues in a comprehensive manner but shied away from making definite recommendations in this regard.

The Government's response to the Report of the Fuel Policy Committee was quite interesting. All the recommendations were accepted in principle but the only perceptible change was the creation of a Ministry of Energy, merging the departments of Coal and Power. Petroleum, however, was left out. Within the Planning Commission the work on matters of energy, i.e., coal, electricity, oil and renewable energy, were integrated under an Adviser (Energy). A decision was taken to set up two low temperature carbonisation plants. The Government also took prompt action in setting up secondary processing facilities in many refineries.

Report of the Working Group on Energy Policy

The next major attempt in energy policy formulation was setting up the Working Group on Energy Policy in December 1977 with a view to

carry out comprehensive review of the present energy situation in the light of recent developments, both within the country and outside, to develop a perspective for the next five to fifteen years and to recommend appropriate policy measures for optimal utilisation of available energy resources including non-conventional sources of energy.

The terms of reference of the Working Group were :

1. To estimate the perspective energy demand in the different sectors of the economy and regions of the country by 1982-83 and a decade thereafter;
2. To survey the present and prospective supplies of energy;
3. To recommend measures for optimum use of available energy resources; and
4. To outline the national energy policy for the next five years, fifteen years and the longer-term conservation policy.

The Committee was headed by the Secretary in the Department of Energy and had three representatives from the Planning Commission and one representative each from the Central Electricity Authority, the ministries of Energy, Coal, Oil and Science and Technology, one technologist each representing coal, oil, electricity and atomic energy, and two academics. The Committee considered the possibility of limiting its work to a review of the findings and recommendations of the report of the Fuel Policy Committee but decided that in view of the steep escalation in oil prices that had taken place since then and the new difficulties experienced in resolving energy issues, a complete re-examination and reassessment of all the issues would be desirable. Though the terms of reference were to set a time horizon of fifteen years for analysing the issues, the Working Group felt that the period should be extended to AD 2000 in order to make a meaningful analysis of the energy issues, especially those relating to new energy technologies. The Working Group pointed out that its approach was influenced by the fact that even during the period when the studies were being made for the Working Group, the international oil market situation changed dramatically due to the disruption of supplies from Iran.

Since the Working Group kept a horizon for the study which was over twenty years, it was unable to get any perspective of economic growth from the Planning Commission or other government agencies; the perspectives developed by the latter were for very short horizons. The Working Group, therefore, adopted a scenario approach and tried to project the energy demand in the household, agricultural and industrial sectors visualising a scenario of growth which would be in keeping with the trends not only of economic development but of Government policies in the past. The demand derived as a result of this was called the Reference Level Forecast (RLF). The Committee then made a study of policy variations in the energy sector and energy-related sectors whose major thrust was to be :

— curbing of consumption of oil to the minimum possible level;
— conserving the use of energy by increasing the efficiency of its utilisation;
— reducing the overall energy demand by lowering the intensity of energy consumption in the economy particularly in the industrial sector;

— an increased reliance on renewable energy resources; and
— a reappraisal of our economic development strategies,
   especially those elements of the strategy which have a direct
   link to energy consumption like technology choice, location
   policies, urban growth, and mechanisation in agriculture,
   with reference to the new awareness of the energy supply
   and demand in future.

The consequences of these policies on the demand for energy were
quantified and the projections obtained in RLF were modified.
The resultant modified energy demand obtained on this basis was
given out as Optimal Level Forecast (OLF).

The methodology adopted for demand forecasting in energy was
innovative for a government report. The energy demand in each
sector was postulated as dependent on a few given parameters and
these parameters were a function of technology and Government
policies. Using these parameters, forecasts up to the year A D 2000
were made. For example, the demand for energy in agriculture is
dependent on the needs for tillage, transport and water-lifting. The
energy demand for water-lifting is a function of the number of
irrigation wells in operation, the number electrified and worked by
diesel engines. Taking the total quantity of sub-soil water available
in the country, the upper bound for the number of wells was
computed. The average rates at which new wells were sunk,
electrified or 'dieselised' were derived from past data. Using the
plans for investment in the agricultural sector, rural electrification
and diesel engine production and the official policy towards rural
electrification, the energy demand was computed. For tillage and
transport in agriculture, it was assumed that the determining variable
was the number of tractors in use; projections were made on the
number of tractors which would be introduced in each year in
future.

This method of forecasting attempted to relate energy demand to
Government policy and as such is of greater value to the policy-
makers.

The Group's broad conclusion was that there was great potential
for improvement in the efficiency of energy use; however, as such
improvements would require replacement of capital stock which
was currently in use, the targets for efficiency increase would
gradually pick up over time if appropriate policies were adopted

and were followed by the installation of more efficient equipment over time. The Group concluded that the pattern of growth in the industrial sector that has been pursued during the past three decades was based on the assumption of continuous availability of cheap energy. The Group felt that within the overall industrial production targets, there was too large a share of intensive electricity consuming industries. The Group therefore recommended that there should be a serious consideration of the measures to restructure the industrial strategy so that the sector could move towards a lower energy intensity.

The Group deviated from the pattern of the earlier reports and considered non-commercial energy *not* as significant only in the household sector, but as more relevant for examination of rural energy issues. It suggested that agricultural waste and firewood should be increasingly used. This recommendation is at variance with the earlier reports inasmuch as those reports assumed and accepted the gradual phasing out of non-commercial energy. The WGEP has argued that agricultural waste was expected to increase in quantity due to increased agricultural production and that supplies of fuel-wood could be augmented through forest plantation. Given these, there is a case for not reducing the level of use of non-commercial energy.

The major thrust of the policy prescriptions is towards reducing the consumption of commercial energy per unit of increase in GDP. While conceding that more studies are required in this regard, the Committee has made the recommendation that detailed studies of the specific operations which should be mechanised in agriculture or industry, and the type of technology to be chosen and the extent of desirable urbanisation, should be undertaken so that the overall economic growth strategy could be consistent with the current expectations of increasing scarcity and rising prices of all energy products in general and oil in particular. The Group has drawn attention to the fact that though India's oil requirement is very small compared to the international trend in that commodity, in the nineties, when oil production declines, India may not have the leverage to obtain even this limited quantity in the competitive market. The Group urged that the nation should prepare for the contingency of not being able to import oil needed even at the reduced levels recommended in the *Report.* In the case of coal and hydroelectricity the recommendations of the EPC were reiterated.

The Group has also ventured to make a more comprehensive recommendation towards reorganisation of the institutional arrangements for energy sector management as it was felt that the energy policy formulation and implementation should be a continuous exercise in the new context.

Comparative Evaluation of Energy Policy Studies

It is interesting that though the subject of the three studies was energy policy, the initiative to set them up came from three different departments of the Government of India and the focus of each Report seems to vary accordingly. The Energy Survey Committee (ESC) was set up by the Ministry of Irrigation and Power and its report is oriented towards the supply of electricity. Sponsored by the Department of Coal, the Fuel Policy Committee (FPC) highlights the importance of coal, recommending a supply strategy based on the utilisation of coal as the substitution fuel for other forms of energy. The Working Group on Energy Policy (WGEP) was set up by the Planning Commission and has taken a more balanced view of the overall energy needs and dealt only with the broader aspects of Energy sector management.

The composition of the committees has also influenced the scope and the analytical approach of these reports. In the case of ESC, the work was done mostly by expatriate advisers and the interaction with the Indian officials was at a very high level. The Committee, as a whole, met only a few times with long intervals. Except in the case of power generation requirements and non-commercial energy computations, the methodology adopted was very simple and no better than what could have been done in the concerned ministries of the Government. But some of the basic assumptions on which the major policy prescriptions were made were questionable even at that time. There was no attempt to examine these in depth. In many instances, the *Report* states that judgements have been used without explaining the basis of these judgements. The FPC was manned entirely by Indians and was headed by a brilliant economist and also had an independent secretariat. Most of its members were technical experts. The recommendations of the FPC were derived from fairly detailed exercises. It has also the merit of attempting to explain in its *Report* the methodology adopted and its limitations.

The WGEP consisted of officials at a higher level (except the Chairman) and had a short period to complete the report. It has attempted to go beyond the terms of reference in respect of the time horizon and issues, but has not undertaken studies in depth as was done in the case of the FPC. The fact that some of the members of the WGEP were earlier members of the FPC had made it possible to draw on the earlier studies in arriving at the policy conclusions.

In terms of substance, ESC and FPC perceived energy policy in Inida as essentially a supply-oriented policy. The energy needs of the future were taken as being defined somewhat immutably by a specified rate and pattern growth of economy. The ESC took three levels of economic growth and calculated for each one a unique composition of fuel demand. The FPC, however, had assumed that the level of total energy required would be determined by the rate of total growth of the economy but the composition of fuel consumption could change by adopting different techniques and policies. Only the WGEP had felt that the same level and patterns of growth of the economy could be achieved by different levels of energy demand if certain economic policies and energy related policies are adopted. In effect, the policies of the ESC, FPC and the WGEP were, respectively, supply, substitution and conservation-oriented.

All the three reports had to consider that the energy sector policies depended on policies adopted for the energy-using sectors, namely, household, agriculture, industry and transport, and there were no clear articulations of even the current policies, let alone the long-term policies in these sectors. The time horizon for a meaningful energy policy is longer than that for most of the other sectors. The reports had desisted from attempting to visualise drastic changes in the policies of the energy-using sectors without having recourse to the necessary data and skills. The WGEP has attempted to overcome this in an ingenious way projecting sectoral scenarios which are based on different policies that could be adopted for each sector.

All the reports give the indication that while the power and coal departments appear to have participated more fully in the work of the committees, the agencies concerned with oil and nuclear power have not done so. A large amount of information and data available with the Ministry of Petroleum does not appear to have been reflected in these reports, though the WGEP has been able to capture the broad trend of work of the Petroleum Ministry. In the case of nuclear power, all these reports show a tendency to shy away from a deeper and relevant analysis of the issues involved. The ESC had accepted without examination the costs furnished by the Department of Atomic Energy and based its recommendations on those figures. The FPC seems to have compromised its judgement with the aspirations of DAE in projecting a very rapid growth for nuclear power beyond the period 1982-83 without substantiating the rationale for this. The section on nuclear power in the WGEP *Report* reads like a public relations brochure of the Department of Atomic Energy and does not really examine any of the basic issues. It is obvious that the agencies concerned with the nuclear power programme are being treated as a somewhat independent subsector in the energy sector, though for long-term energy supply solutions it is of utmost importance that these be integrated.

The Government response to the recommendations of the three reports is also interesting. Formally, the Government had accepted in principle almost all the recommendations of the reports. The Energy Survey Committee had given its *Report* at a time when there was no wide understanding of the energy issues in managing economic development. It is not surprising that the ESC *Report* had very little influence on the energy supply agencies. The agencies concerned with power relied on the recommendations for projecting the resource requirements. But the Government accepted the data base collected by the ESC and used it in all further studies. Secondly, the power projection methodology and procedure, as suggested by the ESC, was accepted and the Annual Power Survey Scheme was implemented. The Government, somewhat inexplicably, accepted the ESC's recommendation for the two-product washery. The FPC recommendation had a sound impact on the energy sector when their emphasis on the importance of coal was accepted by the Government; this was partly due to the timeliness of the *Report* which came out in the year 1985. The Ministry of Energy was formed by the Government but with only coal and electricity as the two departments; the Planning Commission created the post of Adviser (Energy) dealing with all energy issues. The three-product washeries became the rule in the coal sector and the petroleum industry started seriously examining the potential for setting up secondary processing facilities. Two large low temperature carbonisation plants were approved by the Government. The Working

Group had led to initiating a study in different departments of possible energy conservation efforts; though fragmented in approach it is a good starting point. While the recommendations of all these committees were accepted almost in full and in principle, the required follow-up action has been inadequate. No implementation cell or other devices have been observed in any department. While reports are commissioned on the ground that the energy related issues should be viewed in a comprehensive manner, the same anxiety does not seem to be there while pursuing action on the reports received.

Limitations notwithstanding, India's efforts to formulate an energy policy can be reckoned as the most serious effort made by any developing country in this direction. While the results of the reports discussed might be inadequate, the whole exercise has deepened the perception of institutions and agencies concerned with energy-related issues

Notes

1. 'The Role of Atomic Power in India and its Immediate Possibilities,' *Peaceful Uses of Atomic Energy*, Vol. 1, United Nations, 1956. Paper originally presented at the 'First Geneva Conference on the Peaceful Uses of Atomic Energy' in 1955.
2. National Council of Applied Economic Research, *Domestic Fuels in India*, Delhi, 1959.

G. GIRIDHAR • J. K. SATIA •
ASHOK SUBRAMANIAN

5 Policy Studies in Health and Population — A Review

I. Introduction

Since independence three factors seem to have dominated the population scene. Mortality decline, which began sometime before independence, has continued although recently its rate is much less. There is some dispute about what has led to such decline — nutrition and general development or public health measures; but both are likely to have contributed to it.

Fertility also has begun to decline; the most recent estimate of the birth rate is about 34 per thousand compared to more than 40 per thousand in 1951. There is no agreement about the magnitude of the contribution made by the family planning programme to the decline in the birth rate. As a consequence of the differential decline in mortality and fertility, the population has increased considerably from 360 million in 1951 to about 680 million in 1981. Finally, the percentage of urban population in the total has been increasing, somewhat slowly but steadily. In 1951 the urban population was 17.3 per cent but it had increased to about 20 per cent by 1981. What the percentage may not reveal is that the number of people living in urban areas has increased from about 62 million in 1951 to about 136 million in 1981.

In this paper we propose to review the policy studies in the area of population. The United Nations defines population policies as

.... measures and programmes designed to contribute to the achievement of economic, social, demographic, political and other collective goals through affecting critical demographic variables, namely the size and growth of the population, its geographic distribution (national and international) and its demographic characteristics ....

This definition is rather broad, in that it defines government population policies as those actions of the government that affect or attempt to affect the balance between births, deaths and the migration of human beings.

The purpose of the review is to briefly present major conceptual frameworks and methodological approaches used by the policy studies and their influence on the development of policies and programmes. The review is stylistic in nature, for it does not attempt to be comprehensive, rather it is limited to studies which are judged by the authors to be important ones. Second, as it was not clear what attributes would lead to classifying a study as a policy study, we have interpreted the term broadly to mean policy relevant studies. The distinction between policies, strategies and programmes is also not always well defined. One can view the policy as a system made up of two sets of inter-related elements — objectives and instruments — both of which are necessary for a policy to exist. But in practice, several difficulties arise in the use of this definition. The 'health goals' are only being set now but health programmes have existed for a long time. Similarly, the first formal statement of population policy was made in 1976 but the national family planning programme had been launched in 1952. The clarity of objectives and instruments in terms of migration to date remain unclear. We have therefore used many indicators of policies which include *inter alia* goals, programmes, laws and statement of intentions in plan documents.

We discuss studies in the area of health, fertility-influencing and migration-influencing policies in Section II through IV respectively. The review leads to an identification of neglected policy issues, approaches and methodologies and some suggestions on how these gaps can be filled. Section V concludes the paper with suggestions on strengthening the policy formulation processes.

II. *Health Policy Analysis*

Three-and-a-half decades have gone by since the Health Survey and Development Committee, popularly known as the Bhore Committee, offered its prescription of good health to a nation in the fever of a recently achieved independence. Many other 'doctors' have since been consulted, the last of them being the Working Group on Health For All by AD 2000, set up in July 1980. They have, in turn, offered their diagnoses and prescriptions. Like the proverbial patient — the bane of all physicians and presumably of policy advisers — who does not 'obey' all the doctor's orders, the government and its policy-makers have accepted some of the treatment, ignored some and have possibly even forgotten a part.

It is with the doctor — or the series of doctors — and the process of their diagnoses and prescriptions that we are concerned in this paper. Our aim is to consider the approach and method pursued by various study groups in understanding and analysing the health situation and in recommending action to policy-makers. The policies themselves and their impact on health are not the focus of the paper, and are viewed only in relation to the framework or methodology adopted by a study group.

The terrain is risky because it is mainly through documents and commentaries that this review has been attempted. For every written statement, there may be many unwritten views and analyses. Detailed interviews with some of the participants of the study groups would surely have enriched the review and, time and cost permitting, perhaps this can be undertaken as the next step.

Building a Hierarchy : The Early Years

Independent India had the benefit of the first comprehensive study of the country's health status in the Bhore Committee report of 1946. One of its two objectives was to survey the health scene in the mid-1940s. On the basis of this survey, it was to make recommendations for the evolution of a national health care system. Over three years, the twenty-six member committee, which included six non-physicians, worked with five advisory groups organised from among its members. Two of the groups or sub-committees concentrated on the primary services in health care (Medical Relief and Public Health) and the other three on supportive functions such as education and research. Some 450 individual or organisational depositions and 200 memoranda were received by the Committee whose mobility was constrained only by the war conditions.

The Committee stressed that suitable housing, sanitation and safe drinking water were primary conditions for good health and health was not to be equated with health services nor with 'illness-care'. As for the services, effective means for the early detection, treatment and prevention of epidemic and communicable diseases were to be their focus. Hence the Committee's plea for social medicine, to be offered through a front line team of doctor, nurse, social worker, nutritionist, public health engineer and statistician *and* a hierarchy of area-based health services ranging from a primary unit, a secondary unit for a cluster of primaries and the district headquarters hospital. The beneficiary was identified clearly as the 'tiller of the soil' and the Committee drew pointed attention to his plight. Specific groups — such as, women and children and industrial workers — were also to be paid special attention. Community involvement was to be sought through village health committees and the national health programme was to be led by popular elected representatives of the people.

It is remarkable that the *diagnosis* of the need of the country in terms of rural health care (minimum health needs for all) and the *response* in terms of social medicine with peoples' involvement were articulated long before primary health care and community health became prominent in the planner's repertoire.

Notwithstanding its vision and the consideration given to various aspects of policy and strategy — such as, the target group, types of service, the organisation of services, the manpower and other resources required for the organisation, the necessary leadership and relations between the centre and provinces, the need for a pilot project (Delhi was suggested for trial), the need for sequencing (targets for the first ten years and for a longer period) — the report was mainly useful as a framework for health services organisation and was later found to be 'too optimistic' (Mudaliar, 1961) and 'unrealistic' (Rao, 1966).

It is difficult to pin down the critical factors which may have led to the somewhat unrealistic expectations of the Bhore Committee. Some of them would surely have been the *assumptions* underlying the collective analysis of the group largely based on each member's experiences. In fact, the dissenting note on the item of discontinuing the licentiate course complains that the 'decisions of bodies like the Health Survey and Development Committee are often taken not so much on facts garnered or their evaluation but on ideologies which dominate the minds of the members' (Bhore, 1946, Ch. XVIII). The bureaucratic administrative model was to provide the organisational framework. While this would offer a regionalised *structure*, it was not clear how regionalised *strategies* would be evolved. It is quite likely that the performance of the state directorates and the district agencies did not encourage those who would have supported greater decentralisation in planning. Later, the compulsions of unifying a diverse nation may have encouraged further centralisation.

A second assumption relates to the technology. While the diagnosis mentioned community-based problems and the need for minimum needs, the response in terms of the technology of health care was along familiar western lines. The ratios of hospital beds and professionals per population unit (e.g., two beds for 1000 in ten years) indicate the choice of a type of health care technology, which did not seem to have invited adequate deliberation.

The third major assumption relates to resources. Although there is appreciation of the constraints, finally desirability rather than feasibility seems to have won the day. Tax revenues were to be the only source, users' capacity to pay for services being difficult to determine. But competing interests for the nation's revenues seem to have been underestimated.

The assumptions and the gaps in the Committee's efforts are also a *likely product of the bewildering size of the canvas*. The entire range of planning instruments, from goals to methods and procedures, are touched on. For instance, with reference to medical education, the principle of the social physician as well as a detailed curricula for medical education are discussed. There is even a section on co-education! Thus, at a time when policies were not quite clear, the staggering range of advice on objectives, strategies, programmes and procedures may have been far too overwhelming.

The Bhore Committee — as many others — seems to have approached the study more in the role of a policy-maker than an analyst; that, too, a policy-maker cast in a judicial mould since the process used — oral and written evidence, depositions, investigatory field trips and scope for collegial dissent leading to 'verdicts' of plans — appears to leave little room for further debate. The question then arises whether the desire of a Committee to present a final 'consensus set' of recommendations forecloses the chance of offering alternatives which policy-makers and the people can discuss and debate.

Some of the assumptions and approaches of the Bhore Committee were also the basis of the deliberations of the Health Survey and Planning Committee, popularly known as the Mudaliar Committee. Appointed in 1959, the sixteen-member group was to review the progress since the Bhore Committee, assess the implementation of the First and Second Plan health measures and make recommendations for the future. It worked through six sub-committees — two service related (medical relief and public health), two problem-specific (communicable diseases and population) and two functional (education/research and stores).

The first two five-year Plans had provided an outlay of about Rs. 415 crores or about 5.5 per cent of the total public sector outlay, in spite of the Central Council of Health asking for 10 per cent. The Committee was torn between continued expansion and consolidation of facilities already set up. It chose the latter and wished to improve the quality of services by strengthening the district hospital.

Wrestling with the problems encountered in the implementation of the two Plans appears to have given the Mudaliar Committee a much greater *operational focus.* It talked of the importance of 'arrangements for medical care of the people', not merely the provision of hospital beds. The shortage of professional staff led to its recommendation of 'conserving the more qualified for tasks they have to do'. Paramedical training was considered seriously by the group. Some operational problems were identified (lack of linkage between MCH and school activities) and an organisational solution (Health Advisory Board) offered. One of the subcommittees was formed around the materials management function — Drug and Medical Stores. Free care no longer seemed feasible; plan outlays also left much to be desired — hence an attempt was made to examine the policy of raising funds through a cess, fee for service, insurance, etc. Thus the *historical context provided a focus different from that of Bhore.*

Issues such as revenue raising and the relationship between general and special programmes (vertical unipurpose programmes were considered a myopic response) offered good scope for tackling policies, both operational and strategic. Again, the very width of the canvas — the nation's health services — may have been an obstacle to pursue some of these in depth.

A Committee's composition can encourage it to analyse a particular topic in depth. For instance, both Bhore and Mudaliar paid a great deal of attention to medical education. The number of doctors in the committees and the perception of the doctor as the health team leader would have contributed to the keen interest in this topic. At the same time, apart from the contextual demands of operations management posing certain larger questions, the presence of a significant number of medical administrators (twelve out of sixteen members) and the absence of popular representatives in the Mudaliar Committee may have led to a lesser interest in the area of community participation and popular leadership.

Strengthening Linkages : The Middle Years

In its broad aims, the Third Plan (1960-61 to 1965-66) reflected the concerns of increasing coverage and improving the 'supply side' of health services. The removal of shortages and deficiencies in institutional facilities, personnel distribution, equipment and personnel for programmes in communicable diseases, in drinking water supply schemes and urban drainage were its goals. This concern continued in the Fourth Plan (1969-74) which took upon itself the task of implementing the Mudaliar Committee's recommendations. Even the modified one bed per 1,000 population by the end of the Fifth Plan period seemed ambitious given that only about 4 per cent of the Plan public sector outlay was allocated for health.

The concern for the implementation of special programmes became pronounced in the Fourth Plan, which must have seriously considered the Mudaliar Committee's caution. In the early years, the effort to respond to varying needs led to a series of disease-specific programmes in the nature of campaigns to control/eradicate malaria, small pox, filariasis, tuberculosis, leprosy, trachoma and cholera. They were implemented alongside the general health services provided at the primary health centres. The Third Plan speaks favourably of the impact of the malaria programme on life expectancy at birth. It also recognises the need for new problem-specific campaigns in nutrition and family planning. While reinforcing the effects of campaigns, the Fourth Plan desired to bring the PHC back into focus so that the success or partial success of the campaigns could be consolidated at the level of the general health services organisation. The issue of *an appropriate structure through which to offer needed services* was demanding attention.

To investigate the problem at the peripheral and supervisory levels, the eleven-member Kartar Singh Committee was appointed in October 1972 at the initiative of the Executive Committee of the Central Family Planning Council. The Committee was to assess the feasibility of multipurpose workers and their training needs and the wider use of mobile service units set up under the Family Planning programme. Even at its first meeting in March 1973, the Committee 'unanimously agreed that the concept of multi-purpose workers at the periphery was both feasible and desirable. It seemed to have seriously considered the operational research experience of Narangwal, Gandhigram, Wardha and later Maharashtra and of the National Institute of Health Administration and Education in coming to this conclusion. The Committee then mainly saw its role as evolving a strategy for implementing this decision. Field visits in eight states and interviews with field staff, health administrators, PHC doctors and members of the community (villagers, teachers, panchayat leaders) were utilised in formulating the strategy, particularly of sequencing the coverage of the scheme.

District-level integration was the concern of an earlier study group, the eight-member Jungalwalla Committee on Integration of Health Services. It was appointed in 1964 at the initiative of the Central Council of Health. The members were experienced medical administrators from the Central and State Directorates of Health. Its terms of reference were rather broad such as the investigation of various problems including those of service conditions. Perhaps its understanding of the administrative burdens at the state level enabled the Committee to articulate the need for integration between the medical work and public health arms of the health services. Its suggestions include not only structural devices such as coordinating bodies, but also changes in the process of planning and execution such as the creation of a strong district health manager. Comprehensive health work was to be considered at the district level, but this was not possible without requisite resources and skills. While the Committee appears to have underestimated the availability of resources for district level planning in the context of the institutional framework of the earlier committees and national developmental priorities, its stress on *technical and administrative capabilities in the planning and management of integrated services* is to be noted. For the first time since Bhore, the Committee also indicated the need for the district level 'manager' of health services to have *experience in community organisation.*

Pushing the planning process vertically down seemed to have got lost in the more immediate concern of linking the several arms of the general health services and the special programmes. The Draft Fifth Plan (1974-79) devotes considerable space to inter-programme linkages. It is critical of compartmentalisation, reviews the role of the Directorate of Health Services and speaks of inter-departmental committees. The Minimum Needs Programme, a package of services, was proposed. Thus, considerations of services and structure over-rode those of *processes by which local action could be generated.* The Jungalwalla Committee had sounded an early alarm.

Some studies of the sixties and early seventies were the first attempt to include social scientists and lend an interdisciplinary approach and an empirical base to the problems under study. The Johns Hopkins Project around Narangwal was a broad-based study over ten years covering a methodology of understanding health needs and services, the orientation of health centre personnel and the integration of family planning and health services. It involved the collaboration of Indian medical colleges with the Johns Hopkins University team. It is difficult to trace the policy impact of the findings. Although the conceptual base methodologies of these externally funded and long-term studies have been criticised (Banerji, 1981), an interesting feature is *the impact sought through the presentation of the study findings in many forms and forums.* At least in the Narangwal case, the involvement of policy-makers in framing recommendations regarding the role of the health centre doctor (Takulia et al., 1967), participation in conferences and policy analysis efforts (Taylor, 1980) ensure that some bridges were built between those who 'study' and those who 'act'. The National Institute of Health Administration and Education's projects (NIHAE, 1971; 1972) to investigate the integration of health services in India and district health administration by a multidisciplinary team are also among the first such attempts in the field of general health services in India. As noted earlier, the Kartar Singh Committee did consider the 'integration idea' but it is not quite clear, as in the case of the Jungalwalla Committee, how far the attempts to strengthen the district level management were pursued by policy-makers. The studies of the tuberculosis programme carried out by the National Tuberculosis Institute in the 1960s offered an example of a multidisciplinary programme and problem specific approach to investigating implementation. Some myths about the absence of felt needs, need for specialised services, difficulties in diagnosis, etc., were questioned. In this genre, but more general and less interdisciplinary in nature, must be mentioned the studies of Seal and team (1950-58) in the fifties and sixties which pointed to a methodology for comparing the health services and health status of a population over time. The lessons of these studies seem to be that *epidemiology and social sciences have a definite contribution to make to policy and that their actual use in studies and analysis is less than desirable.*

The Years of Discontent

In the health manpower field, medical education has been subjected to the largest number of analyses. The assumption, of course, is that the leadership of the physician at the unit level is crucial to the performance of the unit itself. The Medical Education Commission's committee on undergraduate medical education (GOI, 1969) lamented that the five-fold increase in the number of doctors in twenty years had not helped the vast majority of people in rural India.

The Government of India speaks of similar problems five years later (GOI, 1974) while appointing the Srivastava Committee on Medical Education and Support Manpower. The seven-member committee consisted of five physicians, with a great deal of experience in health administration; a generalist administrator, again with insight into the working of the health bureaucracy; and an eminent educationist and builder of institutions in the social sciences. Its report was ready in six months.

The Committee met in the years when development programmes had experienced the limits of the larger bureaucracies and innovations were being attempted at a micro level and being documented. Alternatives were already in the air. On the one hand, there was the pull of the alternative image — community-based, deprofessionalised, integrated (holistic) and autonomous — and on the other, the realities of the situation. The per capita income in the early seventies was Rs. 29 per month at 1960-61 prices and more than 40 per cent of the population lived on less than Rs. 20 per capita per month. There were 0.49 beds for 1,000 population. Furthermore, this does not indicate the skewed nature of the distribution of resources over the rural-urban sectors and between states.

It was only in the number of medical colleges that we were in fact fast reaching the target suggested by the Mudaliar Committee. There were 96 to the 107 recommended. By 1976, there were 106 medical colleges. The growth was not quite systematic and the other facilities could not absorb the increased number (IAMR & NIHAE, 1966; Krishnaswamy Rao, 1980). At the same time, the scarcity of nursing personnel was significant (Rao, 1980). So also was the case with the other manpower categories.

In the light of this situation, it is significant that the Srivastava Committee was asked by the GOI to suggest a curriculum for training health assistants and improve upon medical educational processes — the terms of the Committee were very specific. In presenting its report, the Committee decided to talk of the structure of health services in the context of an alternative strategy and stressed a community-based approach. While there were again recommendations on facilities and structural changes, a major thrust was on the development of para-professional auxiliaries — the community health worker and the health assistant. Thus the 'Support Manpower' part of the study got as much attention as 'Medical Education'. A strong recommendation was made for a Medical and Health Education Commission as an instrument for changing health related education and training towards desired goals. The ghost of the social physician of the Bhore Committee report may be visible in the community orientation called for in undergraduate medical education.

A possible gap was that the strategy suggested for the implementation of the new categories of personnel was not given as much attention as warranted. The MPW, after being unseated during the heydays of the malaria eradication drive of the fifties, was being reinstated. Soon the CHV was also to enter the scene. Yet another category of health assistant, however desirable, would have meant a great burden for the implementing agencies. The feasibility of new schemes in the light of past experiences of implementation could have made the recommendations more realistic.

The weary planner of the draft Fifth Plan confessed that 'many have criticised implementation;' the changes suggested had been tried out but there seemed to be 'no improvement in the levels of performance'. The draft Sixth Plan (1978-83) was to lament that the achievements were far from the desired levels, especially in the Minimum Needs Programme which was launched with much hope for providing minimum needs and integrated services. Achievements in coverage were eclipsed by the gaps in access for the poor and vulnerable groups. Even before the dust had settled down on the reports and recommendations of the various committees, a well-articulated and attractive thrust towards an alternative mode of health services was gaining ground.

A distinguished group of social scientists and medical administrators proposed an alternative health care system (Naik, 1977). WHO/UNICEF presented a joint study on alternative approaches and later were to document alternative experiences (Newell, 1975) in which the case study of a voluntary agency's effort figured. Lack of a clear national health policy, poor linkage of the health system with other components of national development, lack of clear priorities, and inadequate community involvement in health care were identified as critical issues.

The ICMR's symposium (1977) on alternatives, which was held in 1976, and the National Conference on Evaluation of Primary Health Care Programmes culminated in the ICSSR-ICMR sponsored publication, *Health For All : An Alternative Strategy* (ICSSR, 1981). Perhaps for the first time, three voluntary agency experimenters, a social scientist and a nurse educator were involved. Committee after committee has few women and fewer nursing participants — doctors not only have the major say in the health system but also in committees for policy analysis!

Unlike the Bhore Committee, the fourteen-member ICSSR-ICMR group is no longer trustful of the existing health services as being capable of rendering autonomy enhancing, basic and comprehensive services to weaker sections through a decentralised structure. It rejects with fervour any 'tinkering' or 'minor adjustments'. The call is for a radical transformation in favour of primary health care, by which people assume responsibility for their own health and play a leading role in managing the health services through local representative organisations. This is a forceful plea by a group of renowned field practitioners, administrators and researchers. Much of the desirable state of affairs recommended is not new; the group integrates what other groups and committees have talked about. The strategy for change from the available to the desirable, however, needs to be worked out. An interesting feature of the ICSSR report is that it is *(a)* by a mix of participants, governmental and non-governmental, and *(b)* offered to the people at large for debate and discussion.

The government, as a signatory to the Alma Ata Declaration on Health For All by AD 2000, constituted a Working Group to convert the HFA goals into programmes. Appointed by the Planning Commission, this group was to review past plans and suggest measures for the Sixth Plan (1980-85), in particular, for the weaker sections. It worked through discussions over nine months, in the form of symposia and reports of five sub-groups. For the first time, community participation and voluntary organisations figured explicitly as themes for the sub-groups, indicating the considerable significance attached *to improving the quantity and quality of access to the rural areas and the poor.* There was a cross-section of medical and general administrators (both from the health and other sectors), voluntary agency leaders, members of international agencies and health and general educators. It was truly a gathering of the concerned.

The Working Group asserts that health for all 'is achievable given the sustained will and the supporting efforts to implement the indicated tasks' (GOI, 1981). While this has been said in the past, a difference is that the group has tried to outline alternative objectives and strategies. Indicators are now sought in terms closer to impacts and outcomes of health programmes, i.e., reduction in mortality rate; percentage of pregnant mothers receiving ante-natal care; percentage delivered by trained birth attendants, etc. These are beyond the usual input-oriented criteria suggested. Intermediate time horizons (1985, 1990, 2000) for targets are indicated. The question however arises : Will primary health care go the same way as did Bhore's minimum health care ?

Will other groups and other forums say, thirty years from now, that the radical measures propounded in the seventies were 'unrealistic' and 'idealistic' much as we now talk of the Bhore Committee report ? Like other professionals, the policy analyst would like to believe that his supporting efforts will make the critical difference between a situation of despair and one of hope. Less ambitiously, he might wonder if he can contribute to moving a low performing system to a somewhat better performing one. It is in this light that suggestions for areas of analysis are offered here.

The efforts at analysing policies and strategies related to specific critical programmes (e.g., MNP) need to be strengthened. Here, too, we will have to address ourselves to the problems of *changing organisations and approaches.* While horizontal linkages will need to be understood, the creation of local initiatives by a vertical devolution of the planning process will have to be reviewed. In this context, it is perhaps time for the analyst to compensate his preoccupation with the centre by looking at the possibilities at the state level, particularly at those with the potential for raising resources and planning on their own.

While the various committees and groups have paid a great deal of attention to manpower resources (here, too, mainly the top, i.e., the doctor and the bottom, i.e., the community worker and the next rung auxiliary), it is not so with regard to finance mobilisation. This is perhaps due to the conception of social services as a cost centre in a welfare state. Private expenditure on health, however, is of significance (Montoya n.d.; Rao, 1966). The share of the public system in this is yet to be reckoned. This is not merely an accounting exercise, but also one of understanding the reasons people part with cash or kind to obtain health services. One shot, one village studies such as *Pills against Poverty* may be methodologically impure and exaggeratedly polemical, but may open up new avenues for inquiry. Longer-term, better designed studies (Banerji, 1981) may offer an understanding of people's perception of health and morbidity which influence the choices they make. Peoples' participation could then become a more essential element of the health strategy. Above all, the policy analyst may have to not merely provide 'supporting efforts' but contribute to 'sustaining the will'. Here, he may have to look for roles beyond the conventional rational inquirer to that of a protector and advocate of critical programmes. A search for new roles may enable him to understand the social and political processes which bring about the neglect or even the abandonment of well-intentioned plans.

III. *Fertility-Influencing Policies*

Fertility can be reduced by influencing proximate determinants of fertility — number of years spent in reproductive union, contraception, lactation and abortion. These determinants in turn are influenced by a variety of developmental variables. Although a theoretical understanding of the variables which influence fertility and to what extent is still weak there is a general agreement that the following basic variables affect fertility — life expectancy, infant mortality, adult literacy, school enrolment, non-agricultural labour force, per capita GNP, and never-married females in the age group 15-19. Although a variety of policies influence or can be used to influence fertility, the focus in India has been on increasing the use of contraceptives through family welfare programmes.

Policy and Programme Development

It is difficult to identify points of discontinuity in policies and programmes; but the development of policies and programmes can be broadly discussed under the following heads.

Pre-programme activities (before 1952) : The birth control movement was a part of early social reform movements and birth control clinics were opened in some cities as early as 1925. The Family Planning Association of India, the leading non-government agency, was formed in 1949.

Early phase (1952-63) : Since pre-independence days, there was a general agreement on the desirability of birth control but views differed as to the relative emphasis to be placed on population control for economic development and as a welfare measure, a phenomenon that continues to date.

The National Programme was launched in 1952. The early phase of programme development was marked by slow and hesitant starts. The technology for modern contraceptives was not as yet developed and the influence of Gandhian thought led to eschewing modern methods of contraception in favour of abstinence in the early stages of the programme. The programme was patterned after activities of voluntary agencies and by 1963 a large number of clinics were opened to provide family planning services. During this period the justification for population control was sought from a cost-benefit analysis and acceptability of these programmes by people. The benefits of differential rates of fertility decline (Coale and Hoover, 1958) are usually estimated from a national point of view by constructing macro-economic growth models where population growth is an exogenous variable. Several criticisms have been made of this approach. First of all, only capital is taken as a scarce factor and the contribution of labour is ignored. Second, the cost of the programme has not received adequate attention. Third, several other social-psychological factors influence fertility decisions, and these are ignored. Finally, the view point of families is not considered. Indeed some have argued that it is economically rational to have large families (Mamdani, 1972). How this conflict between desire for larger families at the individual level and a reduced fertility level at the national level can be resolved, continues to be debated.

As in many parts of the world. in the initial stages the acceptability of the family planning programme was assessed by questionnaire surveys of individual husbands and wives on knowledge of, and attitudes towards, family planning, desire for children and practice of family planning (KAP surveys). More than 200 such studies have been carried out in India, but very few at the national level. By and large, the studies revealed that about 50 per cent of couples approved use of family planning methods. When the acceptance of family planning was much lower, questions were raised on both methodological issues and interpretation of data. Methodologically there are problems in measuring complex socio-psychological variables and quality of data. The approval for family planning was interpreted as the motivation to accept family planning. To overcome these problems, some have suggested that the data should be sought at village level by informed observers. Unfortunately, large-scale systematic studies of this type have not emerged.

Extension education and cafetaria approach (1964 onwards) : The extension education component was added to the clinical services starting from 1964. The Department of Family Planning was established in 1966. A network of service centres was also established as a part of the health services. In 1966, subsidised distribution of condoms was undertaken through the established channels of leading consumer goods distributors. IUD was introduced in 1967. Male and female sterilisation services were introduced shortly thereafter. In 1972, the Medical Termination of Pregnancy Act came into effect legalising abortion. Free distribution of oral pills was undertaken in 1978. The basic pattern of the programme — extension education and cafetaria approach — has continued unchanged.

To reduce the extent of the area covered by a worker and to increase his credibility, a multipurpose worker scheme was introduced in 1974 (Kartar Singh Committee Report, 1973). Under this scheme workers of different vertical programmes (health, maternal and child health and family planning) were trained and reclassified as multipurpose workers (see Section II). The implementation of this scheme raised several issues of salary rationalisation and organisational restructuring which are gradually being resolved by various state governments.

The emphasis on economic development leads to a sense of urgency, setting of targets and willingness to accept the need for drastic action. Several demographic macro-simulation type models have been reported (Nortman, 1978) which relate the level of acceptance of family planning methods and demographic characteristics of acceptors to the resulting size of the population and its age-sex composition.

The government uses births-averted calculations for measuring the effectiveness of different methods and for relating family planning acceptance to a reduction in the birth-rate. The method-mix of acceptance, however, has not received adequate attention. No models are available which relate the potential for acceptance and the feasibility of achieving the targets compared to the desired goals for fertility reduction.

Programme : The development of the programme has been greatly influenced by pilot projects, international agencies and various committees appointed for this purpose. The evolution of the programme has been almost always influenced by pilot projects, although it has not been possible to replicate them with the same degree of effectiveness. The extension education pattern used by the national programme seems to have been influenced by the Gandhigram experiments in the Athoor block (1952-71). Mass vasectomy camps were launched after the successful Ernakulam camps (1970-72). The integration of health and family welfare services was tested by such pilot schemes in Uttar Pradesh and the Haryana and Narangwal experiments (1966-74). Most recently, the Jamkhed experiment (1970-76) has shown how primary health care can be developed with the participation of the community.

The performance of the national programme is usually much lower than that of the project areas. One may speculate as to why the shortfalls in performance occur. One explanation may be that while the structural part of the programme is implemented, the process part is neglected. The focus becomes what is to be done and not on how it should be done. Second, the interaction between community, bureaucrats and politicians is taken care of by experimenters but seems to be neglected in large-scale implementation. Research is needed in identifying managerial processes for the large-scale implementation of strategies which are found effective in small-scale experiments.

Several committees have also influenced the programme. Notable among them are annual Central Family Welfare Council meetings, the Kartar Singh Committee and the Planning Commission Working Group on Population, 1980. These committees are used for various purposes such as to pool collective wisdom from diverse sources, use an interdisciplinary approach and to evolve consensus among diverse sets of views. Apart from political commitment, five-year plans seem to have played the most important role in policy and programme development. First, they have served to highlight the impact of population growth on other sectors of the economy. Second, goals for reducing the birth-rate have been set through successive plan documents. Finally, the directions of programme development and availability of resources have been determined by plans because the programme is fully supported by central government assistance.

Campaigns : Campaigns for a single method, whenever contraceptive acceptance did not increase, has been a continuing feature of the programme. With the advent of the IUD shortly after 1960, the political leaders, seeing the prospect of success, shifted to launching IUD campaigns. When in practice the method was found to have side effects, the programme implementation faltered. Mass vasectomy camps were launched in 1971-72. Two major factors accounting for the overwhelming success of these camps were intensive organisational effort and increased monetary compensation to acceptors. However, the poor quality of services and questionable motivational practices led to the discontinuation of the camps During the emergency, the programme of sterilisation was vigorously implemented. About 8.3 million persons were sterilised during the period 1976-77 as compared to a total of 18.9 million persons prior to that date. Finally, the coercion used in family planning became an election issue in 1977 and may have contributed to a change in government at that time.

The bureaucratic influence seems to have led to the emphasis on sterilisation as a method of contraception. Apart from cost considerations, the need for only one time contact with client and easy accountability may have resulted in this emphasis. Some observers of the Indian family planning programme have criticised this phenomena of single method campaigns by labelling the programme as a sterilisation programme.

Evolution of comprehensive population policies (1976 onwards) : Although the goal of reducing the birth-rate were set as early as 1961 and revised on several occasions, the first formal population policy statement was not issued until 1976. This policy statement listed sixteen specific population related measures, which included increasing the minimum age of legal marriage, making the volume of the central government's financial assistance to state governments partly dependent on family planning performance; freezing representation in Parliament and the state legislatures on the basis of the 1971 Census; according higher priority to female literacy; increasing the amount of monetary compensation for individual sterilisation acceptors; and permitting interested state governments to propose legislation for compulsory sterilisation. After the elections in 1977, the new government issued a fresh population policy statement which re-emphasised voluntary acceptance and rejected coercion in matters of family planning. The need for integrating family planning with other welfare programmes, particularly maternal and child health, was emphasised. The name of the programme was changed from Family Planning to Family Welfare. No new policy statements have been issued since then. While comprehensive population policies are being evolved, corresponding changes in organisation have not been brought about. The population programmes continue to be linked to the health services.

Population and development — debates and options : According to Mitra (1978) the history of the population policy shows an alternating emphasis between development measures leading to fertility reduction and family planning efforts. He says that during periods of relatively higher economic growth, family planning recedes into the background. When the economic situation is poor, family planning is the emphasis. In the Bucharest Conference (1974), India took the development approach and is credited with coining the now famous slogan 'development is the best contraceptive'. In 1976, the population policy said that it was not possible to wait for development to take place but a frontal attack on the population problem was necessary. The population policy of 1977 again reversed the situation by emphasising family welfare.

The reviews by Cassen (1979) and Mitra (1978) suggest that a consensus position seems to be emerging. Cassen says :

> But it is possible for India to improve employment prospects, health, education and social equality — if that were to happen, the family planning program could make greater headway .... And even in existing conditions India's family planning program could be somewhat more effective.

Mitra concludes his book by saying :

> Family planning must form an important element of the total package of the development and democratic processes. They are two legs on which the country must walk towards a time-bound goal.

While a general consensus seems to emerge that development facilitates fertility reduction and the family planning programme accelerates the decline in fertility, there is very little research on determinants of fertility. The policy-maker cannot take the stance that development policy is also a fertility policy. The latter should address the question of selective developmental interventions which are feasible and will result in a significant decline in fertility. While the debate on population and development issues has attracted considerable attention, the research into hard choices of various different population policies has been neglected; an unfortunate omission considering the importance of the issue and its impact on the future of the country.

Degree of Compulsion — Some Ethical Issues

The National Population Policy of 1976 stated that where a state legislature, in the exercise of its own powers, decided that the time was ripe and it was necessary to pass legislation for compulsory sterilisation, it might do so. The National Population Policy of 1977 said that compulsion in the matter of family planning should be ruled out for all time to come.

Instances of coercion by over-zealous officials in attempting to fulfil targets have been recorded by several observers, first in 1971-72 in the mass vasectomy camps and later in 1976-77 during the emergency (Gwatlein, 1979). Some have argued that positive incentives or negative disincentives are also a form of coercion because poor people are influenced/affected more by such measures than are others. The ethical issues involved in the measures that the state should or should not take on demographic grounds (with the ultimate objective of larger concerns of human welfare) have never been subjected to a high quality of policy research. Rather, it is discussed in terms of political ideologies and parties.

Berelson and Lieberson (1979) suggest that in this case, the familiar choice presented in the policy literature — that voluntarism is good and coercion bad — is clearly simplistic. We have to examine issues involved in each approach to judge its ethical case. The question regarding incentives/disincentives is whether they serve to enlarge individual options rather than diminish them either in the short or long term. They would become permissible if indeed options increased but we do not have any studies in this regard. A myriad of complex ethical issues are involved in the compulsion issue as Berelson et al. say :

> The problem arises precisely because public and private goals are, or are perceived to be, in disharmony. Private decisions about fertility do not add up to the net, let alone the optimal, benefit of the collectivity. How to balance them out, in a politico-ethical as well as an efficient manner, is the task.

The issues which arise, therefore, are :

1. Whether those affected by such policies are adequately involved in the process of formulating such policies.
2. How does one take into account the views of those as yet not born ?
3. How does one balance the real freedom options open to the individual consistent with the liberties of others in society ?

One thing, however, is clear. Given the moral risks that attend the use of compulsion, one should ensure that every reasonable effort has been made to exhaust the possibilities of using voluntary measures. A debate on ethical issues may never result in a satisfactory resolution of all issues for most people, but it will help focus on the questions : How effective are our voluntary measures ? If a voluntary programme can yield results, what would that programme be like and what resources would be required to implement it ?

Neglected Issues, Approaches and Methodology

A summary of policy studies is given in Table 1. Some of the neglected policy issues were pointed out earlier. Some of the other issues that require attention are :

1. What types of incentives/disincentives are feasible and effective ?
2. How can the community level organisations be effectively involved in the programme ?
3. How can the organisational arrangements be coordinated with policies ? For instance, should there be a population commission ? What should be the centre-state relations ?
4. Are the formulated policies programmable and implementable ?

A serious gap is the view-point used in policy studies. Most of the studies take either a national or an individual point of view. There are very few studies which take the family or community point of view. Questions such as 'Is a small family a happy family' are not investigated in depth.

There is an undercurrent of communal and religious politics on the impact of differential acceptance and its effect on the resultant size of the population for various segments. However, no serious studies are available in this regard.

When one examines the studies dealing with the future scenario, one finds an overwhelming bias in favour of impressionistic discussion. Rigorous, analytic and interdisciplinary approaches are frequently not used. This may also reflect the poor quality of basic research.

To strengthen the processes of policy formulation and the resulting policies, two types of measures may be necessary :

TABLE 1
Summary of Policy Studies

Issue	Studies	Major Conceptual Framework	Methodological Approach
Justification for population control	Coale & Hoover; several others	National point of view; economic considerations; growth as an objective of national development	Macro-economic growth models, investment analysis, cost-benefit
	KAP studies	View-point : adoption process models	Survey
Goals and targets	Exercises by the department; Nortman; Census report	Demographic; convert population growth goals into contraceptive acceptance goals	Demographic macro-simulation approach
Programme development	Several action research experiments	Implement programme in limited geographical areas and evaluate results	Action research
	International agencies;	Evaluation missions, studies and projects	Visit-observation, evaluation-comment
	Study-group such as Planning Commission working group, MPW committee, CFW councils	Review & discussion; use of interdisciplinary group of experts	Meeting-consensus
Population and development	Banerji, Desai, Mitra, Cassen	Book-length reviews of literature; frameworks varied in terms of their emphasis on a Marxist concept of society	Varies : selective use of studies and literature

1. Willingness and openness on the part of policy formulators to subject policy decisions to serious debate; and
2. Further strengthening of organisational/institutional capabilities for policy research.

One final note of caution is necessary. Policy research cannot be devoid of issues of implementation, for this is the area — implementability of policies — which deserves most serious attention.

IV. *Migration-Influencing Policies*

In this section, we discuss policies and relevant studies in the area of population distribution over space. We propose to include some conceptual discussions on factors affecting the distribution of population, review some policy-relevant studies and bring out some of the policy instruments and approaches in India as included in the five-year plans.

A blanket statement that rural to urban migration is bad is indeed simplistic, since distribution is a natural concomitant of development. Therefore, planners and policy-makers must decide simultaneously to encourage urbanisation and derive the benefits thereof and also formulate policies to keep people in agricultural communities and avoid what is called the backwash effects. There are some known policy options in this context. Locating industrial centres in the rural environment as a way to expand the work horizons of rural people and thereby reduce their propensity to move to the city is one option. Related to this is the development of small and medium-sized towns for a more even distribution of the population and to avoid pressures on major cities. A second option is to establish satellite towns around or near existing large cities. The creation of an urbanised 'spoke' extending from a major centre, with the amenities of urban life provided along the spoke can be a third option. A fourth option is to upgrade those rural centres that have the potential to become urbanised. Relocating administrative units outside cities, developing major schemes to exploit presently underutilised resources, etc., are also policy options which affect population distribution. The twin-city plan of Bombay, supplemented by schemes for self-financed housing and industrial land-development, is one example in India of an effort to influence population distribution.

Policies and Programmes Influencing Internal Migration

Not all policies influencing migration are intentionally designed to alter the distribution and movement of population. In fact, the unintentional policies in the form of general development programmes probably have a much greater influence on migration than intentional policies. For example, rural development strategies — including policies concerning land reforms, availability of bank loans, availability of specialised agricultural inputs, labour-intensive agricultural innovations, improvement in rural health care, education and housing — are all policy components of a rural development strategy which have an impact on rural-urban migration. In addition to programmes focused directly on the rural sector, there are a number of national economic policies which support rural development efforts. Policies with regard to price support or controls, taxation, return of revenues to rural areas, urban minimum wage-levels and all other policies concerning redistribution of wealth from urban to rural areas and from rich farmers to landless and marginal farmers have an individual or collective impact on population distribution between rural and urban areas.

There are also strategies focused on urban development as a means to influence the population distribution. For example, the dispersed urbanisation strategy combines the integrated rural development approach with an explicit focus on developing rural service centres, market towns and small cities. This strategy recognises that there will always be individuals who wish to leave rural areas and offers them nearby regional centres and market towns as alternatives to major metropolitan areas. Realising the importance of spatial linkage, the Government of India set up a Rural-urban Relationship Committee in 1971.

The policy of the Government of India on decentralised urban development is reflected in the setting up of various urban development authorities. The focus here is beyond the core city and involves the identification of growth centres and developing them through shifting 'propulsive' firms, linked to other enterprises in the region. The policy thrust should be considerable in strength to first identify and then attract such firms to the newly identified centres. In his study on land policies for urban development, Ved Prakash (1971), for example, points out that a major obstacle to rationalising urban development is the property tax system. At times certain policies meant to stimulate industrial growth really tend to perpetuate the rural-urban differential. For example, in his earlier work on developing countries, Johnson (1970) specifically talks of the metropolitan bias in the provision of the infrastructure in India. He observes that while the availability of all kinds of facilities attracts and serves industrial enterprises, it also attracts migrants — and indeed one job created may attract several migrants.

Policy Effects, Goals and Mechanisms

A variety of policies tend to slow down **migration** from rural areas, slow down urban in-migration, encourage migration from rural areas or in fact encourage migration to **urban** areas. Some policies also help to channel migrants within metropolitan areas to satellite areas, new towns, etc. Many a time, the consequences of such policies may turn out to be incongruous with their explicit goals. One can think of a host of policies which are not formulated to explicitly influence population distribution but which nonetheless quite strongly influence the patterns of distribution. It is this missing link which perhaps leads to incongruity between goals and consequences.

The explicit policy goal of expanded crop output through the mechanism of small farm development, increased income to small farmers without decreasing employment opportunities, employment generation by increasing labour intensity of production, etc., will have the effect of reducing migration from rural areas. In a democratic country like ours, people are free to choose where they want to live and no legal restrictions can be placed on this. But explicit policies of increasing the financial resources available to cities through charges on the use of services, higher levels of taxation for urban residents, income taxation, reducing economic location advantages in cities, etc., are some of the policies which have an effect of slowing urban in-migration. When agricultural mechanisation and the adoption of capital-intensive innovation is on a large scale, it will tend to reduce the demand for labour; when small farmers sell out to large farmers then such policies will tend to encourage migration from rural areas. Concentration of economic and employment opportunities in urban areas encourage migration to urban areas. India had a colonial heritage of a limited number of large cities at the time of independence. Consequently, industrial location policies were solely on considerations of economies of scale leading to the concentration of industry in a few limited locations. This led to the expansion of the construction industry, a concentration of financing available to large urban areas and the rapid spread of information on the employment available in urban areas.

The industrial policy in India is the classic example of channelling migrants to satellite areas. Urban development authorities were set up in India for land development notifications such as housing areas, market and storage areas, transport links and other service centres. Large projects, such as, developing river basins, are also included in this category.

All these indicate that population distribution, migration and urbanisation are influenced by a large range of governmental policies. Even in the absence of conscious population distribution policies, various agricultural and urban development policies may indicate our strategy on migration and urbanisation. The evolution of urban growth policy in India clearly indicates all the above features.

Urban Growth Policy in India

In earlier years, spatial planning was conceived as a social welfare element in development programmes (Jain, 1976). In the first two five-year plans, India's policy in this area was indicated only as housing, slum improvement, development plans for the capital, industry and some new towns. The Third Five-Year Plan for the first time stated that urbanisation is an important element of the process of economic and social development and is closely linked with many other problems, such as, migration from villages to towns; levels of living in rural and urban areas; relative costs of providing economic and social services in towns of different sizes; provision of housing, water, sanitation, transport and power; location of industries; civic administration; and planning land use. The broad objective of the policy was to secure a balanced development between rural and urban areas. While the Plan admits that this is by no means an easy task, it includes the following as the main ingredients of such a balanced development policy :

1. As far as possible, new industries should be established away from large and congested cities;
2. The concept of a region should be adopted in planning for large industries, which should only serve as a focal point;
3. Rural urban linkages have to be kept in mind and in each development plan, schemes for strengthening economic inter-dependence between town and surrounding areas should be incorporated; and
4. In each area, occupational patterns should be diversified in place of the present dependence on agriculture.

The Fourth Five-Year Plan by and large had the same approach to the problems of spatial planning. This Plan also stressed the need for the development of state capitals, adoption of a concrete housing policy and extension of civic amenities and services. The establishment of HUDCO is a major policy mechanism in this context. The Fifth Five-Year Plan includes the following objectives in the chapter on urban development :—

1. Tackle the problem of metropolitan cities on a regional basis;
2. Promote the development of smaller towns and new urban centres.
3. Assist implementation of national and inter-state projects concerning urban development and to enlarge industrial townships;
4. Strengthen the financial and organisational set up of local administration; and
5. Formulate an urban land policy including land-use control, restriction of plot size, restriction on transfers of land, and betterment levies.

Jain (1976) observes that India's industrial investment has two broad categories — capital-intensive industries, whose location is based on resource efficiency, and labour-intensive industries, whose location decisions are based on a balanced distribution of employment opportunities. Industrial estates have been located in industrially backward regions and there has been a gradual shift towards locating them in rural areas. Again during this period, the planning of growth centres has been accepted as a policy in India in order to transmit the facilities of 'minimum needs' in the rural areas. This approach integrates various programmes — such as, irrigation, communication, education, health, transportation — and hence should be linked with health and other related policies.

The Sixth Five-Year Plan states that despite the slow rate of urbanisation in India, all the urban problems still exist due to the sheer size of the urban population. It also points out that the process of urbanisation has been relatively balanced but yet it is important to distinguish problems as they occur between different regions and different cities. Hence the national urbanisation policy should consider regional problems. Urban development should be viewed in the context of its relationship with rural development in each region. The thrust of this policy is to concentrate in the next decade on the provision of adequate infrastructural and other facilities in the small, medium and intermediate towns which have been neglected hitherto in this respect. The policy also calls for the improvement of slums rather than their massive relocation. All other aspects of the Fifth Five-Year Plan have by and large been retained in this plan. While there is now ample evidence of a national urbanisation policy, the evolution of this policy has been very slow. In fact, most of the components of this policy come under the responsive category. This evolution presumably is based on some policy-relevant studies in India. While there is no dearth of urban-related studies, not many studies can be strictly termed as policy-relevant. A quick review of some of these studies follows.

Policy-Relevant Studies — A Short Review

There have been several studies analysing and presenting various dimensions of the process of urbanisation. These predominantly include migration studies in terms of the factors influencing city-ward migration by volume, the composition of migration streams, and the impact of such migration on the areas of origin and destination. After analysing the current patterns of migration, these studies by and large indicate the difficulties that exist now and are likely to arise in the future if such a trend continues, perhaps with increased vigour. Such analyses perhaps contributed to some of the urban-related policies indicated in the five-year plan documents.

Several surveys indicate that the dominant reason for migration in India has been employment. The Thirteenth National Sample Survey (NSS) of urban households during 1957-58 indicated that employment-related reasons account for three-fourths of male migration, while female migration is more associational in nature. Short-distance migration was mainly because of marriage whereas out-of-state migration was more for job-related reasons. Long-distance migration was predominantly to big cities. The eleventh and twelfth rounds of the NSS indicated that proportionately more migrants to rural areas went for reasons other than those related to jobs or education than migrants to urban areas. Lakdawala's survey of Bombay city primarily during 1955-56 supports the NSS's findings that 71 per cent of the migrant earners in Bombay came solely for job-related reasons (such as, insufficient land to cultivate, meagre income, unemployment, insufficient employment and prospects for better employment) while 14 per cent came for a combination of job-related and other reasons. A survey of Poona in 1954 by the Gokhale Institute of Politics and Economics also indicated similar factors. A combination of the traditional push-and-pull factors seem to operate together in inducing migration. The usefulness of such studies is to emphasise the fact that a government considering programmes and implementing policies to influence population redistribution must first examine the causes and consequences of migration.

The most popular explanation among economists is the expected income model which in its simplest form postulates that an individual or family would migrate if the expected income from moving was greater than the sum of the expected income from staying and the costs of moving. While providing economic interpretations of some migration studies, Brigg (1973) points out that national economic and other policies have a powerful influence on redistributing population among different regions and between rural and urban areas. Among these are the industrial location and trade policies protecting the manufacturing sector, credit allocation, public investment and subsidy or pricing policies. Often rural education reinforces urban cultural values. Rural youth, after going through such an educational system, do not prefer to stay in the rural areas.

Oberoi and Singh (1980) did a case study of Punjab trying to see linkages between migration, urbanisation and fertility. The main finding of this study was that the fertility patterns of similar population groups are significantly different in rural and urban areas. Age at marriage, mortality levels, education of both husband and wife, etc., have a considerable influence on fertility. Even though such studies may not be classified as policy studies, their results are policy-relevant.

Jakobson and Prakash (1971) point out the role of the largest cities in the urbanisation process by showing a marked decline in the index of urbanisation if the largest city or cities are excluded from individual state totals. This decline was highly correlated with the size of these large cities in each state. By using the Census data for Calcutta as an illustration, they propose the selective development of certain areas of the urban system to reduce/control the primacy of Calcutta city. Such studies also have considerable policy relevance.

There was yet another effort towards this direction. The National Institute of Urban Affairs and the Town and Country Planning Organisation of the Government of India held a meeting in Delhi in mid-1977 to discuss urban issues and to indicate directions in which urban policies and programmes must move.

The planning response to rapid urbanisation and the growth of large cities has typically involved a set of policies which includes resettlement schemes, creation of new towns, industrial and administrative decentralisation, integrated rural development programmes, and urban policies designed to encourage or discourage migrants into urban areas. So far in India, these policies have only had a limited success. There are many reason for this, the most important of which is the lack of high level political commitment. Second, the fact that a variety of other policies influence population distribution has not been explicitly built into such policies. Third, more emphasis was placed on the symptoms and not on the causes of the misallocation of resources and severe regional disparities. All these call for a national migration policy — explicitly stated and with its objectives clearly defined.

In summary, policy-relevant studies in the area of population distribution concentrate on three major dimensions, namely composition, direction and rate. Studies on composition focus on the occupation, class and ethnic, sex, and age characteristics of migrants. Studies relevant to the policies on influencing the direction of migration focus on places of origin, destination and their interactions. Studies on the third dimension focus on in-migration and out-migration rates and the duration of migration. While these studies are relevant to policies affecting migration and population distribution, the factors that contribute to these three dimensions are often the unintended consequences of various other policies. The intervention through policies comes from an assessment of the consequences of migration while the instrument of intervention comes from our understanding of the determinants of migration. Studies relevant to the former type describe the problems encountered in major cities, such as, inadequate housing, poor living conditions, traffic congestion and poor civic services. Studies concerning the latter investigate why people move to cities and how factors related to origin and destination affect their decisions.

On the one hand these policy-relevant studies serve as guides in reducing the undesirable consequences of migration to cities (say in forming policies to revitalise civic services, housing for the poor or slum clearance). Simultaneously they could be employed to reduce the relative attraction of the city (such as, dispersing employment through policies on industrial location, and investments in rural and urban areas). Again, there are studies which show that policies on the issuing of industrial licences based on their location have not worked very well since economic forces governing location (backward and forward linkages, transport, infrastructural costs and so on) were stronger than the policy forces.

While some macro-level data are available in India on these, there is a severe lack of information on factors determining a person's or a family's decision to move — and this is true also for many other countries. Special surveys are required to list these elements like choice of destination, personal factors and flow of information. Such surveys are very few and indeed very difficult as also expensive to carry out. Migration data from the Indian Census are fraught with problems of definition and presentation for serious use in policy analysis. While micro-level data on migration are almost impossible to extrapolate from the national Census, an attempt should be made to collect such data for carefully selected areas, as there is a heavy dependence on even the existing inadequate information from the Census. However, improving such data systems for policy analysis and providing systematic survey data will get a boost only if the Government seriously adopts a policy on population distribution through the development of alternative growth centres, or concentrating growth on small and medium-sized cities or emphasising rural development or even a combination of all these.

V.   *Strengthening Policy Formulation*

Our review has identified different types of lacunae in policy studies. The committees are usually burdened with divergent points of view and seek to arrive at a consensus, neglecting analytical approaches. The committees normally tackle a broad range of issues and usually have to rely on available material whereas some issues may require additional information. The Government is also usually selective in accepting the recommendations of the committees. Since the inter-relationship of various recommendations may not be always explicit, the effectiveness of the committee approach because of selective acceptance is reduced.

Several issues have also been neglected in policy-relevant studies as already discussed. This may be primarily because the studies are not carried out from a policy perspective. Some issues require an interdisciplinary approach and research organisations may not have the requisite capabilities. Some policies are also controversial and ideological biases may play a prominent role in the way these policies are analysed. The perceived lack of objectivity leads to the reduced utility of researches and a reluctance on the part of many researchers to study these areas.

The data base available for policy analysis is usually weak. First, the data requirement for the analysis of policies is usually large and not easily available. Second, the collectors of data may not always have a policy perspective. Finally, the data needed often would be on the 'soft' dimensions of human behaviour, raising difficult problems regarding the methodologies used for the collection and interpretation of data.

Often the policies are implemented without recognising the organisational and resource requirements for implementing them. While comprehensive population or health policies are evolved, the necessary organisational forms and processes are not created. For example agencies or authorities entrusted with urban development tasks often lack the resources to implement their plans. Thus, an inadequate appreciation of the implementation aspect and the neglect of structural and resource constraints contribute to the ultimate ineffectiveness of policies.

However, as already discussed, the development of programmes has been considerably aided and affected by pilot or action research experiments. Thus one could plead for more pilot projects though good pilot projects are difficult to implement, are expensive, and may not always reflect the critical constraints in implementation. Even when programmes are developed based upon such experiences, their effectiveness during large-scale implementation is usually lower than that of the pilot experiments.

While population policies are supposed to include a balance between births, deaths and migration, the policies and policy studies related to these three dimensions of population are invariably treated separately. There is a need for a more integrated look at the population scene.

These lacunae need to be remedied if policy formulation is to be strengthened. This review suggests a likely agenda for future research, the need for the development of an adequate data base, and the necessity of an increased analytic content in whatever approaches are used for policy formulation. Finally, the direct or indirect involvement of implementors in policy formulation is necessary if good policies are to ultimately emerge.

References

Arole, M., and **Arola, R.** (1975), 'A Comprehensive Rural Health Project in Jamkhed (India),' *Health by People* (ed.), K. W. Newell, Geneva, WHO, 1975, pp. 7-90.

Banerji, D. (1971), *Family Planning in India : A Critique and a Perspective,* People's Publishing House, 1971.

——————— (1978), 'Health and Population Control in the Draft Plan,' *Economic and Political Weekly,* Special No.

——————— (1981), 'Challenge to Social Sciences in Formulating Alternative Health Services in India,' paper presented at the Medical Sociology Seminar, Jodhpur, 15-17 January 1981.

Berelson, Bernard and **Lieberson, Jonathan** (1979), 'Governmental Intervention on Fertility : What is Ethical?' Centre for Policy Studies, Working Paper No. 48, October 1979 (The Population Council, New York).

Briggs, Pamela (1973), *Some Economic Interpretations of Case Studies of Urban Migration in Developing Countries,* World Bank, Working Paper No. 151.

Cassen, R.H. (1979), *India : Population, Economy, Society,* Delhi, Macmillan, 1979.

Coale, Ausley J., and **Hoover, Edgar** (1958), *Population Growth and Economic Development in Low Income Countries,* Princeton, Princeton University Press, 1958.

Desai, A. R. (1980), *Urban Family and Family Planning in India,* Bombay, Popular Prakashan, 1980.

Department of International Health, The Johns Hopkins University (1976), 'The Functional Analysis of Health Needs and Services,' (Monograph), Asia Publishing House.

Djufeldt, G., and **Lindberg, S.** (1975), 'Pills against Poverty — A Study of the Introduction of Western Medicine in a Tamil Village,' Scandinavian Institute of Studies, Monograph No. 23.

Djukanovic, V., and **Mach, E. P.** (eds.) (1975), *Alternative Approaches to Meeting Basic Health Needs in Developing Countries* (a UNICEF-WHO joint study), Geneva, WHO.

GOI (1973), *Report of the Committee on Multipurpose Workers* (The Kartar Singh Committee).

——————— (1961), *Report of the Health Survey and Planning Committee* (The Mudaliar Committee).

——————— (1946), *Report of the Health Survey and Development Committee* (The Bhore Committee).

——————— (1968), *Report of the Committee on the Integration of Health Services* (The Jungalwalla Committee).

_____ (1969), Medical Education Committee.

_____ (1974), *Report on Medical Education and Support Manpower* (The Srivastava Committee).

Government of India, Planning Commission Working Group in *Population Policy Report*, Planning Commission, May 1980.

_____ (1981), *Report of the Working Group on 'Health for all by 2000 AD'.*

Gwatlein, Davidson R. (1979), 'Political Will and Family Planning : The Implications of India's Emergency Experience', *Population and Development Review*, Vol. 5, No. 1, March 1979.

Indian Council of Medical Research (ICMR) (1977), *Alternative Approaches to Health Care*, New Delhi.

Indian Council of Social Science Research (ICSSR) (1981), *Health for All — An Alternative Strategy*, Report of a Study Group, New Delhi.

Institute of Applied Manpower Research (with National Institute of Health Administration and Education, NIHAE, now NIHFW) (1966), 'Development of Modern Medical Education in India,' Manpower Group Survey, Working Paper No. 4.

Jain (1976), 'Evolution of an Urban Growth Policy for India,' *Ekistics*, No. 249, August 1976.

Jakobson and Prakash (1971), *Urbanisation and National Development*, Sage Publications.

Johnson, E.A.T (1970), *The Organisation of Space in Developing Countries,* Harvard University Press.

Mamdani, Mahmood (1972), *The Myth of Population Control, Family, Caste and Class in an Indian Village*, New York, Monthly Review Press, 1972.

Maru, Rushikesh M. (1976), 'Birth Control in India and in the People's Republic of China : Comparison of Policy, Evolution, Methods of Birth Control and Program Organisation : 1949-1974,' Doctoral dissertation, University of Michigan.

Mitra, Ashok (1978), *India's Population : Aspects of Quality and Control*, Family Planning Foundation, ICSSR.

Montoya, Aguilar (n.d.), 'Health Planning in India,'. New Delhi, National Institute of Health and Family Welfare, mimeo.

Naik, J.P. (ed.) (1977), *Alternative System of Health Care Services in India*, New Delhi, ICSSR.

Narangwal Population Study (n.d.), 'Integrated Health and Family Planning Services,' Rural Health Research Centre, Narangwal, Punjab (undated).

Newell, K. (ed.) (1975), *Health by the People*, Geneva, WHO

Nortman, L.L. (1978), 'India's New Birth Rate Target : An Analysis,' *Population and Development Review*, Vol. 4, No. 2, June 1978, pp. 277-312.

NIHAE (1972), 'Study of District Health Administration (Phase 1),' Research Report No. 7, New Delhi.

Oberoi and Singh (1980), 'Migration, Remittances and Rural Development,' *International Labour Review*, Vol. 119, No. 2, March-April 1980.

Pai Panandikar, V. A., and Sud., A (1978), *Public Sector as an Instrument of Development*, ICSSR Research Project, New Delhi.

Pisharoti, K. A., Ranganathan, K. V., Sethu, S., and Dutt, P. R. (1972), 'The Athoor Experience : Implications for a Statewide Family Planning Program,' The Gandhigram Institute of Rural Health and Family Planning and Carolina Population Centre, University of North Carolina.

Prakash, Ved (1971), 'Land Policies for Urban Development,' *Urbanisation and National Development*, (ed.) Jakobson and Prakash, Sage Publications.

Rao, Krishnaswamy (1980), 'Development of Health Manpower,' New Delhi, National Conference on the Evaluation of Primary Health Care Programme, ICMR.

Rao, K. N. (1966), *The Nation's Health*, Basant lectures at Calcutta University, 1961, New Delhi, Publications Division, revised edition, GOI.

Seal, S. C., and R. B. Lal (1944), General Health Survey, Calcutta, Singur All India Institute of Hygiene and Public Health (AIIH & PH).

Seal, S. C. and team (1955-58), *Report of the General Health Survey*, Calcutta, AIIH & PH.

Taylor, C. E. (1980), 'Policy Relevant Findings from Narangwal,' National Conference on the Evaluation of Primary Health Care Programme, New Delhi, ICMR.

Takulia, H. C. *et al.* (1967), *The Health Centre Doctor in India*, Baltimore, Johns Hopkins.

Tiwari, T. R. *et al.* (1971), *An Exploratory Study of Integrated Health Services in India*, New Delhi, NIHAE Research Report, No. 4.

WHO (1978), 'Financing of Health Services,' Technical Report, No. 625, Geneva.

III

Case Studies
on Policy-making
and Implementation

T. V. RAO

6 Specialists, Bureaucrats and Politicians in Social Development : The National Adult Education Programme

Illiteracy can be a great impediment to the development of any individual, society or nation. If a person does not know how to read and write, he may not be able to receive, perceive and make use of the various developmental opportunities. In 1947, illiteracy was as high as 86% in India. This came down to 65.5% in 1971 (excluding the 0-4 age group). However, due to rapid population growth the absolute number of illiterates has gone up from 247 million in 1951 to 307 million in 1971. According to the census of 1971 the total number of illiterate persons above 14 years age was 209.5 million of which 97.1 million were in the age group 15 to 35. Considering the seriousness of this problem, a massive effort to increase adult literacy was launched in October 1978 in the form of the National Adult Education Programme (NAEP). A policy statement NAEP was prepared and widely publicised and discussed *(Appendix)*. The outline of NAEP issued by the Ministry of Education envisaged the following :[1]

1. In a phased way starting from April 1979 all the 100 million people in the age group 15 to 35 years will be covered by the NAEP by the year 1983-84.

2. Starting with a coverage of 4.5 million illiterate adults in 1979-80 (the coverage was estimated to be 1.5 million for 1978-79) a capacity for covering 35 million adults every year through adult education centres was envisaged. Starting with the initial aim of eradicating illiteracy, the adult education centres would be subsequently used to strive for a learning society in which life-long education is a cherished goal.

3. The outline also envisaged the creation of a favourable environment through the involvement of political leaders and mass media, the holding of seminars and symposia, and the participation of voluntary and various governmental agencies, etc. The year 1978-79 was declared as the year of preparation for this.

4. The outline envisaged the involvement of a number of agencies in the implementation of the programme. These included voluntary agencies, Nehru Yuvak Kendras and educational institutions. The role of the government was envisaged mostly as that of coordination and taking the entire responsibility whenever needed.

5. Resources like teaching-learning materials, training designs and materials for instructors, and evaluation feedback were to be developed by the State Resource Centres to be established in each State. The Directorate of Adult Education and the National Resource Group at the central level consisting of experts and expert agencies were expected to provide national level resources for the programme.

6. The involvement of all agencies including SRCs, educational institutions and others was envisaged in the evaluation, monitoring and administration of the programme.

Adult education activities were proposed to be carried out through Adult Education Centres (AECs) in the villages. Each AEC will have an instructor who is paid a salary of Rs. 50 per month. Each centre is expected to enroll about 30 adults and conduct classes at night. A period of 10 months was thought to be sufficient to impart literacy and numeracy at the same time focusing on functionality and social awareness components. A group of 30 AECs would have a full-time supervisor whose function is to identify instructors through community participation, train them, initiate classes, supply materials, assist the centre with educational resources and evaluate the progress.

By the middle of 1979, 94,181 AECs were reported to have been set up by the State governments, voluntary agencies, Nehru Yuvak Kendras, universities and ICDS workers all over the country. Thus, between 2.5 to 3 million adults were getting educational facilities through AECs.[2] Several teaching materials were developed by the State Resource Centres and other voluntary agencies. Fifteen SRCs were established which catered to the needs of nineteen States. Four of them were set up with the help of universities and the rest with the assistance of voluntary agencies.

In terms of programme management, the National Board of Adult Education was established in August 1977. It was comprised of State education ministers, and the heads of organisations like the UGC, Central Social Welfare Board, Khadi and Village Industries Commission, Federation of Indian Chambers of Commerce & Industry, Indian Adult Education Association, and a number of other non-officials and field workers. It met four times and set up several task committees to work out details. The Central Ministry started coordinating with other ministries, like the Health and Family Welfare Ministry and Ministry of Agriculture, to participate and make use of the Adult Education Programme. In six States, full-fledged Directorates of Adult Education were set up to administer the programme. In other States special cells were created in the Directorates of Education. State Boards of Adult Education and steering committees were set up. The State Boards were headed by the Chief Ministers and included the Secretaries of various departments. The steering committees were headed by the Chief Secretaries. To coordinate and administer the programme at the district level, District Adult Education Boards were set up with the Collector as the Chairman having responsibilities to steer the committees. By August 1979 administrative units had been established in 163 districts covering thirteen States.

In addition, the Central Government felt that it would be useful to involve reputed national institutions in external evaluation and experimentation. As a step in this direction six institutions were assigned the task of evaluation and experimentation through adult education cells. These included the Indian Institute of Management, Ahmedabad, Sardar Patel Institute of Economic and Social Research, Tata Institute of Social Sciences, Madras Institute of Development Studies, Institute of Economic Growth and the ANS Institute of Social Studies.

Some Achievements of the NAEP

By 1980 about 130,000 AECs were reported to be functioning with an enrolment of about 3.64 million adults — 55.8% of them were women, 19.1% from Scheduled Castes and 15.1% from Scheduled Tribes. This figure is fairly impressive when compared with the estimated enrolment of 4.5 million by 1979-80. According to the 1981 Census the percentage of illiteracy decreased to 59% (excluding the 0-4 age group — it was 65.5% in 1971). The contribution of the NAEP to this drop in illiteracy is not known and it is probably being too optimistic to expect any dramatic contribution from the NAEP when its design was not followed to its logical end.

However, independent evaluations carried out by various institutions indicate that the NAEP can be considered as having enjoyed a fair degree of success during the initial years (recent evaluation studies are not complete). From a review of ten appraisal studies by seven different institutions conducted up to 1981 in the States of Rajasthan, Bihar, Gujarat, Maharashtra and Tamil Nadu, Mathur and Premchand made the following observations :[3]

1. On an average only 12% of the AECs were closed before completing ten months of instruction.
2. The mean enrolment was about twenty-nine adults per centre as against thirty as envisaged in the design.
3. Average daily attendance in the centres varied from fourteen to twenty-five.
4. A large portion of adults attending the AECs have become literate as measured by simple tests. For example, in Bihar 60% of learners could fill a form designed to test their reading-writing abilities; in Gujarat 60% of learners were found to acquire reading and writing skills; in Maharashtra about 80% of learners were found to have acquired literacy and in Rajasthan about two-thirds of the learners were found to acquire reading-writing skills. The overall assessment indicates that more than 50% of those who attend the AECs acquire reading, writing and numerical abilities. However, achievements in the areas of 'functionality' and 'social awareness' are poor.
5. Voluntary agencies have been found to do good work in adult education in spite of very meagre resources given to them by the government.

Historical Influences

In a document entitled 'Planning and Administration of India's National Adult Education Programmes : A Personal Case Study' prepared for the International Institute of Educational Planning, Anil Bordia traces the history of adult education in India.* The milestones in the history of adult education as indicated in this paper are as follows :

1. The British period saw the emergence of a wide variety of adult education programmes in India. The Indian Education Commission (1882-83) found that there were 136 and 223 night schools in the Bombay and Madras Presidencies attended by about 4000 and 5000 adults respectively. In Bengal there were over 1,000 night schools. Besides, schools were also started in 1865 for inmates of jails.

2. In 1927 there were 288,932 adult pupils attending 11,171 literacy classes of which over 80,000 pupils and over 3,000 classes were in Punjab alone.

3. Some of the most impressive adult education programmes ·were launched at the beginning of the century in the princely states of Mysore and Baroda. M. Visveswarayya established a massive programme in Mysore State where nearly 70,000 literacy classes used to be run regularly. Visveswarayya also set up a public library system and sponsored publication of a magazine, *Vigyan*, to popularise scientific knowledge among the neoliterates.

4. With the establishment of popular ministries in 1937, several States evinced extraordinary interest in adult literacy. Under the leadership of Dr. Syed Mahmud, a most impressive campaign was conducted in Bihar. Mass literacy committees were set up at the State, district, subdivision and village levels.

5. What political commitment can do was demonstrated by the Gram Shikshan Mohim (Village Education Movement). This programme was launched on an experimental basis in Satara district of the then Bombay State in 1959 and extended to the rest of the State two years later. During its peak years (1961-63) the Mohim covered twenty-five districts and made all persons

* This section is an abridged version of the historical account presented by Anil Bordia in his paper.

in the 11-50 age group literate in 1,109 villages. The number of persons made literate was over a million and the percentage of literates increased from 34.27 to 44.94 in Maharashtra between 1961 and 1971 although the average increase in the whole of India was from 27.76 to 34.08.

6. The Farmer's Functional Literacy Programme was launched in 1967-68. This was an inter-ministerial programme with the Ministry of Education having responsibility for functional literacy, the Ministry of Agriculture for farmer's training and AIR for farm broadcasting. This programme was evaluated in 1977-78 by a committee which observed that the basic idea of integrating literacy with functional training and the use of mass media as a support activity was still valid. It recommended a substantial enlargement of the programme and widening of its linkage with the main schemes of rural development. Many areas which required improvement, including interdepartmental coordination and monitoring, were pointed out by the committee.

7. A major programme, called Non-Formal Education, for the 15-25 age group was launched in 1975-76 with the object of providing meaningful education to the young. It envisaged setting up 100 non-formal education centres in each district by the end of 1977-78 and intended to serve the weaker sections of society who had been denied the benefit of formal education. Although conceptually this programme incorporated recent thinking in the field of adult education, in practice it was seldom distinguishable from a routine literacy programme.

8. Apart from the programmes implemented by the government, the Ministry of Education and Social Welfare has been promoting adult education through voluntary agencies since 1953-54. About twenty-five agencies were being funded for this purpose up to 1976-77.

9. One of the noteworthy precursors of the NAEP was the emphasis laid on literacy by the Youth Congress — the youth wing of the AICC (I). Literacy was one of the points in the five-point programme championed by the Youth Congress. Although the Youth Congress lacked conceptual clarity with regard to its literacy programme, their efforts did engage the attention of the central Education Ministry as well as the State governments.

Views of Technicians

The Directorate of Adult Education was the technical wing of the NAEP. The Directorate played an important role in assisting the Ministry of Education in the design, monitoring and continuous review of the programme. It also provided assistance to the States in effective implementation of the programme through continuous review, guidance and dissemination of information. The views expressed by three experts* who have been associated with the Directorate are summarised in the following pages.

Dr. A. K. Jalaluddin, Dr. Anita Dighe and Mr. R. S. Mathur are authorities in the field of applied adult education in rural India. They have been closely associated with the planning and implementation of the National Adult Education Programme as senior functionaries at the Directorate of Adult Aducation, New Delhi. They were interviewed with regard to the development of the adult education programme in India, the people associated with it from different parts of the community, the role played by them and the future of the programme in India.

According to Dr. Jalaluddin, the programme existed in the country much before the NAEP was introduced. The introduction of the NAEP was with the sole objective of providing an umbrella for innovative programmes of adult education in the country. Dr. Jalaluddin felt that no one person could be credited with pushing the NAEP in 1978. He felt that it was more a creation of the prevailing political climate than anything else. The government at that time believed that adult education was needed for the process of democratisation. The bureaucracy, seeing the politician's keenness, worked for the programme in their own interests. Dr. Jalaluddin added that the same bureaucracy is presently hesitant to wholeheartedly work for the programme. He felt that more credit should be given to those who took it up at the grassroots level — the people who learnt and the field level functionaries who taught. He cited the incident of a young instructor in Orissa who contributed Rs. 10

* Dr. Jalaluddin, Dr. Dighe and Mr. Mathur were interviewed by Mr. R. Harihar, Adult Education Cell, PSG, Indian Institute of Management, Ahmedabad. Dr. A. K. Jalaluddin, currently a Professor at the NCERT, New Delhi, was directing the activities of the Directorate during the initial years of the NAEP. Dr. Anita Dighe was a consultant at the Directorate of Adult Education while Mr. R. S. Mathur was Deputy Director in the Directorate (and still continues to be actively involved in adult education).

to the region's adult education association from the payment of Rs. 50 made to him.

Dr. Dighe expressed similar views. However, she felt that due credit should be given to some people who worked hard for the programme. She praised the efforts of Shri Anil Bordia during whose tenure as Joint Secretary in the Education Ministry the adult education programme progressed tremendously. She also credited Dr. Jalaluddin with revitalising the working of the Directorate of Adult Education in New Delhi. Mr. R. S. Mathur added that the entire governmental machinery had been behind the programme during the Janata government. Now, the same climate did not exist any more and it was difficult for the people administering the programme.

Commenting on the role played by intellectuals, Dr. Jalaluddin said that the academic community had taken it far more seriously than before. At one time it was thought that the increasing Gross National Product would take care of the problems faced by the country. When no solution to the problem materialised, the intellectuals began to look for what was fundamentally wrong. Two schools of thought emerged at this juncture. The first school wanted to increase participation at the village level to ensure and distribute equity. The second school believed that there can be no success in this effort. Political and social awareness were more important. However, more intellectuals belonged to the first school than the second and for the first time political, religious, social and intellectual leaders joined hands for a cause. Mr. Mathur also felt that the intellectuals have realised that they have a responsibility towards those who have been deprived of education. Students, teachers, intellectuals — all are more involved in the programme now than before.

The Directorate functioned as a technical wing. Dr. Jalaluddin said that it was modelled after the National Adult Education Board (NAEB) created in 1969. The Directorate was initially involved in developing expertise at the State and district levels. It also printed illustrated material including posters, made slides and provided a great deal of technical inputs. Mr. Mathur traced the history of technical bodies from the National Fundamental Education Centre of 1956, the National Adult Education Board of 1969 and finally to the present National Directorate. The Directorate was initially detached from the NCERT to perform a secretarial role for the

NAEB. Subsequently, it became the main body for directing adult education in the country, and the NAEB is now an almost defunct body which needs to be restructured. Mr. Mathur listed the following functions of the Directorate.

1. All technical support including planning, organising, directing;
2. Helping the State ministries;
3. Preparation of the curriculum;
4. Preparation of broad guidelines;
5. Monitoring, evaluation and research;
6. Preparing answers to questions raised in Parliament;
7. Deciding policies;
8. Conducting evaluation studies on its own;
9. Preparing statistics;
10. Financing research;
11. Dealing with the Urban Adult Education Programme;
12. Publishing literature;
13. Preparing a policy for follow up; and
14. Experimenting with the materials used in the AECs.

Mr. Mathur said that politicians played a big role initially as motivators at the policy-making level. Their statements in the press regarding the programme also acted as morale-boosters. The present government does not play any such role, he added.

Talking about the role of voluntary agencies Dr. Dighe felt that they play the most vital role and they should be given increasingly more responsibility for the programme. Mr. Mathur also felt that the voluntary agencies had played a vital role for the first three years of the programme. He felt that their role was being largely ignored now. The voluntary agencies were also responsible for many innovative programmes at the state level. Dr. Jalaluddin mentioned in particular the programmes in Kerala. These were the science movement and the library movement. Though not in the NAEP framework, they achieved the same objectives as the adult education programmes. Dr. Dighe mentioned the use of development theatre, social awareness songs, etc.

Speaking of the role of the State governments, Mr. Mathur said that they were sceptical initially but became more responsive as the programme advanced. States are now picking up momentum though motivation is lacking at the national level. He made special mention of the states of Bihar, **Gujarat**, Uttar Pradesh and Jammu and Kashmir.

Coming to the future of the programme in India, Dr. Jalaluddin felt that the NAEP as such does not exist now. It had been envisaged as a national development strategy. The sixth plan placed more emphasis on physical resource development than on the development of human resources. Man as a focus of development is no longer visible. He, however, felt that while the programme run by the government can contribute in a small way to the improvement of the total delivery system, improving the total system and resolving the problems besetting it cannot be done by the adult education programme alone. He saw the changing process within the community as the greater force. The NAEP will not now get much money but when the change agents in the community bring about greater awareness then the government will have to sit up and take notice. Talking about objectives and their achievement, Dr. Jalaluddin felt that quoting figures and targets was foolish right from the start. He had tried to discourage this but he did feel that the programme had achieved some of its qualitative objectives in creating an awareness among the people. The greatest achievement was the establishment of the importance of adult education. There has been a complete change in the attitude towards the NAEP in many quarters.

In contrast, Dr. Dighe foresaw a 'depressing' future and Mr. Mathur did not foresee a very dull future. Mr. Mathur felt that while its dimensions have to be broadened, the programme has a bright future in its scope for achieving results. While there exists a status quo on the government's part at the moment, things will begin to move soon.

Insights from Bureaucracy

The bureaucracy in New Delhi played a very important role in the NAEP. The Joint Secretary, Adult Education at that time played an important role in the programme from the civil servants' side — in formulating the policy, designing the structure, and implementing and monitoring the NAEP. Discussions with him and some other officials associated with the NAEP are summarised in this section.

**The Youth Congress, Adult Education Programme and
the Janata Government**

Sanjay Gandhi emphasised literacy as an important aspect of the
five-point programme. This was given great publicity. So some
efforts were made indirectly to create an awareness among the
people about the need for literacy. Dr. Nurul Hasan, Education
Minister at that time, used this to give it a push. However, apart
from strong sympathy not much took place during the Congress-I
time. During the Janata regime, P.C. Chunder, the Education
Minister, instinctively pushed adult education. In fact, he wanted
everything to be done in five years. Although suggestions were
made by the bureaucracy to develop a ten-year porgramme so as to
cover the entire population, the Prime Minister, Mr.Morarji Desai,
wanted everything to be done in five years. In fact in the first
meeting of the National Board of Adult Education the question of
whether it should be a five-year programme or a ten-year one
was put to vote. Even those who were in favour of a ten-year
programme earlier voted for the five-year option after
they knew the Prime Minister's inclination.

The Education Minister at that time played a very important
role. He gave all the support. The Prime Minister prodded the
Education Minister now and then. The Education Secretary
(Mr. Shabanayagam) also encouraged the efforts.

The momentum for the NAEP would not have been possible but
for the Janata Government; they promoted NAEP. They wanted to
make it a movement.

**Is Janata Government the Main Architect of
the Adult Education Programme?**

NAEP was built on the past. It has evolved as a result of a series of
efforts and studies. Review of farmers functional literacy programmes
was one such effort. The National Board of Adult Education existed
in 1965-66 and was only revitalised during Janata time. The credit
for pushing the NAEP in the form it took in 1978-79 goes mainly to
them, but one should not forget that a climate had already been
created before the Janata's time. They added spirit to it. Many
educationists, social workers, and experts in other fields participated
in an involved way in this process.

The First Policy Document

The policy document was first drafted by Anil Bordia, Joint Secretary in-charge of Adult Education at that time. Asher Delon, UNESCO consultant, assisted him. Bordia used to discuss policy with a number of people — Anil Sadgopal of Kishore Bharati, Malcolm Adiseshaiah, Gabriel Gonsalves (a priest who is actively involved in running adult education centres), Kishore Saint of Udaipur and others were his advisers for this purpose. It was Bordia who insisted on having a policy statement and as a result of the discussions he had with the intellectuals mentioned above, the first draft (three to four pages) was prepared. The present one (Appendix) is an outcome of that though it is drastically different from what was initially drafted by Anil Bordia. The first draft was discussed in the first meeting of the NBAE. They made some changes and wanted it to be brought back to them. Then it was discussed in a meeting of all Education Secretaries and Education Ministers of all the States who didn't make many changes and generally appreciated it. Then it went to the parliamentary consultative committee who made small changes like emphasis on post-literacy work. The NAEP outline was also prepared by the Joint Secretary Adult Education at that time.

After the draft policy statement was prepared it was shown to the Education Secretary and the Education Minister. But they made no comments. They wanted it to be discussed in the NBAE. The Prime Minister saw it only during the discussions in NBAE and made no comments.

Intellectuals who had an interest in and understanding of adult education were very closely associated in this effort. For example, half of the National Board consisted of intellectuals, the other half were politicians and civil servants. Even among civil servants the Joint Secretary, Education Secretary and the Education Minister tried to get those with an intellectual orientation. Most of the informal advisors were intellectuals from voluntary agencies.

However, not many academics were involved at this stage. This was because the bureaucracy in Delhi felt that university teachers were preoccupied with formal systems of education and their vision was limited to their immediate concerns like teacher-training. However, the draft was discussed in the conference of Vice-Chancellors. They did not make any changes although they discussed it for half-a-day. Although the officials in the Ministry felt that the university system is not geared to understand mass-oriented programmes, they took it to the universities in order to involve them. It was discussed in the University Grants Commission and a few small changes were made on the basis of its suggestions. Dr. Madhuri Shah and Malcolm Adiseshaiah were two people who were actively involved from the beginning. The officials in the Ministry could not think of many academics who could make a real contribution to this kind of thing.

There is nothing controversial in the document (except one statement about the past efforts). It is a reasonably well-drafted statement. Although it was discussed at length in several forums generally nobody said very much against it or even modified it. For example, it was discussed in 3,200 of the 4,000 colleges of the country. Apart from occasional, casual suggestions like '50% of education budget should be for adult education', and 'We should start it after every child is brought to school', no concrete suggestions were made. The discussions helped people to understand and reflect on adult education. For example, statements in the policy document like 'that the illiterate and the poor can rise to their own liberation through literacy, dialogue and action' may have generated enough thinking. In fact statements of this kind were prepared after considerable thought, debate and discussions in the Ministry. On this statement alone several pages of notes were prepared and discussed and the analytical discussions centred round what Paulo Freire said or what the Gandhian perspective was.

In sum, the politicians decided that there should be an Adult Education Programme. All details regarding its framework and implementation, however, were decided by intellectuals, professionals, civil servants, experienced adult educators, university professors and leading voluntary organisations like the Indian Adult Education Association. The idea of the State Resource Centre was entirely the idea of the bureaucracy. They felt that there was a need for an agency to develop learning materials, conduct training and provide resources. Thus it is one thing to give a political directive, and quite another to prepare a nationwide structure and organisation and to implement it. The bureaucracy played an important role in this case with the help of several others.

National Board of Adult Education and its Role

The idea of the NBAE is not entirely new. There was such a Board in the past. In 1965 when Dr. V.K.R.V. Rao was the Education Minister and when the fourth plan was being prepared, he wanted to give adult education a great deal of importance and convened one meeting of the NBAE. It was a very different kind of Board. It comprised of the ministers from all the States and was like an assembly, not a deliberative body. Eventually, adult education did not get as much attention as was intended. The officials in the Ministry of Education took the idea from there and formulated the NBAE. It has a different composition now and its functions have become different. It was constituted to be more professional. It has for its members the chairman of the UGC, professionals, and a select group of representatives from States, among others. Only five States were represented and the Ministry wanted the membership to rotate. The total membership of the NBAE was about thirty. Nine non-officials were members. The basic idea was that the real decisions on adult education must be taken not by politicians alone or by civil servants, but by a combined group of politicians, civil servants, intellectuals, thinkers, professional adult educators and field workers. This rationale was taken down the line to the States and districts in order to create mechanisms for the involvement of different sections of the community.

When the NBAE was constituted, the Ministry decided that all policy decisions should be taken by the NBAE only. The Board met four times, twice every year. The ministry officials felt that all the meetings were very useful. Members were very punctual and they were kept informed of the progress in implementation. There were occasions when the Ministry's thinking did not agree with the Board's, but they went by the Board's decision. For example, some officials in the Ministry were opposed to giving any education activity to trade unions. But the Board decided to involve the trade unions and therefore they tried to involve them. Of course, they did not respond positively!

Role Played by Colleges, Voluntary Agencies, and Bodies like AVARD

The colleges took a lot of interest. In Tamil Nadu about 70 colleges were running regular projects of sixty AECs each. About 600 to 700 colleges in the country had regular programmes. Thus they did a good job in their own way in the first year itself. Out of these about one-third were very innovative programmes. Some of them linked it up with theatre, family planning, and the like.

AVARD unfortunately got alienated from the beginning from the programme as it wanted to be recognised as a central agency for involving the voluntary agencies. The Ministry did not want such a super-voluntary agency as they wanted the State governments to be involved. The Gandhi Peace Foundation participated. The Indian Adult Education Association discussed and prepared a statement which the Ministry took into consideration while discussing the programme in the NBAE.

Besides being a very neatly designed programme, the NAEP has several strengths. These include : (a) the use of voluntary agencies; (b) the idea of State Resource Centres; (c) involvement of external institutions for evaluation, research and monitoring; (d) the scope provided in the programme for experimentation and innovation; and (e) the attempt to make it a mass programme. One keeps wondering how all these things got built into such a well-knit programme and who is the main force behind the entire thing.

An investigation into this reveals that Anil Bordia was one of the important forces behind this, although in an interview with the case-writer Bordia stated modestly that he played only a limited role. According to him, the ideas came from many people — all that he was able to do was to mobilise these ideas through discussions with hundreds of people. He was one of the very strong protagonists of voluntary agencies. He did not think that we could have an adult education programme in this country without them. He felt that there is a basic fatality about government programmes. He felt that people like Mohan Singh Mehta and J.P. Naik contributed a great deal towards highlighting the role of voluntary agencies.

There were certain coincidences also. Bordia, for example, was connected with a voluntary agency called the Rajasthan Adult Education Association. As a result of several discussions regarding the role of this agency it was decided to start a State Resources Centre and the Government of India was able to fund it. So they submitted a proposal and got the SRC sanctioned. This was much before the NAEP started. Similarly, the Indian Institute of Education, Pune, also became an SRC. So when the NAEP came into existence the Ministry easily adopted this idea.

The RSS and Jana Sangh Involvement

The officials in the Ministry associated with the NAEP at that time emphatically denied that the RSS and the Jana Sangh were involved in the NAEP. In fact there was a deliberate policy to debar communal agencies from funding. Some of the officials themselves had negative attitudes towards communal organisations and felt that they can do more harm to this country than anybody else. So, they excluded them all. For example, a big agency was set up in Rajasthan and application was made for 3,000 centres. The Ministry sanctioned only thirty centres. The Ministry officials felt that under those circumstances not to sanction any centre was impossible. So they felt that out of 3,000 centres sanctioning thirty was like sanctioning zero. In Madhya Pradesh the RSS group had set up a voluntary organisation and wanted it to be recognised as the state Resource Centre. The Ministry had to put up a hard fight with that State. They did not recognise this SRC and in fact the programme in Madhya Pradesh suffered a lot due to this. There was no SRC in Madhya Pradesh. There were problems in Andhra Pradesh in the beginning more because of a particular person in the Directorate of Adult Education rather than any one higher up.

Karnataka wanted the entire thing to be given to the Karnataka Adult Education Association which was headed by a political person. The Ministry wanted them to review it. Subsequently they took more interest. West Bengal took a good deal of interest. Similarly, Jammu & Kashmir. Apparently there was never a problem with the two Congress-administered States, but Janata States did create problems.

Bureaucracy and NAEP — the Political Aspect

A Joint Secretary in the Ministry meets the Minister practically every day. So the Education Minister used to make informal enquiries and whenever there were problems the Joint Secretary used to go to him. There were seldom any formal meetings. The Education Minister used to invite other Ministers to come to the Education Ministry and discuss the programme. One of the interesting things about this programme is that it is not a programme of the Education Ministry alone. All other ministries were involved and have set up adult education cells. The Joint Secretary from the Education Ministry worked with other civil servants to keep them acquainted. He personally preferred not to deal with politicians directly either in the States or at the centre. He always dealt with them through the Education Minister only. If any state education minister or chief minister had problems the Education Minister used to invite them for informal discussions at the Ministry and sort them out.

From the States, only Mr. Sheik Abdullah used to ask for the presence of Ministry officials whenever he reviewed the progress of adult education in his State. He only used to convene meetings after making sure that the Joint Secretary from the central Ministry was available.

Other Mechanisms used by the Ministry

In order to obtain a first hand experience of the problems involved in implementation and in order to do some intensive work, the Joint Secretary adopted Bihar State. He used to visit one district every month. Bihar seemed such a challenge. He took it as a learning experience. He was very interested in knowing why everybody says that nothing can be done in Bihar. He felt that if we can spread adult education in Bihar it can become a beginning for doing other things.

Education Minister and the States

The Education Minister did a lot to influence the State education ministers. He used to write letters regularly. Whenever they came to him he used to first ask about how adult education is going on. Whenever he went on tour, he discussed adult education. The Ministry officials used to brief him for these discussions. The Ministry officials also used to organise regional meetings on adult and primary education convened by the Education Secretary. He used to call the Chief Secretaries and others.

Participation of other Departments

The NAEP was a cabinet decision, and it clearly stated that every department had to participate in it. The Education Ministry conducted a survey about what role which ministry could play in adult education. They prepared a compendium of these activities and published it. The Agriculture Minister was a member of the NBAE and in every meeting of the NBAE he had to give an account of the contributions of his departments in various States. Similarly, bodies like the UGC, Central Board of Workers Education and National Cooperative Union — the whole network of official, non-official and semi-official organisations — had to give an account of their work. For example, SAIL, Coal India Ltd., and others undertook adult education activities.

This is one level of involvement. However, more important than this is the coordination and linkages at the field level. For example, workers from different areas like agriculture, health and family welfare should have participated and used this opportunity for developing people. No such thing happened at the field level and this is one of the major weaknesses of the programme. In fact, the review committee report also identified this lack of linkage with developmental sectors as a major weakness in the programme. It was possible to focus on social awareness aspects in a state like Bihar. But even in that State there was a failure on functionality. This may be because of the excessive reliance on the bureaucratic structure. The Education Ministry did press all these ministries to introduce awareness training for all their functionaries. However, sometimes they ran into serious problems. For example, when the Education Ministry identified CHV, milk collectors of cooperatives, and others to conduct adult education classes, they did not receive enough cooperation. For example, the Health Ministry did not agree to the idea of CHVs becoming adult educators. There was a basic mental block in the leadership of the Health Ministry to these kind of ideas. Although the Health Minister at that time was willing to pick it up, one of the civil servants in the Health Ministry strongly opposed this. The officials in the Education Ministry did not want to get any orders passed for this, because they wanted voluntary and committed involvement rather than forced involvement. Similarly, at the district level they relied heavily on District Collectors. The Ministry officials thought that they would see NAEP as an important development programme. Unfortunately, they lacked the orientation required to take this programme seriously. This is probably a basic problem with our development efforts.

Of course, there were a few District Collectors who took active interest, particularly in Bihar. For example, one of the District Deputy Commissioners in Bihar used to function as the District Adult Education Officer. He mobilised workers from all departments and got them to work in this programme. Some voluntary agencies have done an excellent job. For example, one agency used voluntary health workers, retired doctors, etc. The whole programme has become a 'Chetna Sangh'.

Mass Media and the Ministry

The officials in the Ministry did not miss any opportunity. For example, on every special occasion a reference was made to the NAEP. The Convocation addresses, addresses of the Education Minister to Vice-Chancellors as also his discussions with bodies like UGC were used as opportunities to discuss the NAEP. Wherever the Minister went to address (including teachers rallies),the address of the Prime Minister, President, Vice-President and others were used as opportunities to talk about the NAEP. The briefs were prepared by officials in the Ministry. The mass media were also used. The wall paper of the Ministry of Information and Broadcasting called 'Hamara Desh', for example. Films were also made. The Ministry arranged to include the item in the news reviews. Similarly there were regular programmes on TV and radio. The Education Secretary met editors of newspapers and magazines and requested them to publish items about adult education. The Ministry even paid them travel expenses and did not want to bother about what they wrote as long as they wrote something.

The mobilisation of financial resources was monitored through the Planning Commission. The Education Secretary used to sit with every Chief Secretary and make sure that funds were allocated for adult education. He took a very active role in this aspect.

NAEP During the Time Charan Singh was PM

It appears that Charan Singh did not believe in NAEP. During his tenure Mr. Karan Singh was the Education Minister. He also was not quite involved in adult literacy. The then Education Minister wanted to reduce financial allocations to adult education and put it in higher education. Some of the Ministry officials were worried and went to Dr. D. S. Kothari for whom the Education Minister had great respect. As a result of these discussions a review committee was set up and it was decided that nobody would touch the NAEP till the review committee submitted its report. So the review commitee was in a way an outcome of the thinking of the bureaucracy committed to the NAEP. The review committee idea also gained momentum partly because some of the committed bureaucrats started seeing several weaknesses in the programme and thought that the review committee would come up with suggestions. The officials in the Ministry thought that it should seek the views of people outside the programme. For example, Ila Bhatt and D.S. Kothari had very little to do with the NAEP. Since science and technology were not well represented, they decided to have a Scientist as Chairman of the group. Thus the committee came into existence with Dr. Kothari as Chairman.

For the Success of Social Development Programmes is it the Political Commitment or the Bureaucracy and its Commitment or both that are Important?

What lessons can be drawn from the NAEP ?

According to Anil Bordia who studied the development programmes in other countries subsequent to his experience in NAEP :

It is difficult to give any clear answer. It depends on what you want to organise. If you want to organise a political movement like in Ethiopia, Tanzania etc. then you need political leadership, political cadre including village level leaders become important and that is it. And mind you in countries like Cuba, Ethiopia, Tanzania etc. there are two principal characteristics. One is a one party authoritarian system of govt. The second characteristic is that a programme of this kind is accompanied by fundamental changes in socio-economic structure, class system etc. So the whole thing becomes different. In India you can look at any program — NAEP, Health Care, Dairy Development etc. You cannot bring about fundamental changes in the economic, class and caste relationships. What you can do is only to make the lives of poor people a good deal more dignified and better — healthwise, nutritionally, educationally, economically etc. You cannot change the agrarian relationships. You cannot run the programme without money. In the countries I mentioned above you can close all the schools for a year and ask every one to go and work for adult education. In India you cannot do that. Money has to be provided and allocation of money depends on political commitment.

You cannot run a programme of this kind without a number of important decisions being made and number of agencies being involved. A source of all these decisions is political support and will. But, I believe that these are two other things that are important. One is that political support and decision is not enough to run a long term programme. Education can never be a short-term programme. Primary and adult education is a very long term programme. This kind of long term programme requires careful design, planning and administration. That is where the Bureaucracy becomes important. So, I would say that political commitment is indispensable — but not necessarily political commitment of the kind in Ethiopia and Tanzania where the political party takes over everything.

Anyway one needs to give a lot more thought to this aspect !

Notes

1. GOI, *National Adult Education Programme : An Outline,* New Delhi, Ministry of Education and Social Welfare, 1979.
2. GOI, *NAEP : The First Year,* New Delhi, Ministry of Education and Culture, October 1979.
3. R. S. Mathur and Premchand, *Adult Education Programme : Analysis of Strengths and Deficiencies — A Critical Review of Appraisal Studies,* New Delhi, Directorate of Adult Education, December 1981.

APPENDIX

Adult Education — A Policy Statement

Exclusion of a vast majority of the people from the process of education is a most disturbing aspect of educational and social planning. This has been uppermost in the consideration of the present Government ever since it assumed office in March 1977. While determined efforts must be made to universalise elementary education up to the age of fourteen years, educational facilities must be extended to adult population to remedy their educational deprivation and to enable them to develop their potentiality. Indeed, universalisation of elementary education and of adult literacy are mutually interdependent.

2. The Government has resolved to wage a clearly-conceived, well-planned and relentless struggle against illiteracy to enable the masses to play an active role in social and cultural change. Literacy ought to be recognised as an integral part of an individual's personality. The present thinking on adult education is based on tha assumptions (a) *that illiteracy is a serious impediment to an individual's growth and to country's socio-economic progress;* (b) *that education is not co-terminus with schooling but takes place in most work and life situations;* (c) *that learning, working, and living are inseparable and each acquires a meaning only when correlated with the others;* (d) *that the means by which people are involved in the process of development are at least as important as the ends;* and (e) *that the illiterate and the poor can rise to their own liberation through literacy, dialogue and action.*

3. Adult education should emphasise imparting of literary skills to persons belonging to the economically and social deprived sections of society. However, such persons often lack motivation for sustained participation in literacy and follow-up programmes. In this context, stress should be laid on learning rather than teaching, on use of the spoken language in literacy programmes and on harnessing of the mass media. Motivation also depends on an awareness among the participants that they *can transform their destinies and that the adult education programmes will lead to advancement of their functional capability for the realisation of this objective.* Moreover, a literacy programme unrelated to the working and living conditions of the learners, to the challenges of the environment and the developmental needs of the country, cannot secure an active participation of the learners;

nor can it be an instrument of development and progress. Adult education, therefore, while emphasising acquisition of literacy skills, should also be

— relevant to the environment and learners' needs;
— flexible regarding duration, time, location, instructional arrangements,
— diversified in regard to curriculum, teaching and learning materials and methods; and
— systematic in all aspects of organisation.

4. Highest priority in adult education needs to be given to the illiterate persons. In the post-independence period, the achievements in the field of literacy have been far from satisfactory. In 1947, the rate of literacy was 14 per cent, which rose tc 34.45 per cent (excluding the age-group 0-4) in 1971. Yet, owing to population increase and half-heartedness of the past effort, the number of illiterate persons has risen from 247 million in 1951 to 307 million in 1971. According to the Census of 1971 the total number of illiterate persons above fourteen years of age is 209.5 million, of which 97.1 million are in the age-group of 15-35, which is likely to be about 100 million at present. A massive programme should be launched to cover this vast segment of population in 15-35 age-group as far as possible within five years of its launching. This implies organisation of special programmes for women and for persons belonging to Scheduled Castes and Scheduled Tribes. The regions which have a concentration of illiteracy will also require special attention.

5. While the conceptual position stated in paragraphs 2 and 3 needs emphasis, the need to view the programme as a mass movement must also be underlined. From the organisational point of view it is of utmost importance that elaborate preparations are made before launching a massive programme. Identification and motivation of the instructors, preparation of curriculum and teaching/learning materials and training have been the main areas of deficiency in adult education programmes in the past. A satisfactory level of preparedness in these areas must be reached before the programme is to be launched. *Besides, adult education must cease to be a concern only of the educational authority. It should be an indispensable input in all sectors of development, particularly where participation of the beneficiaries*

is crucial to the fulfilment of development objectives. A pre-requisite of an adult education movement is that all agencies, governmental, voluntary, private and public sector industry, institutions of formal education, etc., should lend strength to it. Voluntary agencies have a special role to play and necessary steps shall have to be taken to secure their full involvement. Instructional work shall have to be done by the teachers, students and unemployed men and women. It would be of great advantage if unemployed or under-employed youth having the potentiality to organise adult education programmes are provided necessary training and then entrusted with the responsibility for organising such programmes. To ensure effectiveness and systematic analysis of the problems, the programmes should have built-in mechanisms for monitoring and evaluation as well as for applied research. *Finally, importance must be laid on follow-up measures such as production and distribution of reading materials, organised learning and group action.*

6. Adequate financial and administrative support will be essential for organisation of the massive programme. Provision shall have to be made for a programme comprising literacy as well as environmental and social education, extending to approximately 300-350 hours or about 9 months, and also taking into account other costs. The required resources shall have to be provided by the Government, local bodies, voluntary agencies, trade and industry, etc. A realistic assessment should be made of the size and capability of the administrative and professional apparatus which would be necessary for the programme and necessary steps taken to create it.

7. In addition to organising a massive programme for adult illiterates, it is necessary to provide special programmes for special groups based on their special needs. For example, programmes are needed for

— urban workers to improve their skills, to prepare them for securing their rightful claims and for participation in management;
— Government functionaries, such as office clerks, field extension workers and police and armed forces personnel, to upgrade their competence;
— employees of commercial establishments, such as banks and insurance companies, to improve their performance; and
— housewives to inculcate a better understanding of family life problems and women's status in society.

Programmes for these and several other categories of persons could be organised through class-room participation, correspondence courses or mass media, or by a combination of all these.

8. It is of the greatest importance that implementation of adult education programmes is decentralised. It would also be necessary to establish agencies of coordination and catalisation. A National Board of Adult Education has been established for this purpose by the Central Government and similar Boards should be established at the State levels. Suitable agencies should also be created at the field level for coordination and for involvement of the various agencies in the programme.

RUSHIKESH M. MARU

7 Policy Formulation as Political Process — A Case Study of Health Manpower : 1949-75

The capability of health programmes to effectively reach the vast majority of the rural masses depends on the quality, distribution and utilisation of health manpower.

The evolution of the Indian health manpower policy has been characterised by two different models of health manpower development. One model is based on primacy of quality considerations in design of health care programmes, concentration of health personnel in urban areas, unwillingness to recognise indigenous medical practitioners as participants in the regular health care network, and opposition to delegation of the primary curative functions to para-medical personnel. For the sake of brevity, we shall call this a 'professional' model of health manpower development. An alternative model emphasises redistribution of medical manpower and physical facilities in favour of rural and poorer sections of the society. This, in turn, requires a rapid increase in admissions to medical colleges, shortening the duration of medical courses and greater emphasis on the use of para-professionals and indigenous medical practitioners in regular health organisation. The proponents of this model, however, argue that the twin criteria of quality and wider accessibility of health care cannot be fulfilled simultaneously at the present stage of development in poor countries such as India, and that accessibility must get precedence over quality for a certain transitional period of development. In contrast with the 'professional' model, we shall call this a 'populist' model of health manpower development.

It should be made clear that the professional and the populist models are not mutually exclusive. Every society has a different combination of elements from each of these models depending on its needs, resources, and value orientations. The main difference between the two models is in terms of the *predominance* of either professional concern with quality of health care or of the populist concern with serving the largest number of people. When the professional model is predominant, the principal question that policy-makers ask themselves is : 'Which of the manpower strategies are likely to provide the best possible health care?' But when the populist model is prevalent, policy-makers are guided by a different set of questions, such as : 'Which of the manpower policies will enable us to reach the largest number of our clients?' and 'Which ones will provide at least primary health care to the poorest, the remotest, sections of our society?'

In India the professional model was the main framework for health policy until 1966. The populist model has gained increasing acceptance from the Ministry of Health and Family Planning during the late 1960s and early 1970s. Even during the periods of the prevalence of the professional model, certain elements of the popular model were grafted on it in a kind of uneasy alliance. For example, the indigenous systems of medicine had started gaining limited legitimacy from the mid-1950s. Similarly, a rapid expansion in medical education occurred from early 1950s even in the face of repeated warnings from medical professionals about the dangers of diluting the quality of medical training. It is, therefore, important to account for both the dominance of one or the other model as well as deviations from it.

How can we explain such shifts in policies over time? Four clusters of explanatory variables are proposed as relevant to our analysis of specific policy choices and policy shifts over time :

1. Personal socialisation and background of relevant actors in the health policy process, such as education and previous professional and political experience;
2. Attitudes and opinions of the relevant professional and political elites towards health manpower issues;

3. Relative influence of various individual actors and groups in the health policy process; and
4. Environmental influences — such as, resource constraints, popular pressure for redistribution of resources, ideological milieu and external influence. The latter includes both specific influences of foreign agencies and more general western cultural influences.

A brief methodological explanation of the limits of our evidence on elite attitudes is necessary. We have relied mainly on written documents for reconstructing the policy-making process. Most of our evidence is limited and indirect. It is not therefore possible to systematically measure the attitude and opinion of the relevant elites. What we can reasonably try to do is to *infer* attitudes and opinions from indirect evidence regarding the educational and career background characteristics of the elites and some public statements. In other words, we will attempt to develop a plausible explanation for particular policy choices and shifts over time through an analysis of the policy process, roles and values of those exercising the greatest influence over policy determination in the health field, and a set of environmental influences.

Policy-making Arenas

In order to understand the Indian policy process. we must identify the most important policy-making arenas of the Indian political system.

In India, the four most important groups at the central level are the Prime Minister and his cabinet colleagues, the members of Parliament, the Ministry of Health, the Indian Medical Association, and the Planning Commission. The state leaders form a different policy arena, but they participate in central policy-making through coordinating institutions such as the Central Council of Health. The following policy-making arenas are the most important sites of health policy formulation in India.

1. *The Prime Minister's Arena :* This includes the Prime Minister and his cabinet colleagues. As we shall see later, the values and preferences of this arena have varied from Nehru to Mrs. Gandhi.

Mrs. Gandhi has been more favourable to the populist model than her father, Jawaharlal Nehru. Despite these differences, the involvement and interest of the arena in health issues have remained fairly low during most of the period since independence.

2. *The Parliamentary Arena :* Parliament has the authority to approve the budget of the Ministry of Health. The members of Parliament get an opportunity to criticise the Ministry's activities during the debate on demand for grants. The members of Parliament also participate in consultative committees and evaluate the Ministry's performance. The views of the members of Parliament may differ according to their personal backgrounds, but, in general, they have supported the populist model of health care.

3. *The Bureaucratic Arena :* This is under the control of the Ministry of Health. The Minister of Health and his junior colleagues, officers of the generalist Indian administrative service, professional bureaucrats in charge of technical departments are the immediate actors within the Ministry's arena. Until 1966, the Ministry leadership was dominated by ministers who either had a medical background or were highly sympathetic to professional medical values.

4. *The Professional Arena :* This includes all the national associations of western and Indian systems of medicine. The two most important institutions in this arena are : the Indian Medical Association and the Indian Medical Council. While the Indian Medical Association is a voluntary professional society which functions essentially as a pressure group, the Indian Medical Council is a properly constituted authoritative institution entrusted with enforcing standards of medical education throughout the country. The latter is composed of representatives of medical students, faculties, private and government practitioners of western medicine, and state and central governments. Both these groups are distinct entities and have different functions, but in terms of their value preferences and policy positions on health issues, they are the custodians of the interests of the medical profession.

5. *The Planning Commission's Arena :* The Planning Commission is an important body which allocates resources between various ministries during the formulation of the five-year plans. The annual budget is controlled by the Ministry of Finance, but the Planning Commission has a say in the long-term allocation of resources.

6. *Arena under the Control of the State Governments :* The states have control over health manpower resources other than post-graduate education and research. States also have control over the indigenous systems of medicine. The Central Health Council coordinates the interests of the states in the central health policy process; it is composed of the health ministers of all the states. Because of their nearness to field operations in health field, states tend to be more oriented towards populist values than is the case with the distant central government.

Having specified the most relevant arenas of policy-making, we can now turn to examine their roles in the health policy process in India.

Pre-1966 Health Manpower Policies

The first Health Minister of India (1947-56), Rajkumari Amrit Kaur, a Christian by religion, was a member of the royal family of an Indian princely state. Rajkumari had her school and college education in England. She took an active part in the Independence movement under the leadership of Gandhi.[1] The Deputy Minister of Health, Mrs. M. Chandrasekhar, a relative newcomer to politics, was a very well-educated person. She received her Bachelor's degree in science from Madras and then went to London where she got a B.Sc. from King's College. She also attended courses in domestic science and underwent practical training in dietetics at Middlesex Hospital, London.[2] The second Health Minister (1957-62), D.P. Karmarkar, an educationist and a political leader from the south Indian state of Mysore, was trained in India. He held an M.A. and a law degree. There were no junior ministers during his tenure as the Health Minister. The third, and one of the most powerful, Ministers of Health (1962-67), Dr. Sushila Nayar, herself a medical professional, was trained in India and the United States.

Below the level of the Minister, the top level of administration is controlled by two types of administrative elite groups: the Indian Administrative Service and the Indian Medical Service. Secretaries of the Ministry were initially members of the Indian Civil Service (ICS), a predecessor of the post-independence IAS, and were trained under the British colonial rulers. Similarly, the officers of the

Indian Medical Service had close links with the British medical profession because of their training in England and because of their associations with the British rule in their work prior to independence. Even the institutions of medical education were designed on the British pattern; the Medical Council of India, which sets national standards for medical colleges, was a direct descendant of the Medical Council of Great Britain. Thus, the post-independence health bureaucracy was dominated by 'men who were trained in the colonial traditions and whose claim to a number of vital posts in development administration was based merely on their seniority in the cadre'.[3]

We will now construct a plausible basis for policy change through an analysis of the attitudes of the professional and political elites towards problems of medical education, indigenous medicine, and redistribution of manpower between the urban and rural areas. Unlike China, the Indian government has not encouraged the training of an assistant doctor or any other equivalent of the Chinese middle-level physician. This is ironic because India already had about 30,000 licentiate physicians in 1949. These physicians entered medical college immediately after high school graduation and were given medical training for three years. This middle-level medical training course was started by the British during the colonial period. However, immediately after independence, the Government of India decided to abolish the licentiate course and upgrade the skills of the existing licentiate doctors through a condensed degree (MBBS) course. This decision was based on the recommendations of the Health Survey and Development Committee appointed by the Government of India in 1946. The majority of the Committee members arrived at the following conclusion :

We have given serious consideration to a suggestion that in the conditions now prevailing in the country, there is room both for the fully trained doctor and a less elaborately trained type of medical man .... The conclusion which the very large majority of our members has arrived at is that, on the whole having regard to the limited resources available for the training of doctors, it would be to the greater ultimate benefit to the country if those resources are concentrated on the production of only one and that the most highly trained type of doctor, which we have termed the basic doctor.[4]

The six minority members of the Committee who wrote a 'minute of dissent' strongly felt that the majority of the members were influenced by the report of the Goodenough Committee in England which recommended abolition of the licentiate degree in that country.[5] Although there is no clear-cut medical versus non-medical division of opinion on this issue, it is interesting to note that three of the six dissenting members were the only non-medical members. Moreover, all three of them were members of the Central Advisory Board of Health which was composed of representatives of the state governments. To an extent, therefore, they also represented the views of the state governments.

The majority recommendations of the Health Survey and Development Committee were later endorsed by the Minister of Health, Rajkumari Amrit Kaur,[6] the Indian Medical Association,[7] and the Central Health Council. The abolition of the licenciate course was also supported by the licenciate doctors because of differences in pay scales, position, and opportunities for promotions between them and the regular MBBS doctors.[8] Historically, licenciate education was started by the British to fill subordinate positions in the British Medical Service. Licenciate doctors felt that their subordinate position continued after independence.[9] The Planning Commission proposed reviving the licentiate course in 1960 during the formulation of the Third Five-Year Plan;[10] so did some state governments.[11] Both the Planning Commission and a few states which were facing a shortage of trained doctors viewed the problem from the perspective of overall economic planning and were willing to lower the standards of medical education in order to better serve the rural populations. But this was opposed by the medical professionals who dominated the Medical Council of India as well as by the Indian Medical Association.

The Medical Council of India had been intensely concerned during the fifties and early sixties about getting recognition from the international medical community in general and the British Medical Council in particular.[12] These professional sentiments and views were endorsed by the Health Survey and Planning Committee (1961). The Committee was appointed by the Ministry of Health to undertake a review of the developments since the publication of the Health Survey and Development Committee Report in 1946, and to formulate further health programmes for the third and subsequent five-year plan periods. The Committee, which consisted of fifteen

medical professionals and only one non-medical member, overwhelmingly presented the view of medical professionals. The
Committee considered a suggestion to introduce shorter courses in
colleges of medicine, but rejected it on the following grounds:

> We are in a position to state that the profession as a whole and all
> Associations connected with the professional bodies in the field
> of medicine are strongly opposed to the revival of this course.
> Apart from any such protests, we are convinced that the proper
> development of the country in the field of health must be on the
> lines of what we consider as minimum qualification for a basic
> doctor. There is another aspect to be taken into consideration.
> India is no longer isolated and is participating in all problems of
> international health. The WHO has laid down certain minimum
> standards of qualifications .... So far as problems of rural health
> are concerned, it has been our experience that such persons
> trained in short term courses generally concentrate in urban
> areas as the chances of their settling down in rural areas are
> remote ... nor do we consider it right that rural areas should be
> treated on a differential basis from urban areas. If proper care of
> rural population is to be given, they should get as good facilities
> as those in urban areas.[13]

This extract from the Committee's **Report** succinctly summarises
four reasons for not reviving the licentiate course or for that matter
any short-term medical course : (a) Opposition from the medical
profession including the All India Licentiate Association; (b) concern
about keeping up with international standards in medical education;
(c) failure to persuade licentiates to go to the villages; and (d) equal
treatment for both urban and rural areas in the matter of quality of
health services.

While medical professionals opposed the training of middle-
level physicians, at no time did they oppose the expansion of para-
medical training. The Health Survey and Planning Committee
placed considerable emphasis on this aspect when it stated that 'the
suggestions we are making for the training of several categories of
para-medical personnel would justifiably meet these demands and
in consequence thereof there would be no necessity of a short-term
course being revived in any state whatsoever'.[14] Thus, there occurred
a substantial increase in para-medical and auxiliary health personnel

education. It was not, however, adequate to produce a favourable doctor-nurse ratio. We do not have enough information to fully analyse the reasons for this policy outcome. However, there is some evidence to suggest that the Health Ministry was constantly faced with the problem of extremely limited resources. Each of the three Health Ministers during the pre-1966 period complained about lack of resources for health schemes.[15] In a reply to the parliamentary debate on the Health Ministry's demand for grants, Sushila Nayar expressed her perception of the resource constraints in the following words :

There is not enough hospital accommodation, not enough of medicine, and not enough of a number of other things. But, may I say, sir, that we can only do our best within the resources made available to us. In the First Plan, total amount of money made available for health plan was ... 2.5 per cent of the total plan outlay. In the Second Plan [it] was ... 4.7 per cent. In the Third Plan [it] was ... 4.2 per cent. What we will get for the Fourth Plan I am not in a position to say at the present moment. ... The total demand that we put up before the planners was to the tune of Rs. 2700 crores. ... Against that, we were promised in the first instance Rs. 1090 crores. Now we are told that it will be Rs. 949 crores.[16]

Faced with this low priority accorded to health in economic plans and the consequent scarcity of resources, the Ministry followed a strategy of concentrating limited resources on training fully qualified physicians. This was also the main reason why, despite grumblings from high-level medical researchers and educationists, the Indian Medical Council agreed to a rapid expansion of enrolment in medical colleges. The most vocal demand for an expansion in medical education came from the state governments, and was strongly articulated in the Central Council of Health. It seems that the agreement to expand regular medical education was the result of bargaining between various state governments and the Medical Council. When it was realised that the state governments would go ahead and introduce short-duration courses to meet the shortage of doctors, the Medical Council probably thought it was wise to agree to expand regular medical education. This reasoning is implicit in a conciliatory speech by the President of the Medical Council at its fifty-fifth annual session on 24 April 1961.[17] It was in this session that the Medical Council passed a resolution to increase admissions to medical colleges by 50 per cent. The President, C. S. Patel, quoted the Yugoslav experience in support of this resolution. He said that Yugoslavia met her requirements by increasing admissions in five colleges from 500 to 5,000. They did not introduce any short courses or licentiate courses. He, therefore, recommended the same course of action.[18]

The licenciate issue was practically dead by the mid-1960s. Regular medical college education had expanded considerably, but the problem of unequal distribution of medical manpower between urban and rural areas was still defying solution. During the period 1949-65 two important solutions were debated, and one of them was haltingly implemented. The first solution suggested by some of the political leaders in Parliament was to introduce some type of compulsion for doctors to serve in rural areas for a specific period of time. The second suggestion was to train practitioners of indigenous systems of medicine in modern medical practice for short periods of time, and utilise them for rural health service. There was also a group of unqualified rural practitioners of western medicine who were officially recognised in many states of India because of their experience in the delivery of medical care. Many of these Registered Medical Practitioners (RMPs) had some previous experience of working as drug dispensers or assistants to local government or privately qualified doctors. When some of the qualified doctors moved to urban areas, these assistants continued to serve the local community and took over most of the curative functions. Both these kinds of health manpower, the RMPs and indigenous medical practitioners, are generally grouped together in policy proposals for rural health care.

We shall first discuss the policy proposal regarding compulsory rural medical service, which was often suggested by many political leaders, including Jawaharlal Nehru, the first Prime Minister of India. In his various addresses to medical professionals, Nehru always stressed the need for compulsory rural health service.[19] The Planning Commission also revived the idea of making a minimum period of service in rural areas a precondition for public employment.[20] The seventy-second report of the Estimates Committee presented to the Lok Sabha on 21 March 1960, criticised the government for dealing with the question of extending medical aid to rural people 'in a halting manner'.[21] Thus, non-professional groups consisting of some political elites and economic planners were demanding that something drastic needs to be done to redistribute medical manpower in favour of rural areas. But the Indian Medical Association and the Health Ministry were still not prepared for such drastic solutions. D.P Karmarkar, the Minister of Health, articulated his own definition of the problem:

> Now people say that doctors do not go to villages. . . . I do not see any reason why doctors should be blamed for not going to the villages, because they find it difficult to educate their children there, because they find it difficult to find proper accommodation there. We should create proper conditions for them in the villages . . . . What I really believe is that the State should step in, instead of trying to put some compulsion upon the poor doctor. I do not know what sin he has committed. If engineer can live and enjoy in town, and a politician can live and enjoy in town, in fact, everybody else can enjoy in a town and doctors can not do that . . . . Let us take it that unless we want to compel him in a totalitarian regime and make him stay there for three years — and in that unwilling mind he is likely to kill more patients than to cure . . . . I cannot think of a scheme of conscription for doctors.[22]

Thus, the problem was defined as not one of incorrect attitudes (as Mao did in China) but of lack of proper physical facilities and incentives in rural areas. Sushila Nayar, who succeeded Karmarkar as the Health Minister, did not, at least in principle, oppose a policy of sending fresh recruits to rural health centres for an initial period of three years, but her definition of the problem and its solution also emphasised the physical environment and facilities.[23] The following quote from the President of the Indian Medical Association brings out a similarity of approach between the Ministry and the IMA

> I am sorry to remark that even our topmost leaders often advise medical men to develop a missionary spirit. But I fail to understand how you can expect me to have missionary spirit throughout my life when I am neither a missionary nor I am in a mission. . . . The medical officer must be adequately remunerated which will compensate other losses which he will have to undergo.[24]

The *Journal of Indian Medical Association* published an editorial on 'Rural Health in India' which further elaborated the position of the IMA. It listed unattractive terms of employment, unfavourable environment of the villages, poor prospects of private practice, lack of educational facilities, and lack of facilities to practice the most advanced medical science as some of the most important reasons for doctors' unwillingness to go to rural areas. The same editorial reflects the professional values that form the western-style physicians' orientation towards rural service :

Moreover, most of the young doctors are ambitious to attain high standards in respect of their qualifications, knowledge and experience and execution of diagnostic and therapeutic steps with the help of modern appliances, and they eagerly look forward for applications of their newly gained knowledge from teaching institutions and recent books and journals for which the village offers little prospects. If the instruments of precision and appliances of modern techniques are rendered available along with the current medical literature in the most peripheral villages, much of the disinclination of the young ambitious doctor to work in rural surroundings will melt away.[25]

It is interesting to note that the medical profession in India never seems to have attempted to do any soul searching. I have read through all the addresses of the Presidents of IMA during the last two decades, and all of them, with one exception, repeat the same arguments and reflect the same professional values. The one exception was the Presidential address delivered in 1967 by Dr. Bhola Nath, who for the first time recognised the problem of the wrong social orientation of the profession acquired through a western-style education. He expressed his views with refreshing frankness and humility when he said that

With a sense of shame I have to point out that even after 19 years of independence, we are still *de facto* guided by the General Medical Council of Great Britain for working out the curriculum, teaching programme, methods and standards of examinations. It is done so that our degrees are recognized by them and our students are allowed to appear in their examinations.[26]

Given this confluence of interests and orientation between the medical profession and the Ministry of Health, the official policy was one of persuading the state governments to provide better facilities to doctors serving in rural areas. Under the Indian Constitution, health is a state subject and the major responsibility for raising additional resources for this purpose was initially placed on the states. We have already discussed the central Health Ministry's concern over the low priority attached to health in overall economic planning. Most of the state health ministries faced similar problems and were unable to provide enough facilities to attract doctors to serve in rural areas. Similarly, state politicians were even less willing than the central leaders to impose compulsions on doctors.[27]

Before we turn to the next policy area of indigenous medicine, there is one unresolved question in our explanation of rural health policy which needs to be addressed. We have shown that the Ministry and the medical profession were opposed to the idea of compulsory rural health service, but it was advocated by some top political leaders, including Nehru, some members of the Planning Commission, and members of the Parliament's Estimate Committee. How can we explain the relative ineffectiveness of these non-professional political elites? It is difficult to answer this question without in-depth interviews with the leaders of these various groups, but a reasonably logical explanation can be given. While the Planning Commission and the Prime Minister felt strongly about these issues, they did not exert their full power to back their stand on the rural health issue because health was never considered to be among the core sectors of national economic planning. Also, health was viewed as the responsibility of the state governments and not the central government. The parliamentary committees are advisory in nature and they do not constitute a strong influence on policies which require a major shift from the *status quo*. This lack of strong political commitment and interest in health in India provides a major contrast with China where Mao's personal interest at the highest level brought health issues to the centre of the policy debates.

The question of using indigenous medical practitioners for rural health services is closely linked with elite attitudes towards the development of indigenous medicine and its integration with western medicine. Initially, indigenous medicine was given symbolic support by all sections of Indian society on the grounds of national pride and the practical need for using all existing health resources.

The real conflict arose when the relationship between the indigenous and the western medical systems had to be worked out. The Health Ministry and the political leaders cherished the idea of synthesising the two into a new single system of medical science. However, this goal was interpreted differently by different elite groups. The political leaders, mainly members of Parliament and state leaders, saw integration as a process of mutual learning on the part of practitioners of both systems. The medical professionals, on the other hand, emphasised the reform of the indigenous medical system. As the latter interpretation was shared by the Ministry of Health, it placed state-run institutions of indigenous medicine under the leadership of western style physicians. Indigenous medical practitioners saw, this development as a threat to their own identity and, therefore, advocated a change in the government policy. By the late 1950s, they brought pressure on the government to stop integration and promote *shuddha* (literally, 'pure') Ayurved. This proposal was accepted by the Health Ministry in the early 1960s.

One of the consequences of the promotion of *shuddha* Ayurved was an increasing emphasis on high-level education and research in indigenous systems of medicine. Thus, it did not encourage the development of middle-level health manpower for rural areas. The pure systems of indigenous medicine had to justify their excellence *vis-a-vis* the western system of medicine, and this was sought through an emphasis on high-level training and research.

What we have described so far is the policy of the central Health Ministry. The state governments were much more receptive to the indigenous systems of medicine and, by 1957, many of them had established Boards of Ayurvedic Medicine or Departments/Bureaus of Indian Medicine. Registration Acts were also passed to set standards for the practice of indigenous medicine. There were fifty teaching institutions and 5,469 hospitals of Ayurved and Unani medicine in 1957 which were supported by various state governments. The governments of Madras, Orissa, and Uttar Pradesh started colleges of integrated medicine (both Ayurved and western).[28] Most of these integrated courses were discontinued in the early sixties when the central government adopted a new policy of encouraging *shuddha* Ayurved. There were three reasons for the encouragement given to indigenous systems of medicine by the state governments. First, the top political elites in many of the states were less westernised than the elites at the centre. Second, health being a state subject, states which were short of qualified doctors were more willing to use indigenous practitioners than the central government and those states which had an adequate number of doctors. Third, historically, popularly elected ministries were formed in India in 1938 when the British granted limited provincial autonomy. In this pre-independence environment of a strong nationalistic revival, the leaders of Congress ministries in the states recognised Indian systems of medicine and enacted legislation to support them.[29]

While the states continued to encourage Ayurved, Unani, and Homoeopathy, the central government followed a policy of verbal support but gave little material support. *India 1954,* an official publication, presented the Government of India's position as follows: 'Since the existence of the several systems of medicine in the country was a source of confusion, the government felt that only one system of medicine should be recognized, although contributions from other systems could be incorporated'.[30]

As a result of this policy, the central Health Ministry and the Indian Medical Association supported research in Indian medicine for the most part of the fifties, but discouraged any official recognition of degrees in Indian medicine. Both the IMA and the Health Minister Amrit Kaur were of the opinion that anyone who wanted to practise medicine must first obtain a basic degree in western medicine, and then if he/she wished to pursue further studies in Indian medicine, that should be done through specialisation at the post-graduate level. Amrit Kaur made the following remarks during the state Health Ministers' Conference in 1950 :

The organization of parallel health services based on indigenous systems, homoeopathy, and modern medicine which has developed in recent years in different parts of the country, is I feel, a definitely retrograde step. These systems lack some of the essential elements of a complete service to meet the total health needs of the people. For instance, Ayurved and Unani have no surgery, preventive medicine, obstetrics, radiology and all the more modern developments which are of great importance in the diagnosis, treatment and prevention of disease. ... It is recognized that Ayurved and Unani do contain certain valuable drugs and medical procedures and it is most desirable that such of these which can be tested by modern scientific methods and proved to be of value should be made available to all mankind. Government is only anxious to ensure that all future medical practitioners shall have a complete course of training in the basic modern sciences, before they take up training in any other system of medicine.[31]

D.P. Karmarkar shared the basic value premises of the medical profession. In his reply to the debates in Parliament, Karmarkar stated :

We do believe in trying to encourage Ayurved to the extent it deserves. I am quite sure in my mind that if Charaka and Sushruta were alive they would not be urging the case for Ayurveda with greater vehemence than is justified. ... Charaka, Sushruta and Vaghbhata would find in our science, in the institutes and laboratories, how through microscopes microbes and other things are found much better. Living at the time that we do, it is a marvel how they associated mosquito with malaria, how they found out that infection spreads from man to man, breath to breath, from sweat to sweat. All these things are marvels of modern science. We would be guilty if we do not take from medicine the best it can give us.[32]

Karmarkar encouraged the integration of indigenous and Western systems of medicine, but it was more in the spirit of recasting the Indian systems in the mould of modern medical science. Integration did not work because the graduates of the integrated schools continued to practise mainly western medicine. This was opposed by the medical profession.[33] Also, integrated doctors were not accorded the same status and salary as the western-style doctors. The integrated doctors, therefore, demanded that the government should start condensed MBBs courses to help them become fully qualified doctors of modern medicine. Integration was opposed by practitioners of indigenous medicine because it led to the domination of medical institutions by western-style doctors. Karmarkar's successor, Sushila Nayar, abolished integrated medical education and instead supported the claim of shuddha Ayurved. Committees were established to work out curricula for shuddha Ayurved and Unani education.[34] Despite her public support for shuddha Ayurved, Sushila Nayar is not viewed by the proponents of indigenous systems of medicine as their well-wisher.[35] Without in-depth interviews with the actors in this policy process, it is difficult to reconcile this contradiction between her favourable public posture and its completely opposite evaluation by the proponents of indigenous systems of medicine. One hypothesis suggested by one of my respondents, who was a participant in this decision, is that Nayar's support for *shuddha* Ayurved was a strategic move on her part to isolate indigenous systems from the main trends of modern scientific investigation, and thereby take away their opportunity to scientifically prove their worth.[36]

Much before the development of barefoot doctors in China, a committee of the Government of India had recommended a similar scheme for India (1948). The Chopra committee had suggested that practitioners of indigenous medicine in the rural areas may be trained for six months in western medicine and then systematically absorbed into the rural health network.[37] This whole issue was, however, neglected in the great debate and political conflict between proponents of indigenous and western medicine. To summarise this debate, we may emphasise two major factors responsible for this neglect.

First, both due to professional competition and the pressure to keep up with international standards in medical education, medical professionals consistently opposed the use of western medicine by indigenous practitioners. The competition with indigenous practitioners was cited as an important factor by the President of the Indian Medical Association in 1960 when he observed that 'one of our main problems today is quackery and competition we have from Ayurvedists, hakims, homoeopaths and quacks . . .'.[38] Many statements can be cited to bring out the medical profession's concern with western standards. However, the following extract from an address by the President of the Indian Medical Council is representative of the professional view. Referring to the demand for giving condensed courses in western medicine to students who had qualified in indigenous medicines, he warned that 'there is great danger that our medical qualifications may face a great deal of difficulty for recognition by the other countries in the world'.[39]

Second, faced with the need to justify their legitimate role in a system dominated by modern medical science, the proponents of indigenous medicine tended to emphasise research and long-term education. Most of the courses offered in Ayurvedic colleges were of four or five years' duration. Research in various non-western systems of medicine was encouraged from the beginning. In

1952-53, a Central Institute of Research in Indigenous Medicine was started in Jamnagar in Gujarat. A post-graduate training centre was also started at the same Institute in 1955. An advisor in indigenous systems of medicine was attached to the central Ministry of Health in 1956; and three different advisory committees for Ayurved, Unani, and Homoeopathy were established. By the end of 1959, the advisory committee on Ayurved was replaced by a Central Council of Ayurvedic Research which was chaired by the Health Minister. Many post-graduate training centres were upgraded in the early sixties. In 1962, a committee was constituted within the Health Ministry to coordinate research on Ayurvedic drugs at the Indian Council of Medical Research and the Central Council of Ayurvedic Research. Also, a unit to survey medicinal plants in the Himalayan region was established, followed by the formation of the Ayurvedic Pharmacopoeia Committee in 1963. A composite drug research scheme with ten regional centres for different aspects of research in Indian medicinal plants came into existence by 1966.[40]

Post-1966 Developments in Health Manpower Policies

Although there were no dramatic departures from past policies, by the late sixties the Health Ministry had recognised the inadequacy of the professional model and, by the beginning of the seventies, it came up with a plan for rural areas based on the populist model. Let us very briefly sketch some of the salient developments. Parliament approved the setting up of a Central Council for Research in Indian Medicine and Homoeopathy in March 1969. Moreover, for setting standards of education, the Central Council of Indian Medicine — including the Ayurved, Unani, and Siddha systems — was established in 1970. In August 1974, a similar Central Council of Homoeopathy was also constituted. Both these councils have, in their respective medical spheres, the same power as those accorded to the Indian Medical Council in western medicine. But the most important change was ushered in by the Health Ministry's rural health scheme which is based on the utilisation of existing paramedical personnel, indigenous medicine practitioners, and Registered Medical Practitioners. It is significant that this scheme was proposed by the Ministry of Health.[41] How can we account for these changes in the official position of the central Health Ministry? Among other factors, changes in the leadership of the Ministry of Health after 1966 were congenial to the populist model. We will first analyse the leadership changes, and then discuss contextual factors.

In March 1967, S. Chandrasekhar, a prominent demographer, was appointed as the Minister for Health and Family Planning. Chandrasekhar had no strong professional tie with the medical community. In fact, he is known to have advocated many unconventional measures for family planning which went beyond a purely medical approach. Satya Narain Sinha, a senior political leader of the Congress party, took over as the Minister of Health with cabinet rank in November 1967; Chandrasekhar continued as his junior colleague in the Ministry. Sinha, a law graduate from Patna, was an experienced politician. He had held many important positions within the Congress party since 1920, and had been a central Minister since 1948. Sinha was replaced by K.K. Shah in February 1969. Shah, a veteran of the freedom struggle, was a lawyer and a senior leader of the Congress party. He had held various positions within the Congress including that of its General-Secretary in 1962-63. Shah was succeeded in 1971 by another veteran politician and a labour leader, R.K. Khadilkar. He was replaced by Karan Singh, who assumed office in November 1973. Singh, a former ruler of Kashmir, has been active in politics since the fifties. He holds a Ph.D. in literature from Delhi University.

At the junior level, Chandrasekhar continued as a Minister of State for Health until 1970. He was replaced by Professor Debiprasad Chattopadhyaya, a graduate of the London School of Economics and Political Science, and a prominent Gandhian. B.S. Murthy took over in 1966 with the title of the Deputy Minister. He was an arts graduate with a degree in education; he was also a prominent trade unionist and a veteran Congressman. In 1971, Murthy was replaced by A.K. Kisku who had studied at Calcutta University and the University of California, Berkeley, but whose past political and educational work was related to the uplift of tribals and poorer sections of society in Western Bengal. He was formerly a Minister in the West Bengal Government in charge of education, social welfare, and tribal welfare.[42]

As can be seen from the above, the political leadership of the Ministry since 1967 was dominated by either veteran politicians or scholar-politicians with a strong social science background. Both these groups had no medical constituencies, but they were more responsive then their predecessors to populist pressures which were gaining strength in Indian politics during late sixties. This brings us to a contextual factor of increasing demands on the Indian political system for equal distribution of economic resources.

The 1960s in India was marked by two divergent trends : (a) increasing issue orientation of the electorate due to political mobilisation ;and (b) mounting economic pressures due to stagnation in the rate of economic growth. A succession of events were responsible for the poor economic performance. Two successive wars (one with China in 1962 and the other with Pakistan in 1965) were followed by a temporary discontinuation of foreign aid and two bad years in agricultural production. This poor economic performance had already created pressures for change in economic policies. During the 1967 general elections, for the first time since independence, the Indian electorate registered its protest by substantially reducing the ruling Congress party's overwhelming majority in Parliament and replacing it with opposition governments in a number of states. A national sample survey of voting behaviour underscores the saliency of economic issues to the electorate, e.g., 61 per cent of the respondents 'strongly agreed' that the Congress had failed to keep prices down and 52 per cent that the Congress had failed to distribute food properly.[43]

The Congress party responded to these economic pressures by intensifying the debate within the party. In 1969, the ruling Congress was split into two factions : a left-of-centre group led by the Prime Minister Indira Gandhi, and a relatively conservative group led by the Deputy Prime Minister Morarji Desai. Although one can debate whether the split was primarily a result of ideological or personality conflicts within the party, it definitely forced the ruling elite to radicalise its ideological rhetoric. The ideological context of policy formulation had changed and popular pressures were mounting for equal distribution of resources. All areas of social and economic policies were affected in varying degrees by the new rhetoric of socialism and redistribution.[44]

Both these factors — change in leadership and growing economic pressures — were reflected in the changed attitudes of the Ministry towards the populist model. As can be seen from the following extract from Pandit Shiva Sharma's speech in the Parliament in 1968, the proponents of the indigenous systems of medicine perceived the new political leaders of the Ministry as supporting their own cause.[45]

> Ayurved is alive today not for a want of effort to kill it during the days of the first three Health Ministries of the Government of India. It is only with the advent, first of a scientist Dr. Chandrasekhar, and subsequently a well-wisher of Ayurved, Satya Narayan Sinha, that the era of the release of the Ayurved from the clutches of its enemies can be said to have begun .... After a very long period, a set of fair and just Ministers have come into Health Ministry. All the three of them, Shri Satya Narayan Sinha, Dr. S. Chandrasekhar, and Shri B.S. Murthy — it is a pure but welcome accident — happen to be well-wishers of Ayurved.[46]

The Indian systems of medicine were also supported by the Prime Minister Indira Gandhi. Inaugurating the Forty-fourth All India Medical Conference Allahabad in December 1968, Mrs. Gandhi said : 'I, as a lay woman, naturally do not know whether there is anything in them (ancient systems of medicine) or what the value is, but I certainly feel that we have not done enough to investigate the matter.'[47]

On another occasion, speaking to a conference of Unani physicians at Bangalore in 1973, the Prime Minister reiterated her belief in the simultaneous development of all systems of medicine :

> In India, it is specially necessary for us to advance the different systems, because our modern medicine, allopathic medicine, has not been able to reach 75 per cent of our population .... We want lakhs of people's doctors who are ready to live where the poor live.[48]

Mrs Gandhi is also said to have initiated the idea of rural doctors following the Chinese model. She instructed the Planning Commission to study the feasibility of working out a scheme for the development of 'peasant doctors' through re-training of allopaths, homoeopaths, hakims (Unani doctors) and vaidyas (Ayurvedic doctors).[49]

It was in early 1972 that the central Ministry of Health circulated a bill which provided for the registration of all unqualified medical practitioners who had a minimum of five years' practical experience. A few states opposed the bill, but majority of the states endorsed it.[50] While the bill and the Ministry's National Health Scheme for Rural Areas were being discussed, the National Service Bill was approved by Parliament in May 1972. Nationalistic feelings generated during the short war with Pakistan over the Bangladesh issue in 1971 helped to mobilise support for this bill which empowered the government to conscript any qualified engineer or doctor for four years' national service in conditions of war as well as for essential social services in remote areas.

Two other factors may have further facilitated this change in the government's policy towards the populist model of health manpower development. First, in the face of growing pressure for the redistribution of health manpower, the Indian Medical Association faced a serious dilemma. Although it opposed the government's populist policies, the Association could not reject the demand for extending health services to rural areas. But, at the same time, the Association could not persuade its own members to go and serve in those areas. Popular pressures for redistribution were also affecting the medical profession. In 1971, there were many cases of public assaults on doctors for failure to attend emergencies and provide adequate services, or for excessive fees. The President of the Medical Association, Dr. A.K.N. Sinha, voiced this concern at the Forty-sixth All India Medical Conference at Bikaner in 1970 :

Everyday we are subjected to criticisms and have often been called 'murderers,' 'traders in flesh,' 'demons,' etc. .... Sometimes our members are at fault too. Some of us practise while holding non-practising posts, neglect patients, earn money by unfair or unethical means. ... It will be, however, unwise to condemn the entire medical profession for the faults of a few misguided persons.[51]

The Indian Medical Association, therefore, was divided between the need to maintain professional standards and the need to serve the people.[52] Consequently, its opposition to the government's policies lacked the past assurance and confidence. It did not oppose the National Service Bill and the development of indigenous medicine as a separate scientific tradition. However, when it came to the National Health Scheme for **rural areas**, the Association publicly protested because it threatened **the** very essence of its professional value system. We will discuss this issue later as one of the factors which has hindered the implementation of the rural scheme. But, before turning to that issue, let us briefly consider one more facilitating factor.

The acceptance of the populist model by the ruling elite may have been facilitated by a change in the value preferences of the World Health Organisation. The leadership of the Health Ministry as well as the professionals in charge of medical education looked up to the international medical community in general, and the WHO in particular, for guidance on standards of medical education and services. By the late sixties, the WHO had started soul searching which resulted in its increasing endorsement of the populist model of health care. S. Btesh, Director of Research, Planning and Coordination in the WHO, articulated this changing mood in 1967 :

> Twenty years experience in the World Health Organisation has shown us the mistaken approach of trying to attack disease by disease, of trying to eradicate yaws in countries where there were no basic health services. ... I should like the representatives of the developing countries to realize the mistake that WHO has made. ... Developing countries should avoid the trap of trying to build their health services piecemeal. They should try to avoid the big beautiful hospitals in the main towns and leave areas without minimum health services. How can we avoid the trap ? ... I only see one priority : in the field of health there is just one thing to do, to build your basic health services ... no matter how simple, no matter how unsophisticated, provided they give enough coverage.[53]

Despite the changes mentioned above, except for the development of the indigenous systems of medicine, other policies have either faced stiff opposition from the medical profession or they have not been implemented effectively. As we have documentation on the IMA's opposition to the National Health Scheme for Rural Areas, we shall focus on that issue for analysing the factors hindering its implementation.

The Indian Medical Association opposed the National Health Scheme in the following words :

The Indian Medical Association is totally and fundamentally against the proposed scheme. ... Whereas the qualified and trained medical practitioners in indigenous systems of medicine may be utilized in specially prepared schemes as pilot projects with the objective of providing relief within the scope of their individual systems, no 'cocktail' or mixing up of the system be allowed under any circumstances.

The Indian Medical Association is totally against the continuance of practice of medicine by the unqualified quacks who are neither educated nor trained nor qualified. ... Their being labelled as Rural Medical Practitioners with abbreviation 'RMP' would be nothing but throwing dust in the eyes of the people. ... Their backdoor recognition is bad; their involvement in rural medical relief is worse.[54]

This verbal protest was followed by strikes and public protest marches by the doctors. This militant strand in the IMA's public posture on the rural health issue must be placed within the context of changed economic prospects for doctors. The rapid increase in medical education had, by 1972, saturated most of the cities with medical graduates. Consequently, as stated by the President of the IMA, there were about 15,000 to 20,000 unemployed medical graduates in 1972.[55] Another reason for unemployment was that while some states had a shortage of doctors, others were finding it difficult to employ all their graduates. The regional imbalance was further accentuated due to the lack of inter-state mobility. On the one hand doctors were unwilling to migrate to another region of the country where they may have had to face a different language and culture, on the other hand, many states were unable to employ outsiders due to local opposition. The Indian Medical Association, therefore, urged the government to 'appoint a Commission to explore the possibility of nationalising health services on a phased basis'.[56] This changed economic context of the medical profession further strengthened the Medical Association's opposition to the rural health scheme. Faced with unemployment, doctors were not prepared to let a whole new class of para-professionals enter medical practice and compete with them. The National Health Scheme threatened the very essence of professional organisational interests.[57]

The IMA's views on the National Health Scheme have considerably slowed down the process of decision-making. The President of the IMA was a member of the Planning Commission's Task Force on Medical Manpower. He also presided over the Study Group of the same Task Force which was entrusted with the task of examining the feasibility of the scheme. The Annual Report of the IMA for the year ending 30 September 1972 claims that 'as a result of discussions, the scheme was considerably watered down'.[58]

In conclusion, let us briefly recapitulate the major factors which contributed to the change in the ruling elite's attitude towards the populist model in India : shift away from the dominance of the professionals in the Ministry; personal support of the Prime Minister; predominance of the redistributive ideology due to popular pressures generated by economic failures; change in the international professional community's views towards the populist model; and growing public challenge to the legitimacy of the professional model as the main basis of the Indian Medical Association's organisational ideology.

The manpower policies pursued in the past had led to certain outcomes which posed considerable constraints on the Ministry's ability to implement new policies. Rapid expansion in the output of fully trained western doctors and resultant regional imbalances and partial unemployment in some parts of the country had created tremendous counter pressures. It is natural that the policy area which has been least affected so far by the new orientation in health policy is medical education.

Notes

1. S.P. Sen (ed.), *Dictionary of National Biography*, Vol. 1, 1972, pp. 53-54. On the one hand, she inherited ground, on the other, she also came under the strong influence of Gandhi. These two very different sources of influence were apparent in her policy postures. It is interesting that while she opposed the introduction of chemical and mechanical contraceptives for birth control, she was sympathetic to western medical values regarding medical education and health policy. Given her Christian upbringing she must have found it easier to hold simultaneously these different value orientations.

2. Trilochan Singh (ed.), *Indian Parliament 1952-57*, New Delhi, n.d., p. 54.

3. D. Banerji, 'Social and Cultural Foundations of Health Services Systems,' *Economic and Political Weekly*, Special No., August 1974, p. 1335.

4. GOI, *Report of the Health Survey and Development Committee*, Vol. 2, *Recommendations*, Delhi, Manager of Publications, 1948, pp. 339-40.

5. *Ibid.*, pp. 349-55.

6. *The Times of India,* 6 July 1952.
7. *Journal of Indian Medical Association,* Vol. 22, No. 6, March 1953, pp. 255-56.
8. *Ibid.,* Vol. 26, No. 6, 16 March 1956.
9. *Ibid.,* Vol. 30, No. 6, 16 March 1958, pp. 183-84.
10. *Ibid.,* Vol. 35, No. 9, 1 November 1960, p. 429.
11. In 1961 the government of Mysore State decided to start the licenciate course to meet the rapidly increasing demand for health services in rural areas. This move was strongly opposed by the Medical Council of India which finally forced the Mysore government to abandon the idea. See address of the President of the Medical Council of India, *Journal of Indian Medical Association,* Vol. 37, No. 2, 16 July 1961, pp. 86-97.
12. This observation is based on my analysis of the Indian Medical Council's presidential speeches delivered at its annual meetings over 1955-65. These speeches are regularly reported in the *Journal of Indian Medical Association.*
13. GOI, *Report of the Health Survey and Planning Committee,* New Delhi, Ministry of Health, 1961, Vol. 1, pp. 349-50.
14. *Ibid.,* p. 349.
15. The first Health Minister, Amrit Kaur, expressed her disappointment in a speech she delivered to the All India Medical Conference in 1953. *Journal of Indian Medical Association,* Vol. 22, No. 5, February 1953, pp. 212-15.

    D.P. Karmarkar, the second Health Minister, also expressed similar sentiments in a speech to Parliament. *Lok Sabha Debates,* Vol. 42, 6 April 1960, Cols. 9849-50.
16. *Lok Sabha Debates,* Third Series, Vol. 53, 15 April 1966, Cols. 11129-30.
17. *Journal of Indian Medical Association,* Vol. 37, No. 2, 16 July 1961, pp. 86-97.
18. *Ibid.,* p. 86.
19. *Ibid.,* Vol. 23, No. 2, 16 July 1954, pp. 468-74; *ibid.,* Vol. 30, No. 12, 16 June 1958, p. 420; *ibid.,* Vol. 34, No. 7, 1 May 1960; *ibid.,* Vol. 38, No. 1, 1 January 1962, p. 42.
20. 'IMA on Third Five-Year Health Plan,' *Journal of Indian Medical Association,* Vol. 35, No. 9, 1 November 1960, p. 429.
21. *Journal of Indian Medical Association,* Vol. 34, No. 8, 16 April 1960, p. 325.
22. *Lok Sabha Debates,* Vol. 52, 21 March 1961, Cols. 6308-9.
23. For an excellent statement of her attitude towards this issue and definition of the problem, see *Lok Sabha Debates,* Vol. 53, 1966, Cols. 11138-40.
24. B.P. Tribedi, 'Presidential Address,' *Journal of Indian Medical Association,* Vol. 40, No. 6, 16 March 1963, pp. 259-67.
25. *Journal of Indian Medical Association,* Vol. 40, No. 3, 1 February 1963, pp. 126-27.
26. *Ibid.,* Vol. 48, No. 7, 1 April 1967, p. 321.
27. There were, of course, a few states — such as, West Bengal — which had given high priority to health and were able to develop a good network of rural health care. West Bengal is a special case because its first Chief Minister, Dr. B.C. Roy, was a highly effective political leader and a respected physician. He took deep personal interest in the development of the health services.
28. GOI, *Annual Report of the Director-General of Health Services,* Central Bureau of Health Intelligence, 1957, Ch. 14.
29. *Journal of Indian Medical Association,* Vol. 22, No. 5, February 1953, p. 195.

30. As quoted in *ibid.*, Vol. 26, No. 5, 1 March 1956, p. 177.
31. As quoted in *ibid.*, Vol. 20, No. 5, February 1951, p. 184. The President of the IMA strongly supported this position during his address to the Twenty-seventh All India Medical Conference in 1951 (*ibid.*, p. 185).
32. *Lok Sabha Debates*, Second Series, Vol. 42, 6 April 1960, Col. 10015. Charaka, Sushruta and Vaghbhata were the three foremost authorities on Ayurveda in ancient India.
33. *Journal of Indian Medical Association,*Vol. 35, No. 5, 1 September 1960, p. 221.
34. For Nayar's statements on this policy, see *Lok Sabha Debates*, Third Series, Vol. 15, 25 March 1963, Cols. 6036-37; *ibid.*, Vol. 53, 15 April 1966, Cols. 1147-51.
35. This view is forcefully presented in the parliamentary debate on the All India Ayurvedic Medical Council Bill, *Lok Sabha Debates*, Fourth Series, Vol. 17, 10 May 1968, p. 3585.
36. Interview with an Indian Ayurvedic physician, October 1975.
37. GOI, *Committee on the Indian Systems of Medicine*, Ministry of Health, 1948; popularly known as the Chopra Committee.
38. *Journal of Indian Medical Association,*Vol. 35, No. 5, 1 September 1960, p. 221.
39. *Ibid.*, Vol. 37, No. 12, 16 July 1961, p. 93.
40. All the information contained in this paragraph was collected from the *Annual Reports of the Director-General of Health Services*, New Delhi, Government of India, 1957 to 1966.
41. 'National Health Scheme for Rural Areas : Proposal of the Union Ministry of Health,' *Journal of Indian Medical Association,*Vol. 60, No. 2, 16 January 1973, pp. 75-77.
42. Biographical information about various ministers was collected from a number of different sources : *(a) India's Who's Who* : 1969, New Delhi,INFA Publications; *(b) India's Who's Who* : 1972, New Delhi, INFA Publications; *(c)* Parliament of India, Rajya Sabha, *Who's Who 1974*, New Delhi, September 1974.
43. Rajni Kothari, 'The Political Change of 1967,' *Economic and Political Weekly*, Vol. 6, Annual No., 1971, p. 245.
44. For one of the most insightful discussions of the growing pressures for equity and distribution in the Indian political system, see Rajni Kothari, *Politics in India*, Boston, Little, Brown and Company, 1970, pp. 338-82.
45. Pandit Shiva Sharma, a leading Ayurvedic physician, has been one of the most prominent leaders of the Ayurvedic movement since the fifties. In 1968, he was a Member of Parliament, and also held the prestigious Presidentship of the All India Ayurvedic Congress.
46. *Lok Sabha Debates*, Fourth Series, Vol. 17, 10 May 1968, Cols. 3585-89.
47. As quoted in the *Journal of Indian Medical Association*, Vol. 52, No. 6, 16 March 1969, p. 257.
48. *Journal of Indian Medical Association*, Vol. 60, No. 2, 16 March 1973, p. 212.
49. *Ibid.*, Vol. 59, No. 1, 1 July 1972, p. 28.
50. *Ibid.*, Vol. 58, No. 11, 1 June 1972, p. 432. The states which opposed it were Mysore, West Bengal, Andhra Pradesh and Jammu & Kashmir.
51. *Ibid.*, Vol. 56, No. 6, 16 March 1971, p. 171.
52. *Ibid.*, Vol. 53, No. 12, 16 December 1969, pp. 611-12. There is some evidence to indicate that these growing pressures for redefining the IMA's rationale on rural health policy led to divided opinion within the Association.

53. Moshe Prywas and Michael A. Davies (eds:), *Health Problems in Developing States* (Proceedings of the Fourth Rehovoth Conference, August 1967), New York, Grune and Stratton, 1968, pp. 57-58. For further documentation on the same theme, see WHO Director-General M.G. Gandau, 'Keynote Address : Knowledge, the Bridge of Achievement,' *ibid.*, pp. 23-29.

54. 'Views of Indian Medical Association on the Proposal of the Health Ministry, Government of India,' *Journal of Indian Medical Association* (Supplement), Vol. 60, No. 2, 16 January 1973, p. 79.

55. *Ibid.*, Vol. 58, No. 9, 1 May 1972, pp. 323-24.

56. *Ibid.*, Vol. 60, No. 9, 1 May 1973, p. 333.

57. Morton Halperin has articulated the concept of organisational interests and organisational essence in his study of bureaucratic politics in American foreign policy. Halperin has suggested that most organisations, but more specifically mission-oriented organisations, will fully resist any change that may affect their organisational essence. See Halperin, 'Why Bureaucrats Play Games,' *Foreign Policy*, No. 2, Spring 1971.

58. *Journal of Indian Medical Association*, Vol. 60, No. 9, 1 May 1973, pp. 340-41.

AQUEIL AHMAD

8 The Making of Science and Technology Plan

Historical Perspective

Prior to achieving independence in 1947, India had been taking in the so-called western science and technology in small doses for nearly one hundred years.* But the British government in India did not have a national policy or plan for scientific and technological development. Scientific research and explorations started in response to the interest that some British (or British-trained Indian) scientists and explorers took in the Indian sub-continent, its flora and fauna and diseases, as well as the needs of science-based education in the few universities established by the government. Modern systems of transport and communication were introduced as administrative exigency. Dams and canals were built to check recurring floods and famine. Industrial technology was adopted by affluent entrepreneurs influenced by the West. None of this was, however, done as a planned effort to uplift Indian society out of centuries of stagnation under feudal-colonial rule. The leadership of free India decided at an early stage to change this situation.

* This work has greatly benefited from discussions with, and material supplied by, the following individuals -- the first three of them having been personally involved with NCST in various capacities in the making of the First Science and Technology Plan, 1974-79 : Dr. Hari Narayan, Director, NGRI; Dr. G. Thyagarajan, Director, RRI; Mr. G. Hanumantha Rao, Scientist, NGRI ; and Dr. G. S. Rao, Scientist, RRL, all from Hyderabad.

Starting with Prime Minister Nehru's personal interest and stewardship, national science and technology policy in India has enjoyed the patronage and encouragement of the highest political authority, the central Cabinet, under the chairmanship of the Prime Minister, directly accountable to Parliament. In Nehru's vision, political independence and self-reliance were invariably linked with economic self-reliance for which a strong scientific and technological capability was an imperative. It was generally agreed among the early planners in India that the country's science and technology (S&T) capability was among the lowest in the world. It was also agreed that the major task ahead was to expand the existing scientific and technological infrastructure by way of building new institutions, augmenting the supply of qualified scientists and engineers, increasing financial investments in relevant areas, etc. Three major landmarks in the early days of independent India toward laying the foundations for such developments were the establishment of the Ministry of Scientific Research and Culture in 1948 under the Prime Minister, establishment of the Department of Atomic Energy (DAE) in 1954, and passing of the Science Policy Resolution by Parliament in 1958.

A centralised structure of (governmental) science, such as that initially concieved in India, required that the overall (national) scientific and technological priorities be defined and translated into well-stated R&D objectives to be coordinated at the apex and implemented at various levels of operation. The Ministry of Scientific Research and Cultural Affairs was established with these objectives in view. However, the Ministry's role in national S&T planning remained insignificant. The Planning Commission assumed the responsibility of incorporating S&T concerns in the five-year plans, under the direction of a member of the Commission, P. Mahalanobis, the famous Indian statistician.

It is evident that high-level policy-making structures were lacking in India, until a beginning was made in the mid-fifties by constituting a Scientific Advisory Committee (1956) to the Cabinet (SACC). As a body of scientists and technologists (mostly scientific agency heads), the role of SACC during its eleven years of existence was confined to advising the Cabinet and assisting the Planning Commission in charting out national directions on scientific and technological matters and incorporating them in the five-year plans.[1] The SACC was replaced by the Committee on Science and Technology (COST) in 1968 for a similar, mostly advisory, role. The Planning Commission, SACC, and COST were assisted from time to time by various groups and institutions, including an expert group called Research Survey and Planning Division (now the Planning Division) established by the CSIR in 1963.

In 1971, the Government of India created a separate Department of Science and Technology (DST) with the Prime Minister as its Minister and a Secretary to the government (a scientist by profession) as the chief executive officer. As a permanent bureaucracy, the role of DST has been to assist in the formulation of science and technology plans (to be incorporated in the national plans drawn up by the Planning Commission); compile, collate, publish and disseminate vital statistics on science and technology; initiate, sponsor, implement and monitor a large number of S&T projects of national importance through research institutes (both government and private) and universities; encourage and administer international collaboration; and generally promote science and technology in the country. The most recent and significant offshoots of DST are the departments of Environment and Oceanography established in 1981 and 1982 respectively with the Prime Minister as the Minister and a Secretary to the government as the chief executive officer in each department. (Following the DST tradition, the Secretaries of the departments of Environment and Oceanography are distinguished scientists.)

The government appointed a National Committee on Science and Technology (NCST) through the DST in 1971 with the purpose of writing the first ever Five-Year Science and Technology plan. The creation of NCST was a significant landmark for more than one reason. First, it took India over a decade since passing the Science Policy Resolution in 1958 to consider formulating a science and technology plan in consonance with the national priorities laid down by the Planning Commission (in the Fifth Five-Year Plan). Second, it was for the first time, through the NCST, that a large number of scientists and engineers participated in formulating a national science and technology policy in the form of a five-year plan. And third, the NCST, unlike its predecessors, had a clear mandate as well as an institutional base in the Department of Science and Technology.

The NCST issued an Approach to the Science and Technology Plan in January 1973,[2] and the Draft Science and Technology Plan itself in the month of October 1974.[3] The Plan laid heavy emphasis on R & D in agriculture, industry, electronics, space, nuclear energy, nautral resources, and others; and institution-building in these priority areas. Soon after finalising the Plan, the NCST became inactive. By 1978-79, it had become more or less non-functional, although it did provide some assistance in writing the S & T components of the Draft Sixth Five-Year Plan.

After a lull of almost two years, the government constituted a fresh Science Advisory Committee to the Cabinet in 1981. The membership of the new SACC consists of mainly agency heads in the governmental R & D establishment. It will function under the Chairmanship of the Member (Science and Technology), Planning Commission,* and will be responsible to the Prime Minister and the Cabinet. The exact role of this SACC, besides being an advisory body to the government like its predecessor SACC, is not clear even now.

What has been described above constitutes the top of the structural hierarchy in the field of Indian science policy. Its main role has been formulating a national policy for scientific and technological developments, which includes laying down overall S & T priorities in consonance with the government's socio-economic policies and developmental plans as enunciated by the Planning Commission; suggesting appropriate infrastructures and institution-building; and proposing (subject to the approval of the Planning Commission, the Ministry of Finance and the Cabinet) total as well as sectoral financial allocations for research and development.

This structure would remain incomplete without taking into consideration the role in policy formulation and implementation played by the various ministries and ministerial level departments of the Government of India under which all the autonomous research agencies function. The role of the Department of Science and Technology *vis-a-vis* scientific and industrial research in general has already been mentioned. The DST's bureaucratic counterpart for nuclear research and development is the Department of Atomic Energy; for R & D in electronics, the Department of Electronics/ Electronics Commission (DOE, established in 1971); and for space

* M. G. K. Menon of the DST now replaced M. S. Swaminathan as the Member (S & T), Planning Commission after the latter relinquished office in India to take over as the Director General of IRRI in Manila. The new DST chief is S. Varadrajan, an industrial chemist by profession and formerly, Chairman of the Indian Petro-chemicals Corporation (since 1974).

research, the Department of Space/Space Commission (DOS, established in 1972). LIke the DST, these departments (through their Secretaries) are directly responsible to the Prime Minister and the Cabinet.

There are no DST equivalents for agricultural, medical, defence, and energy-related research and development. These come under the jurisdiction of the concerned ministries — of Food and Agriculture, Health, Defence, etc. The heads of the apex R & D agencies in these sectors* report directly to the respective ministers who are, of course, members of the Cabinet whose Chairman is the Prime Minister. Other ministries also have research establishments relevant to their special needs and areas of operation — some of the them transferred there about three years ago from the Council of Scientific and Industrial Research when it was reorganised by the Janata government (1977-78) headed by Morarji Desai.

There is no national policy or planning for in-house industrial R & D in the public or private sectors. Some public sector undertakings in high technology areas, such as BHEL, have large R & D divisions as part of their corporate policy. Government encouragement and incentives have helped the growth of in-house R & D in private industries, up from 300 units in 1975 to approximately 800-1000 at present. Most of the in-house R & D activity is of an elementary nature confined mainly to product/process testing and modification rather than new product/process development.

The organisational apex for all types of university research is the University Grants Commission (UGC) which comes under the Ministry of Education, although university research may be sponsored by any national or international agency subject to appropriate sanctions at various levels in the educational administration. National level policy and commitment to university research have remained extremely fuzzy over the years.

It may be significant to note that from the point of view of national policy the social sciences in India do not have the same status as the natural sciences or the technical and engineering disciplines. They do not constitute a part of the planned national scientific and technological thrust. One never hears of anything like a social science research policy. The most active and visible aspects of the social science research activities at the national level are carried out

---

* Except the CSIR, which has a ministerial level Vice-President and is placed under the office of the Prime Minister who is the ex-officio President of the Council.

by the research institutions and schemes supported by the Indian Council of Social Science Research (ICSSR), the three national Indian Institutes of Management, the Administrative Staff College of India, and a number of private institutes and colleges throughout the country run by individuals, industries and trusts.[4]

The Making of the First
Science and Technology Plan, 1974-79

It is noteworthy that despite a fairly long-standing, although somewhat erratic, experience of planning for science and technology going back to the early days of independence, our First Five-Year Science and Technology Plan (1974-79) was issued only in the beginning of the seventies. As mentioned earlier, in 1971 the Government of India had constituted a National Committee on Science and Technology for this purpose. The original membership of NCST consisted of ten eminent men of science and technology selected by C. Subramaniam, then Minister for Planning, who had also assumed the Chairmanship of this Committee (Appendix 1).

The NCST went through a very complex and elaborate process for formulating the first comprehensive science and technology plan and took about three years to complete it. Under the able guidance of its Chairman, the NCST was aware of the stupendous task before it. India's first national science and technology plan had to be thorough, broad-based, integrated, specific, and task-oriented. In this effort, the NCST had decided early to involve a large number of scientists and technologists, educationists, industrialists, and others.

From the very beginning, a sectoral but integrated approach was adopted. The entire national S&T thrust was divided into twenty-seven sectors. Specific and time-bound programmes of research, development and design were to be identified in each of the chosen sectors according to the development profiles for these formulated by the task forces of the Planning Commission. Each sector was divided into a number of more specific sub-sectors, totalling 140. In many cases the sub-sectors were further demarcated into more concrete areas or projects, totalling about 100.

Each member of the NCST was assigned the responsibility of nominating a panel of experts to look after a particular sector within his own area of competence and knowledge. Several members nominated panels for more than one sector. A total of twenty-seven panels, one for each sector, were thus constituted to coordinate the sector-wise planning process. The panels in turn formed sub-committees to identify priority areas/projects critical to a particular sub-sector. The work of the sub-committee was reviewed and coordinated by a planning group consisting mainly of the convenors of all the sub-committees of the concerned sub-sector, two members from the sectoral panel, representatives of the Planning Commission and the concerned ministry, plus one or two persons from other relevant organisations. The sub-committees appointed their convenors internally while the planning groups were generally chaired by the Chairman of the sectoral panel. Certain sub-sectors were not divided further into areas or projects to be separately handled by sub-committees and coordinated by planning groups. For these a different methodology was followed as, for instance, in the case of the family welfare and health sector :

> Unlike the other panels of the NCST ... , the panel on Family Welfare and Health did not constitute planning groups (or sub-committees) ... , in view of the fact that the Ministry of Health and Family Planning (Department of Family Planning) had already set up a high powered Coordination Committee for Research in Human Reproduction and Family Control. The Convenor of the NCST Panel was also a member of this Committee and he was of the view that the recommendations of this Co-ordination Committee could form the basis for the formulation of research and development programmes in this vital area. In fact, the NCST has largely drawn up this material for its overall plan in the field of health and family welfare.
>
> However, a separate Task Force on Nutrition was constituted in consultation with the Planning Commission and it was agreed that the Task Force of the Planning Commission and the Task Force of the NCST would work on a complementary basis, [the former] to indicate broad strategies for fighting malnutrition [and the latter] to work out the research and development components for those strategies.[5]

In other similar cases, no sub-committees were appointed; only planning or working groups were constituted to prepare sub-sectoral reports. In others, even planning/working groups were considered unnecessary; the sectoral panels themselves incorporated in their reports the plans already prepared by the apex sectoral agencies — for example, the plans for space exploration, atomic energy, agriculture, and scientific and industrial research, were originally prepared by the concerned agencies and subsequently incorporated in the national plan with slight modifications, additions or deletions. This diversity of approaches seems to have created some confusion of nomenclature, blurring the distinction between planning groups, working groups, and sub-committees. In all, 233 planning/working groups, task forces, or sub-committees are reported to have worked to bring out the First Five-Year Science and Technology Plan. The total membership of this formidable assembly consisted of 1855 distinguished scientists, engineers, industrialists, and other experts, drawn from research laboratories/institutes, design engineering groups, manufacturing units, natural resource surveys, institutions of higher learning, and extension organisations throughout the country. (For details on general classification see Appendix 2.)

The formulation of the Plan was informed and aided by broad-based as well as in-depth methodologies, from the very general to the particular, at various levels. At the highest level of generality, several regional seminars were organised in collaboration with national institutions (including one with the ASCI in 1972) to which large numbers of experts and professionals from different fields were invited to articulate and identify national needs and the corresponding science and technology/R&D priorities. The NCST itself assumed the responsibility of providing broad guidelines and overall coordination. Each sectoral panel, under the chairmanship of an NCST member, met approximately four to six times to focus upon the sectoral S&T priorities. These meetings were sometimes attended by other concerned NCST members as well as by invited experts. The sub-committees and/or planning groups, which actually formulated or coordinated the priority areas or sub-sectoral plans, had similar meetings and discussions to arrive at a consensus regarding operational matters, plan proposals, and other technical details. They were aided in this process by a large number of macro project proposals submitted by various groups, institutions, and ministries on request through an elaborate proposal proforma specially designed for this purpose. The sub-committees or planning groups critically examined these proposals and either approved or disapproved them. If approved, a proposal was included in the sub-sectoral plan under a particular priority area. These proposals contained information on financial outlays, the groups and institutions to carry out the projects (in government, industry, or universities), and the prospective users of the results of the research. The sub-sectoral plans were discussed and reviewed by the sectoral panels and presented to the NCST as sectoral plans. Finally, the NCST took an overall view of the sectoral plans and approved and presented the Plan to the Planning Commission toward the end of 1973. It consisted of two volumes, with a sixty-seven page outline and the detailed sectoral plan consisting of 517 pages. The major sectoral recommendations of the S&T Plan were incorporated in thr Fifth Five-Year Plan which was endorsed, as usual, by the National Development Council and the Union Cabinet. The following quotation sums up the approach to this planning process rather well :

In short, the formulation of the S&T Plan has been an interactive process. It has involved an examination not only of the scientific and technological efforts as also of the policies and procedures necessary for maximising the returns from the existing investments and achieving self-reliance ....

The need for a total systems approach also made the planning an iterative one. For example, the first step of identifying the process or product technology in turn led to the spelling out of the technological skills covering the entire spectrum of engineering design capability, materials knowhow, and production techniques that are critical to the fabrication and manufacture of equipment and machinery. Similarly, emphasis on agriculture brought into focus not only ı on-industrial resources like land, water and seed, but also matters relating to fertilizer, soil nutrients, pesticides, machinery, post-harvest technology, and climate control.[6]

The Lacunae

It is not my intention to suggest that there were no difficulties in carrying out this very complex process of planning. The main difficulties were those of coordinating and integrating the work of a vast number of sectoral panels, planning groups, and sub-committees into a national science and technology plan, both sector-wise and as a whole. Looking at the total profile of the Plan it is obvious that not much integration was accomplished by the NCST at the overall level; for the Plan as a whole is a collection of the sectoral plans with implied but not specifically identified and stated inter-sectoral links. In any case, integration would not be easy in planning as diverse a set of activities as the First S&T Plan attempted to cover through the efforts of such a large number of people, groups, and institutions. While intra-sectoral integration depended greatly upon the efforts of the panel groups and the sectoral panels, whatever integration could be achieved in the total plan was due mainly to the fact that the S&T sectoral plans were complementary to the national plan in that they identified the scientific and technological components/contributions necessary to achieve the main sectoral goals set forth by the Planning Commission.

The sectoral reports generally display a much greater degree of internal consistency and coherence than is found in the total Plan, despite the fact that all the panels, planning groups, and sub-committees did not follow a universal methodology of work.

On a more substantive basis, large portions of the Plan were merely reiterative. For instance, in many sectors there was hardly any original thinking; just reiteration by the panels of data supplied by the concerned ministries and agencies, such as in the case of agriculture, space, nuclear energy, industrial research, electronics, health and family planning.

Form the very beginning, the NCST was concerned about the success or failure of the Plan it was formulating. The Committe did not have any mandate to implement, monitor, or review the Plan. These were to be the responsibility of various ministries, agencies, and institutions of the government, in keeping with the adminis-trative system and traditions in India. The financial 'allocations' indicated by NCST for the identified projects and programmes were merely suggestive, not committed. If these projects and programmes were already budgeted items in the plans of the concerned ministry or agency, well and good; otherwise their fate depended upon the motivation and zeal of the relevant individuals and institutions and their ability to seek funds and carry out the Plan. In the absence of a systematic assessment of the First Science and Technology Plan it would be hard to make generalisations about its successes and failures, but knowledgeable people agree that many of its targets have either been abandoned or remain incomplete due to lack of commitment to them, both financial and motivational. However, in no way do these lacunae mitigate the importance of the Plan as a historic landmark of considerable symbolic and practical significance, or gloss over the fact that it was a grand exercise in planning for science and technology.

Science and Technology for the Sixth Plan :
The Second S&T Plan, 1980-85

The NCST was established primarily for the purpose of preparing national science and technology plans. As described above, the greatest achievement of NCST was the preparation of the First Five-Year S&T Plan methodically and elaborately. The NCST, and its mandate, were the brainchild of C. Subramaniam, its first Chairman. When P. N. Haksar replaced Subramaniam as Deputy Chairman of the Planning Commission during the Emergency, he automatically became the Chairman of NCST as well. The NCST had already begun to degenerate soon after completing the Plan. The sectoral panels became non-functional, with the exception of a specially created, general panel on futurology which continued to be active until lately. Subsequently, the government in Delhi changed hands in 1977. Prime Minister Morarji Desai dissolved the old NCST and constituted a new one under the Chairmanship of Atma Ram, retired Director-General of CSIR. The First S&T Plan was coming to an end in 1979. Preparations for the next plan should have started in earnest at least soon after the NCST had been reconstituted. However, nothing of the sort happened, for reasons largely unknown. The NCST remains functionally non-existent to date, neither formally abolished nor renewed.

Instead, the Planning Commission appointed a Working Group late in 1980 to prepare a 'Plan'/Report on science and technology for the Sixth Plan. The Group was constituted through two office memos: No. M. 12018/83/80-S&T dated 12 and 15 September 1980. Initially, the names of twelve persons from different agencies were announced as members with M.G.K. Menon, Secretary, DST, as Chairman, along with the terms of reference. Subsequently, nine more names were added through the later memo, to include all the agency heads, the Chairman of the University Grants Commission, the Director, RRL, Hyderabad (now DG, CSIR), and the Chief of

Planning, CSIR. (For details, see Appendices 3 and 4). The Group met five times during the months of September, October, and November, completed its work by 6 November, circulated the draft report to all the members, incorporated their comments, and submitted the final report to Narayan Datt Tiwari, Minister of Planning, on 22 December 1980.[7]

It is indeed an incredible accomplishment that a five-year national science and technology 'Plan' could be put together in a short span of three months, and the Working Group must be congratulated for that. However, the shortage of time also proved to be the greatest handicap for the Working Group. Consequently, there were no preliminary meetings with larger participation, regional seminars, brainstorming sessions, etc. There was no assessment of the strengths and weaknesses, the successes and failures of the First S&T Plan. Contrary to the terms of reference, 'sub-groups relevant to the component sectors of the Plan' were not set up 'to assist the core Working Group for a more detailed exercise in the second phase'. Projects of national importance were not identified and specified for implementation by various agencies as necessary components of sectoral priorities laid down in the Sixth Plan. One would expect the nation to have learned through the elaborate formulations of the First S&T Plan and improved upon it in the Second. On the contrary, the entire experience gained earlier seems to have been lost to history in the preparation of the 'Second Plan' which, like the Science Policy Resolution of 1958, ends up being a statement of good intentions, albeit a grander one.*

Compared to the First Plan, the fact that the scientific community was not involved in the formulation of the Second Plan was a serious handicap. It may be noted that at about the time the First S&T Plan was under preparation, a sample survey of scientists' participation in the formulation of the S&T Plan had clearly demonstrated that (a) participation was low, (b) but it was much

---

* This is not to deny some of the unique features of the Working Group Report. For the first time subjects like scientific temper; S & T for weaker sections; women and rural development; involvement of young scientists; S & T administration; scientific academies and professional societies; and working conditions for scientific personnel were given due prominence in the highest national document on science and technology. The document was also relatively more specific on the procedures to be followed while making foreign versus indigenous technology choices.

desired, and *(c)* wherever indicated, it had a positive influence on the perception of the policy, and commitment to it, by the scientists.[8] During 1971-73, the NCST was able to involve about 2,000 to 3,000 scientists, engineers, industrialists, and educators either directly or indirectly in the planning process and one could sense a great deal of awareness and excitement in the involved and concerned sections of the scientific community about the Plan, its formulation and implementation. This was not the case in 1980. The scientific community, let alone the public at large, hardly knew anything about the Plan or seemed to care about it. The only notable exception was a series of seminars and meetings hurriedly conducted in various parts of the country by the Vice-President of the CSIR, S. Nurul Hasan, to obtain the views and sentiments of some scientists, professionals, and others about the role and priorities for science and technology (and scientists and technologists) in the Sixth Five-Year Plan. These were fed into the S&T Plan through the CSIR channels in the Working Group.

Apparently, these shortcomings in the planning process were mainly due to lack of time at the disposal of the Working Group. The questions to be asked, however, are : Why such great haste ? Why was not the planning exercise started earlier and why were the tradition and methodology established by the NCST seven years ago not maintained ? Why was the NCST not reactivated for formulating the Second Plan ? The answers are not readily available although some reflections may be helpful.

First, it seems that the mandate given to the NCST by C. Subramaniam as its Chairman to formulate not only the First Science and Technology Plan but the succeeding ones as well did not last beyond his term of office. His successor for a short interim period, P.N. Haksar, had misgivings from the very beginning about the way the First Plan was prepared and doubted the future role of NCST in science and technology plan formulations. The Committee soon began to lose much of its punch. Second, Haksar's successor, Atma Ram, was the first scientist to Chair the NCST — this was the first time the charge was held by anyone other than the Minister of Planning and/or Deputy Chairman of the Planning Commission. Atma Ram viewed the NCST in a totally different light than C. Subramaniam. The former wanted the NCST to be a promotional and advisory body rather than the formulator of national S&T plans, a task for which he would consider the Planning Commission responsible. Naturally, the Committee under his

Chairmanship functioned the way he wanted it to function. It did not do any preparatory work for the Second S&T Plan, although at one time Atma Ram did express (including to this author) NCST's intention to prepare the first ever national technology plan. The sectoral panels constituted during the preparation of the First Plan were never revived because there was no reason to do so. The old membership of the Committee was neither renewed nor terminated.

Thus, by the time the Congress (I) returned to power in 1979 the five-year period of the First Science and Technology Plan (1974-79) had just about run out without any preparation for the Second Plan to be fed into the Sixth National Plan, which itself had been considerably delayed. In its anxiety to issue the Sixth Plan, the Planning Commission, perhaps on the suggestion of the Prime Minister, appointed the *ad hoc* Working Group in September 1980 to do a quick job of preparing the 'Second S&T Plan'/Report before the year was out. The reasons why the dormant NCST was not reactivated for this purpose still remain obscure.

Conclusion

The experience in planning for science and technology is reflective of the process of national planning in general. The present case study of the formulation of the First and Second Science and Technology plans is a study in contrasts and contradictions in national level policy-making, as much as it is a study of the influence on the planning process of political vagaries and personal styles of men and women at the helm of affairs. It raises certain fundamental issues about our vision of the future, the future of science and technology in Indian society and, more importantly, about the seriousness of the business of national planning. The reader is expected to zero-in on these issues and make his/her own judgement about them with the intention of contributing toward our ability to foresee rightly and plan earnestly.

The question to be ultimately answered is : What makes a good policy/plan as opposed to a bad one ?

Public policy is not and cannot become an end in itself. It is to be judged in terms of its social objectives, in terms of its short- and long-term impact on society; in short, in terms of its values. The other criterion is that of practicality : Is the policy implementable, manageable ? Does it set forth achievable goals ? Is it realistic enough in terms of the human condition and resource constraints to be 'cost effective' and yield results, either partially or wholly ? Does it commit resources to accomplish the stated goals and identify resource mobilisation strategies ? And so on. The further we go in identifying the parameters of a 'good policy or plan,' the closer we come to understanding the relationship between good policy and good policy-making — the axiomatic relationship between process and the product. If the axiom that 'process determines the product' is to be held valid in the realm of public policy, we must ensure sound policy-making procedures, allowing a careful and critical examination of the criteria of values and practicality in order to ensure a good public policy.

This case study on the making of the science and technology plan in India is intended to be a pointer to S&T policy analysts and policy-makers toward identifying the lacunae in our policy-making/planning procedures and improving them for the future. Emerging out of the case study are four critical factors for consideration : political influence on the policy process; the time allowed for policy-making; extent of participation; and identification and commitment of resources to policy implementation.

Notes

1. For a critical assessment of the role of SACC in S&T policy-making, see Ashok Parthasarathy, 'Appearance and Reality in Two Decades of Science Policy' in Rahman and Sharma (eds.), *Science Policy Studies*, New Delhi, Somaiya Publications, 1974, pp. 81-95.
2. GOI, *An Approach to the Science and Technology Plan*, New Delhi, National Committee on Science and Technology, January 1973.
3. GOI, *Science and Technology Plan, 1974-79*, Vols. I and II, New Delhi, National Committee on Science and Technology, August 1973.
4. For the development of management education and research and the performance of management training institutions in India, see S.R. Ganesh, 'Collaborative Institution Building : A Critique of Three Experiences in Higher Education,' *Vikalpa*, Vol. 4, No. 2, April 1979, p. 162; and 'Performance of Management Education Institutions : An India Sampler,' *Higher Education*, Vol. 9, 1980, pp. 239-53.
5. GOI, *Sectoral Science and Technology Plan for Family Welfare and Health*, New Delhi, National Committee on Science and Technology, August 1975, pp. iv-v.
6. GOI, *Science and Technology Plan, 1974-79*, Vol. I, Introduction, pp. 2-3.
7. GOI, *Report of the Working Group on Science and Technology for the Sixth Plan* (1980-85), New Delhi, Planning Commission, December 1980.
8. Aqueil Ahmad, 'Scientists and Science Policy Formulation,' *Journal of Scientific and Industrial Research*, Vol. 37, No. 11, November 1978.

Appendices

APPENDIX 1

List of NCST Members

C. SUBRAMANIAM, Chairman
HARI NARAIN
A. B. JOSHI
A. R. KIDWAI
A. K. MALHOTRA
V. RAMALINGASWAMY
R. RAMANNA
C. N. R. RAO
M. M. SURI
R. V. TAMHANKAR
B. D. TILAK

APPENDIX 2

NCST Panels and Planning Groups

Name of Panel	*Planning Group*
1. Family Welfare and Health	1. TASK FORCE ON NUTRITION 2. CLINICAL TRIALS OF DRUGS 3. NCST GROUP ON PRIVATE RESEARCH 4. COMMUNICABLE DISEASES
2. Natural Resources	1. FOREST, LAND, SOIL AND WILDLIFE (a) Plant introduction, silviculture and management (b) Plant breeding, physiology and ecology (c) Protection from pests and diseases (d) Farm forestry and range management (e) Wood sciences (f) Pulp and paper products (g) Minor forest products (Medicinal Plants, Essential Oils, etc.) (h) Harvesting and extraction (i) Land-use

　　　　(j) Watershed management and
　　　　　　flood control
　　　　(k) Soil and soil plant relationship
　　　　(l) Wildlife and environmental
　　　　　　conservation
　　2. OIL AND NATURAL GAS
　　　　(a) Origin, migration and accumu-
　　　　　　lation of petroleum
　　　　(b) Biostratigraphy
　　　　(c) Sedimentary processes and
　　　　　　formation of deltas
　　　　(d) Exploration geophysics
　　　　　　including well-logging
　　　　(e) Drilling techniques and processes
　　　　(f) Drilling mud and cement
　　　　(g) Production, reservoir studies
　　　　　　and transportation
　　3. GEODETIC AND TOPO-
　　　　GRAPHICAL SURVEYS
　　　　(a) Aerial photo-interpretation
　　　　(b) Cadastral surveys
　　　　(c) Photogrammetry
　　　　(d) Surveying and cartography
　　　　(e) Urban land-use and engineering
　　　　　　surveys
　　　　(f) Printing technology
　　　　(g) Geodesy
　　4. MINERAL RESOURCES
　　　　(a) Atomic minerals
　　　　(b) Ferrous minerals
　　　　(c) Non-ferrous minerals
　　　　(d) Industrial minerals
　　　　(e) Coal and lignite
　　　　(f) Geophysical exploration
　　　　(g) Remote-sensing
　　　　(h) Structure and tectonics of
　　　　　　mineralised zones
　　　　(i) Geochemistry and petrology
　　　　(j) Gaps between exploration and
　　　　　　exploitation
　　　　(k) Economic geology
　　　　(l) Data processing
　　　　(m) Frontiers in earth sciences
　　5. WATER RESOURCES
　　　　(A) Surface Water
　　　　(i) Assessment Sub-sector
　　　　(a) Precipitation, snow and glacier
　　　　　　study

    (b) Evapo-transpiration, run-off, recharge and floods

    (c) Sediment and water quality observation

    (d) Acquifer identification and sub-surface water level logging

    (e) Hydrometry

    (f) Computerisation, mathematical modelling and simulation

    (g) Satellite and remote sensors

    (h) Instrumentation

    (i) Data processing, collation, storage and retrieval

(ii) Utilisation Sub-sector

    (a) Hydraulics, hydraulic structure

    (b) Engineering geology, geohydrology, geophysics, geochemistry, seismology

    (c) Agriculture, soil-water-plant research, irrigation, water management and drainage

    (d) Material, soil, concrete rock

    (e) Water-pollution, control and monitoring water conservation, re-use research

    (f) Sedimentation, watershed management

    (g) Hydro-mechanical equipment

(B) Ground Water

(i) Sub-Committee on Ground Water

(ii) Sub-Groups

    (a) Hydrogeology

    (b) Groundwater geophysics

    (c) Groundwater hydrology

    (d) Groundwater engineering

6. EARTH SCIENCES

    (a) Astronomy and astrophysics

    (b) Palaeogeophysics and geodynamics

    (c) Seismology

    (d) Geothermal resources

    (e) Geomagnetism and geoelectricity

3. Fuel and Power

1. R&D RELATING TO ELECTRICAL SYSTEMS

2. MHD

3. EFFICIENCY OF FUEL UTILISATION

    (a) Power sector

    (b) Industrial sector

	4. INSTITUTE FOR ENERGY STUDIES
	5. SOLAR ENERGY
	6. TIDAL POWER
	7: WIND POWER
	8. GEOTHERMAL ENERGY
	9. CHEMICAL ENERGY
	10. AERO-GAS TURBINES FOR POWER GENERATION
	11. COAL UTILISATION
	12. BETTER UTILISATION OF EXISTING THERMAL STATIONS
	13. COAL SLURRY PIPELINE
	14. HV-DC TRANSMISSION
4. Heavy Engineering	1. HEAVY ELECTRIC EQUIPMENT FOR POWER HOUSE, TRANSMISSION SUBSTATION, MILLS DRIVES, TRACTION EQUIPMENT, STEAM AND WATER TURBINES
	2. HEAVY PRESSURE VESSELS, BOILERS, HEAT EXCHANGERS, DRYERS, ETC.
	3. EQUIPMENT FOR FERTILISER PLANTS, PETROLEUM REFINERIES AND PETRO-CHEMICAL PLANTS, HEAVY DUTY PUMPS, COMPRESSORS AND SPECIAL PUMPS FOR CHEMICAL INDUSTRIES
	4. HEAVY MACHINE TOOLS
	5. STEEL PLANT AND METALLURGICAL PLANT EQUIPMENT
	6. MINING MACHINERY, ORE BENEFICIATION EQUIPMENT, AND HEAVY EARTH MOVING EQUIPMENT
	7. PORT AND HARBOUR MACHINERY
	8. SPECIAL REQUIREMENTS OF DEFENCE
	9. CEMENT, PAPER AND SUGAR MACHINERY
	10. PROCESS CONTROL INSTRUMENTATION
	11. SPECIAL MACHINERY FOR PRINTING, PACKAGING, BOTTLING, ETC.
	12. EQUIPMENT FOR THE MANUFACTURE OF FABRICS, FELTS, FILTERS, ETC.

	13. EQUIPMENT FOR WIRES AND CABLES, WIRE ROPES AND PLASTIC EXTRUSION
	14. INFORMATION CENSUS SURVEYS IN HEAVY ENGINEERING
	15. EXPORT PROMOTION FORE-CASTING POTENTIAL
	16. DRILLING RIGS
	17. CEMENT MACHINERY
5. Chemical Industries	1. BULK ORGANIC CHEMICALS/ PETRO-CHEMICALS, POLYMERS
	2. FERTILISERS AND OTHER NUTRIENTS
	3. INORGANIC CHEMICALS/ ELECTRO-CHEMICALS
	4. ORGANIC FINE CHEMICALS INCLUDING DRUGS AND PHARMACEUTICALS
	5. DYES AND INTERMEDIARIES FOR DYES AND PHARMACEUTICALS
	6. OILS, FATS, SOAPS, SURFAC-TANTS, PAINTS AND VARNISHES
	7. PESTICIDES
	8. MARINE CHEMICALS
	9. CHEMICAL ENGINEERING RESEARCH AND DESIGN CAPABILITY DEVELOPMENT
6. Machine Tools	1. FOUNDRY MACHINERY
	2. FORMING MACHINERY
	3. MATERIAL REMOVAL MACHINERY
	4. HEAT TREATMENT EQUIPMENT
	5. MEASURING AND TESTING EQUIPMENT
	6. PLASTICS MACHINERY
	7. MODERNISATION OF MACHINERY
	8. PRODUCTIVITY OF MACHINE TOOLS
	9. DEFENCE PRODUCTION MACHINES
	10. EXPORT POTENTIAL AND STRATEGY
	11. INFORMATION AND DOCUMEN-TATION IN MACHINE TOOLS
	12. METAL WORKING AND METAL FORMING TOOLS, INCLUDING HAND TOOLS

7. Mining, Steel and Metallurgical
   Industries

   1. ORES AND MINERALS
   2. COAL AND COKE
   3. IRON AND STEEL
   4. SPECIAL STEELS
   5. COMMON NON-FERROUS METALS
   6. SPECIAL NON-FERROUS METALS
   7. RARE METALS
   8. HIGH PURITY METALS AND
      SUPER ALLOYS
   9. FOUNDRY AND FORGE
   10. POWER METALLURGY
   11. REFRACTORIES
   12. FERRO ALLOYS
   13. METALLIC CORROSION AND ITS
       PREVENTION
   14. MINING
   15. METALLURGICAL RESEARCH IN
       EDUCATIONAL INSTITUTIONS

8. Agricultural Equipment

9. Transportation

   1. RAIL SUB-SECTOR
      (a) Operations
      (b) Equipment
      (c) Materials
      (d) New areas of R&D
   2. ROAD AND WELFARE SUB-SECTOR
      (a) Road and terminal facilities
      (b) Inland water transport
      (c) Ship and ship-building
      (d) Road transport and vehicles
      (e) Special modes of transportation

10. Agriculture

11. Meteorology

    1. METEOROLOGY
    2. TROPICAL METEOROLOGY

12. Defence Space and Aeronautics

13. Electronics and Atomic Energy

14. Consumer Industries

    1. GROUP ON TEXTILES
       (a) Agricultural and genetic
           research on jute
       (b) Jute process/products technology
           and machinery development
       (c) Cotton textiles and blends
       (d) Synthetic fibres
       (e) Wool process/products techno-
           logy and machinery development
       (f) Futuristic development in the
           field of textiles

2. GROUP ON FOOD
   (a) Milk and milk dairy products
       and animal husbandry
       including meat
   (b) Fish processing
   (c) Cereals and their processing,
       storage and inspection
   (d) Oils, proteins and other sub-
       sidiary foods
   (e) Vegetables and fruits
   (f) Tea, coffee, spices and nuts
3. GROUP ON SUGAR
   (a) Sugar and sugarcane development
   (b) Sugar technology and processing
   (c) Sugar machinery
   (d) By-product industries
4. GROUP ON LEATHER
5. GROUP ON SALT
6. GROUP ON FILMS AND PHOTO-
   GRAPHIC CHEMICALS AND
   CAMERA
   (a) Films and photographic chemicals
   (b) Cameras
7. GROUP ON TOBACCO AND
   TOBACCO PRODUCTS
   (a) Health hazard on the use of
       tobacco and tobacco products
   (b) Tobacco products and machinery
       development
   (c) Bidi, zarda, hookah and tobacco
   (d) Agricultural and genetic research
       on tobacco

15. Housing and Urbanisation
    and Construction Technology

1. HOUSING AND CONSTRUCTION
   TECHNOLOGY
   (A) Housing and Other Building
       Construction
   (a) Materials of construction
   (b) Construction equipment
   (c) Structural design and cons-
       truction techniques
   (d) Foundation and foundation structures
   (e) Building services (services for
       specific functions and environ-
       mental efficiency of buildings)
   (f) Urban housing and physical
       planning
   (g) Rural housing and community
       development (physical facilities
       for rural development)

(h) Industrial building
(i) Institutional building (Including architecture and physical planning)
(j) Building practices, productivity and management
(k) Education, training and manpower
(l) Extension services for the building industry

(B) Construction Technology
(a) R&D in structural engineering
(b) R&D in soil mechanics and foundation engineering
(c) R&D in earthquake resistant design and earthquake engineering

2. URBANISATION (RURAL, URBAN AND REGIONAL DEVELOPMENT)
(a) Planning standards and planning methodology for Indian conditions
(b) Strategy, planning and implementation, mechanisms for physical plans to get balanced regional development
(c) Planning Group on new towns (including industrial townships)
(d) Rapidly growing towns (other than metropolitan cities); slum improvement
(e) Community wastes/R&D in public health engineering
(f) Socio-technical aspects of urbanisation

16. **Employment of Scientific and Technical Manpower**

17. **Marine Resources**

1. FISH AND FISHERIES
2. MARINE ENVIRONMENT
3. SEA WATER
4. SURVEY OF INSTRUMENTS
5. INFORMATION MANAGEMENT AND DATA COLLECTION
6. EDUCATION RESEARCH
7. EQUIPMENT
8. MINERAL OIL AND GAS
(a) Studies for offshore oil and gas
(b) Studies for offshore minerals
(c) Marine geophysical data acquisition and processing for minerals, oil and gas

(d) Marine scientific instruments for data acquisition of off-shore minerals, oil and gas
(e) Marine technology (drilling and production)

9. COASTAL ZONES

18. Environmental Quality and Pollution Control

19. Research Support, Extension and Education

EXPERT GROUP SET UP TO LOOK INTO THE PLAN PROGRAMMES OF GRANTS-IN-AID TO INSTITUTIONS UNDER THE DEPARTMENT OF SCIENCE AND TECHNOLOGY

20. New Materials

1. CERAMICS
2. MICA
3. ELECTRONIC MATERIALS
4. THICK/THIN FILMS
5. PHOTO MATERIALS
6. FERRITES AND OTHER MAGNETIC MATERIALS
7. COMPOSITE MATERIALS
8. CARBON PRODUCTS
9. LIQUID CRYSTALS
10. CENTRES FOR MATERIALS RESEARCH

21. Group Agreements on Collaboration

22. Instruments

23. Utilisation and Recycling of Wastes

1. AGRICULTURAL AND ANIMAL WASTES
2. MINING AND METALLURGICAL WASTES
3. COMMUNITY WASTES
4. WASTES FROM CHEMICAL INDUSTRIES
5. BUILDING MATERIALS FROM WASTES

24. Khadi and Village Industries

1. KHADI
2. VILLAGE INDUSTRIES

25. Small-Scale Industries

26. Refrigeration and Air Conditioning

27. Information

1. TOTAL OF PANELS   27
2. TOTAL OF PLANNING GROUPS   233
3. TOTAL NUMBER OF MEMBERS 1855

APPENDIX 3

No. M. 12018/83/80-S&T
GOVERNMENT OF INDIA
PLANNING COMMISSION

Yojana Bhavan
Parliament Street
New Delhi 110 001

12th September, 1980

Office Memorandum

SUB : *Core Working Group on Science and Technology*
for the Five-Year Plan (1980-85)

In the context of the preparation of the Five-Year Plan (1980-85), it has been decided to set up and integrate Working Group on Science and Technology. The composition and terms of reference of the Group are as follows :

COMPOSITION

1. **Prof. M. G. K. Menon**   Chairman
   Secretary
   Department of Science and Technology

2. **Prof. B. M. Udgaonkar**   Member
   Tata Institute of Fundamental Research
   Bombay

3. **Prof. Y. Na,udamma**   Member
   Distinguished Scientist
   Madras

4. **Dr. S. Varadarajan**   Member
   Chairman and MD, IPCL
   Baroda

5. **Prof. Rais Ahmed**   Member
   Vice-Chancellor
   Kashmir University
   Srinagar

6. **Dr. H. K. Jain**   Member
   Director, IARI,
   New Delhi

7. **Prof. G. P. Talwar**   Member
   Jawaharlal Nehru Fellow
   AIIMS, New Delhi

8. **Shri T. R. Satishchandran**   Member
   Adviser (Energy)
   Planning Commission

9. **Shri M. Satyapal**   Member
    Adviser (I&M)
    Planning Commission

10. **Dr. G. Rangaswamy**   Member
    Adviser (Agri.)

11. **Shri Lav Raj Kumar**   Member
    Chairman
    Bureau of Industrial Costs & Pricing
    New Delhi

12. **Shri M. R. Raman**   Member-Convenor
    Joint Adviser (S&T)
    Planning Commission

TERMS OF REFERENCE

1. To recommend a policy framework for S&T priorities for the Plan 1980-85.

2. To suggest specific mechanisms for strengthening the following linkages :

    (a) Academic/educational institutions with national laboratories,

    (b) Academic institutions with indust: ≈.

    (c) National laboratories with industries,

    (d) National laboratories/academic institutions with user departments,

    (e) User departments and scientific institutions with Planning Commission.

3. To review the existing organisational struc ures, system for S&T planning, coordination, implementation, monitoring and evaluation and suggest the manner in which the role and structure of NCST, S&T Div. (Planning Commission) and S&T Cell in administrative ministries should be strengthened/reorganised.

4. To recommend on incentives, au…ties and facilities needed by the scientific community for effective functioning.

5. To recommend on proper and full utilization of scientific manpower.

6. To suggest the methodology for adopting an integrated approach in areas in which several agencies/laboratories are operating.

7. To suggest areas of priorities for S&T effort in the seve₁ al sectors of the socio-economic Five-Year Plan (list of sectors given in Annexure I), and further identify major areas for coordinated research thrust in the Five-Year Plan, demarcating clearly the scope of work of the participating agencies.

8. To recommend on the methodology and the setting up of new institutions in the field of S&T to ensure self-reliance on a long-term, continuing basis.

9. Identify requirements of S&T inputs/needs specific to the sectors (Annexure I refers) and recommend broadly the programme content and outlays (Plan/non-Plan) required by the different implementing/participating agencies/organisations/departments.

2.   The Working Group is expected to give its report in two phases. **Phase I of the report** is expected to be furnished by 26th September 1980, covering the policy framework, issues and structures, priority areas and major/important programmes together with indicative outlays for the different sectors/Departments.

3.   For a more detailed exercise in the second phase, sub-groups relevant to the component sectors of the Plan are expected to be set up to assist the Core Working Group.

4.   The expenditure on TA/DA in connection with the meetings of the Working Group will be borne by the parent Departments/Ministries/Organisations to which official members belong. Non-official members will be entitled to TA/DA as admissible to Grade I officers of the Government of India and this will be paid by the Planning Commission.

5.   Any correspondence regarding this Working Group may kindly be addressed to Member-Convenor.

[Sd/-]
Y. MOHAN
Director (Admn.)

To : Chairman and all Members of the Working Group.

A List of Sectors/Sub-Sectors Pertaining to S & T

1.   ENERGY :
   (a) Coal, Petroleum and Alternative Sources of Energy
   (b) Power and Atomic Energy

2.   INDUSTRIES :
   (a) Machinery, Tools, Instrumentation Development, Electronics and Steel Industries
   (b) Mining, Minerals, Non-Ferrous Metals and Ocean Resources Industries
   (c) Consumer Industries (Textile, jute, synthetics, sugar, paper, leather and ceramics), Small Scale and Village Industries
   (d) Chemicals Industries (including fertilisers, drugs, insecticides, pesticides, petrochemicals and polymers, catalysts and corrosion)

3.   COMMUNICATION AND BROADCASTING : Tele-communications; Satellite Communication/Space Science and Technology; Broadcasting (Wireless & TV)

4.   AGRICULTURE AND BIO-SCIENCES :
   (a) Agricultural Research & Education, Forestry, Animal Husbandry, Fisheries and Remote Sensing Applications
   (b) Irrigation & Meteorology
   (c) Biosciences and Biotechnologies, Natural Plant products, Ecology and Environmental Sciences

5.   TRANSPORT : Shipping, Road and Ports, Offshore Facilities, Railways and Aeronautics

6.   BASIC RESEARCH, EDUCATION AND TRAINING :
   (a) Support for Technical Education, Refresher/Retraining, Societies, Academics/Professional Institutions, Grant-in-Aid Funding and Information Science/Systems
   (b) Food and Nutrition, Health and Allied Health Education and Water Supply

APPENDIX 4

No. M.12018/83/80-S&T
GOVERNMENT OF INDIA
PLANNING COMMISSION

Yojana Bhavan
Sansad Marg
New Delhi

15th Sep. '80

Office Memorandum

SUBJECT : *Core Working Group on Science and Technology for the Five-Year Plan (1980-85).*

In partial modification of O.M. of even no. dated 12th September, 1980 it has been decided that the composition of the Core Working Group would be as follows :

COMPOSITION

1. **Prof. M. G. K. Menon**	Chairman
Secretary	
Department of Science and Technology	
2. **Prof. B. M. Udgaonkar**	Member
Tata Institute of Fundamental Research	
Bombay	
3. **Prof. Y. Nayudamma**	Member
Distinguished Scientist	
Central Leather Research Institute	
Madras	
4. **Dr. S. Varadarajan**	Member
Chairman and Managing Director	
Indian Petrochemicals Corporation Limited	
Baroda	
5. **Prof. Rais Ahmed**	Member
Vice-Chancellor	
Kashmir University	
Srinagar	
6. **Dr. H. K. Jain**	Member
Director	
Indian Agricultural Research Institute	
New Delhi	

7.	**Prof. G. P. Talwar** Jawaharlal Nehru Fellow All India Institute of Medical Sciences New Delhi	Member
8.	**Shri Lav Raj Kumar** Chairman Bureau of Industrial Costs & Pricing New Delhi	Member
9.	**Dr. G. S. Sidhu** Director Regional Research Laboratory Hyderabad	Member
10.	**Shri A. Rahman** Chief (Planning) Council of Scientific and Industrial Research New Delhi	Member
11.	**Secretary** Department of Electronics Lok Nayak Bhavan New Delhi	Member
12.	**Secretary** Defence Research and Development New Delhi	Member
13.	**Chairman** Atomic Energy Commission Bombay	Member
14.	**Chairman** Space Commission Bangalore	Member
15.	**Director-General** Indian Council of Agricultural Research New Delhi	Member
16.	**Director-General** Indian Council of Medical Research New Delhi	Member
17.	**Vice-Chairman** University Grants Commission New Delhi	Member
18.	**Shri T. R. Satishchandran** Adviser (Energy) Planning Commission	Member

19. **Shri M. Satyapal**   Member
    Adviser (I & M)
    Planning Commission

20. **Dr. G. Rangaswamy**   Member
    Adviser (Agriculture)
    Planning Commission

21. **Shri M. R. Raman**   Member-Convenor
    Joint Adviser (S & T)
    Planning Commission

The terms of reference, etc., will remain the same.

[Sd/-]
Y. MOHAN
Director (Admn.)

To : Chairman and all Members of the Working Group.

VINA MAZUMDAR

9 Role of Research in Women's Development : A Case Study of the ICSSR Programme of Women's Studies

I. *The Historical Context*

The period was the seventies — the background one of a deepening development crisis across the world — with increasing problems of mass poverty, malnutrition, unemployment, imbalances in socio-economic development, the confrontation between the first and third worlds on the 'population crisis' and growing disillusionment with the 'trickle down' theory of development. Amongst the many groups searching for better strategies which could narrow inequalities within and between nations was a section of the new women's movement which had erupted in many countries of the western world from the mid-sixties. The movement recorded women's protest against their unequal status in society, their image as commodities or sex objects — unproductive consumers with only the biological role of reproduction to perform — and their ineffectiveness in influencing the socio-political process that shaped their own and their children's lives.[1] Pressure from this movement has resulted in a declaration by the UN General Assembly for the Elimination of Discrimination Amongst Women (1967). This was followed by a

UN decision requesting Member States to submit reports on the status of women in their countries.

While India shared the development crisis, there was in fact no women's movement nor any realisation of the interrelationship between the situation of women and developmental trends. The women's movement which had developed along with the freedom struggle had ended by the mid-fifties, with the acceptance of women's claim for complete equality in the Constitution, and the first attempt to apply this principle in Hindu Law.[2] The organisations which had spearheaded the movement remained but most of them accepted their new role as partners of the new government in providing needed services to women, children and other handicapped groups in society. Many of the leaders who had also played significant roles in political parties accepted important public offices. The new generation coming out of the universities benefited from the equality clauses of the Constitution and entered careers in academia, administration and other important professions. To most of these groups it appeared that the women's movement had attained its objectives and it was only a question of time for the benefits to reach all women in Indian society. While some women leaders played important roles in national policy-making and attended international conferences, including the UN commission on the Status of Women, as Indian representatives, one cannot say that they played any important role in the beginning of the women's issue within the UN system, because the complacency of the fifties had not been seriously disturbed for them to challenge any development *from the women's point of view.*

Repeated reminders from the UN for a report lead to the decision of the Government of India to appoint a committee — to review the changes that had taken place in the status of Indian women as a result of constitutional equality, legal reform and educational and other measures introduced by the government since independence. Several chance coincidences preceded this decision. First was the Ministry of External Affairs's puzzled question, 'Who in the government is responsible for women'? Had it been workers or Scheduled Castes and Scheduled Tribes, one knows of agencies like the Ministry of Labour or the Commissioner for Scheduled Castes and Tribes. But there was no such agency within the government which could be considered as responsible for women. A senior officer decided that the letter from the UN had better be sent to the

Department of Social Welfare since they were the only agency which had something to do with women. The Union Minister for Social Welfare was Dr. (Smt.) Phulrenu Guha — an old activitist of the women's movement whose continuous involvement in social and political work and with welfare agencies working for women had not resulted in the complacency shared by many women's organisations. She saw in the UN's request an opportunity for initiating a review of changes in the status of women since independence and sent her suggestion to the Prime Minister. The decision was taken thirteen months later, when the Government of India appointed the Committee on the Status of Women in India (September 1971) under the Chairmanship of Dr. (Smt.) Phulrenu Guha.[3]

By the time the Committee got started there had been a change in the Ministry and Prof. S. Nurul Hasan had taken charge of both the Ministries of Education and Social Welfare. A feeling of discomfort, which was shared by the Chairman, that the composition of the Committee, which included only one social scientist,[4] was not adequate to undertake an investigation of the kind envisaged, resulted in two decisions — *(a)* to induct two more social scientists (one anthropologist and one political scientist) on the Committee, and *(b)* to request the Indian Council of Social Science Research to provide the research support that the Committee might need. The Member-Secretary of the ICSSR, Shri J.P. Naik, accepted this responsibility and offered the Council's assistance to the Committee.

During the first two years of its existence, however, the Committee depended primarily on task forces that it had appointed to assist its work. Only two of these task forces — on legal and social aspects — accepted the Council's offer and requested that a large number of papers be commissioned by specialists on different fields. It was only in 1973, after the reconstitution of the Committee,[5] that the collaboration with the ICSSR took full shape, resulting in the commissioning of a large number of papers as well as empirical studies to gather material for the Committee's investigation.[6] The Committee's own research unit was also strengthened to undertake a critical examination of both secondary data as well as the primary information gathered by the Committee from its rapid tours across the country and discussions with large groups of women from different socio-economic backgrounds. The report of the Committee, submitted on 1 January 1975, while acknowledging with gratitude the most valuable assistance received from social scientists across the country through the intermediacy of the ICSSR, pleaded for the continuous involvement of social scientists since 'changes in the status of women will be a long-term aspect of our social process and will require continuous examination and assessment by persons interested in social change'.[7]

A few weeks before the submission of the Committee's report, the Indian Council of Social Science Research took the decision that in view of the declaration of 1975 as the International Women's Year (IWY), the Council would undertake to publish a summary of the forthcoming report of the Committee on the Status of Women in India (CSWI) and also a series of volumes incorporating the studies that had been commissioned for the Committee. The present writer was appointed (January 1975) as Chief Editor to implement this decision. A small unit was temporarily created to assist the Chief Editor.

The summary of the report was published in May 1975, practically simultaneously with the main report which was published by the Government. A Hindi translation followed and efforts were initiated by the ICSSR to persuade local agencies in different states to bring out translations of the summary in various Indian languages. A small working group was constituted to plan a series of monographs on sources of data for research on women, as the CSWI report had identified considerable ignorance amongst researchers with regard to available data as well as flaws in some of the official data which had influenced many social scientists to avoid any analysis of women's situation, particularly in the economic field.

The CSWI had emphasised the need for primary data with regard to the position of women in unorganised occupations. On the suggestion of the IWY unit, the Research Committee of the ICSSR approved a programme of commissioning a few micro studies of poor women working in various unorganised occupations. It was decided to publish these micro studies in a series titled 'Women in a Developing Economy'.

Since the SNDT Women's University had started a research unit on the status of women from 1974, the ICSSR decided that publication of the series of volumes coming out of the studies commissioned for the Committee on the Status of Women in India (entitled 'Women in a Changing Society') could be entrusted to the SNDT University with partial support from the Council.

II. *Genesis of the Programme of Women's Studies*

The activities undertaken by the ICSSR during 1975 may be viewed as marginal efforts in response to identified gaps in information or the need for research aids to stimulate greater interest among social scientists in this field. The Council did not feel it had any major policy role to perform since the report of the CSWI had been debated in Parliament, leading to a unanimous resolution requesting the Government to 'initiate a Comprehensive Programme of specific legislative and administrative measures aiming at remedying as far as possible the economic and social injustices, disabilities and discriminations to which Indian women continue to be subjected.' An inter-ministerial Empowered Committee was appointed in 1975 to consider the fifty-two recommendations made by the CSWI and to take decisions thereon. Simultaneously, as a follow-up measure to the World Plan of Action for the International Women's Decade (1976-85) adopted by the UN at the World Conference on International Women's Year (Mexico, 1975), the Department of Social Welfare, Government of India, initiated the preparation of a National Plan of Action for Women in consultation with other ministries.

Responding to the recommendation of the CSWI, the Ministry of Labour and Employment established in early 1975 a special cell to give greater attention to women's employment needs and problems and ushered in the Equal Remuneration Ordinance (which was converted into an Act in 1976) to begin the process of removing wage disparities between employment and women in the productive sector. The women's cell began collecting improved data on women's employment conditions and trade union participation in the organised sector of the economy. A new division for Women's Welfare and Development was also established within the Ministry of Social Welfare and entrusted with the task of coordinating, reviewing, and initiating policies for women's development. In September 1976, the Prime Minister announced the constitution of a National Committee on Women — an advisory body under the chairmanship of the Prime Minister herself — to provide a better deal for women. The Women's Bureau in the Department of Social Welfare was to service the Committee and also act as convener of a Standing Inter-ministerial Committee (which succeeded the Empowered Committee) which was established to improve coordination between and joint action by different agencies of the government. In 1976 also came the Report of the National Commission on Agriculture which severely criticised the failure on the part of agricultural and rural development agencies to recognise the major role played by women in the rural economy and society and its recommendation to establish a division within the Ministry of Agriculture and Rural Development to promote the greater involvement of rural women in development activities.

While most of these government agencies referred to the need for better data and information on women and the need for research in different areas (National Plan of Action for Women), there were several disturbing features. It appeared that the Committee's recommendations were being considered piecemeal. While a few of the relatively marginal ones were accepted, most of the major recommendations were being put into cold storage. Agencies such as the cells within the different ministries were being established but with no clear definition of their power or functions. The importance of improving data was mentioned but no operational plan for this purpose was visualised. Above all, the National Plan of Action found no recognition within the Fifth Five-Year Plan or the Planning Commission, but had been prepared on the request of the Department of Social Welfare by the Institute of Applied Manpower Research. The National Plan was thus not linked to the major development strategies embedded in the five-year plans and had no financial backing through allocation of resources. This fact was pointed out in the valedictory meeting of the National Committee appointed for the International Women's Year,[8] but provoked no assurance from the Government. Nor was there any serious evidence of action being taken on the other recommendations of the CSWI, even those which had been accepted by the Empowered Committee. It appeared that in the context of the political emergency issues like women's development had been allocated a low priority.[9] There was the beginning of a new awareness, but no indication of a clear policy legitimised by appropriate decision-making and action agencies. At the same time, commitments to women's equality and development were being renewed in international forums. In addition to the UN's World Plan of Action,[10] India was a signatory to a decision taken by the nonaligned summit held at Colombo in 1976 to integrate women in development. The role of the ICSSR's research programme on women has to be examined in this context.

The separate decisions taken at the end of 1974 and during 1975 to undertake some publication and research activities on women as a gesture of celebrating the International Women's Year was succeeded early in 1976 by a decision on the part of the Member-Secretary, ICSSR, to develop a long-term programme of sponsored research on women with definite objectives.

He believed that the policy of public education and arousing public consciousness that had been initiated with the publication of the summary of the CSWI's report needed to be carried further to develop pressure from below. He was conscious of the need to promote institutionalised action for women's equality and development as well as the need to expand and promote a number of women committed to the same cause. During 1975-77, he assisted some women social scientists to go and observe women's problems inside and outside India, to participate in seminars and conferences so that they would develop both expertise and involvement. Collaboration with the SNDT University and other women's institutions were based on his conviction that without sustained activities no real transformation in women's situation would take place.[11] Research was important and crucial, but unless researchers developed links with individuals, groups or institutions which could organise action or mobilisation, the research was likely to remain confined to the boundaries of academia. It was for researchers to forge alliances with social workers, voluntary organisations, women in political parties and offices, and government agencies responsible for planning and implementing development policies.

I have not altogether succeeded in explaining J.P. Naik's decision to encourage so many of us to develop international contacts. Was it to help change our perspectives and widen our vision? Was it on the other hand to create opportunities for Indian women to make a contribution to the global debate on women's liberation? Or was it to help develop pressures within the country that might encourage the government to take some action in favour of women? The question will have to remain unanswered.

On the issue of women's equality and liberation, J.P. Naik was a Gandhian. He agreed with many of us that the social debate on the women's question which had really begun during the twenties had remained unresolved. The constitutional guarantees only provided a legal framework but the transformation in society that was essential for women's liberation had not taken place. He also believed that women's liberation was a prerequisite of human liberation and that the critical analysis of development strategies from the women's perspective was an essential part of his vision for alternatives in development with which he was becoming increasingly involved.[12]

I must make it clear that this is my interpretation of J.P. Naik's growing conviction that lay behind his decision to ask me to develop a five-year plan for women's studies early in 1976. Before that he had looked at the women's issue as one of the many areas with which the Council should be involved. He had tried to get me involved in his programme of alternatives in education, but when he found that my concern for the women's situation left very little room for involvement in any other area, he gave me full encouragement and considerable freedom to develop a programme within the Council's framework. My colleagues and I had come fresh from the experience of the Committee on the Status of Women and the burden of that experience undoubtedly helped us to define the purpose and objectives of the Council's research programme. But in designing the operational aspects of the programme we drew on Naik's wealth of experience and were guided at every step by his unconventional attitudes. Some of his unconventionality (for example, the need to campaign about the programme, the results of research, and the findings of the CSWI, and to develop public awareness) did not always meet with the approval of the academic community. The Second Review Committee of the ICSSR (1977-78), while complimenting the Women's Studies programme on its success, criticised its 'aggressive promotional activities' and observed that there was no need to maintain a cell within the Council to look after the programme.

The Research Committee of the ICSSR felt that institution building was not a responsibility of the ICSSR, nor could the ICSSR undertake training programmes for development workers or social workers to make them more effective in their functions. The draft programme therefore underwent some modification in the hands of the Research Committee, but was accepted in principle. At the meeting of the Research Committee, Naik explained that as in the case of other sponsored programmes of the Council, an Advisory Committee would be appointed. The Research Committee, therefore, proposed that the programme should be finalised by the Advisory Committee when constituted. The Committee was constituted with an inter-disciplinary membership and a deliberate inclusion of the new officers made responsible for women within the government.[13]

The Programme of Women's Studies: Objectives and Operational Structure

The policy statement of the ICSSR defines the objectives of the Women's Studies programme as follows :

(a) Generation and analysis of data with a view to uncovering significant trends in patterns of social and economic organisation which affect women's position in the long run — *with the specific intent of improving policies for socio-economic development, increasing public consciousness, and assisting the framing and implementation of adequate programmes for women's development and welfare.*

(b) To develop new perspectives in the social sciences — through examining basic assumptions, methodological approaches and concepts used in social science, e.g., the family, household, women's work, economic activity, productivity, etc.; to remedy the neglect and under-assessment of women's contribution to society.

(c) To revive the social debate on the women's question that was initiated during the freedom movement, but has been consigned to oblivion for the last two decades.

These objectives were clearly aimed at policy-makers, with the academic community and the general public as its target groups. Proceeding on the assumption that the previous neglect by social scientists and policy-makers of women belonging to non-elite classes was the result of ignorance, the programme emphasised the study of women in the poorer or less visible sections of our society.

In the first meeting of the Advisory Committee, Prof. B.N. Ganguli and Prof. Ashok Mitra observed that the programme must, while seeking to add to academic knowledge, aim also to change society's attitudes and arouse its conscience. The outrage and shock felt by the members of the CSWI needed to be communicated to people throughout the country — academic communities, women's organisations, trade unions, and the public — to make them more aware and active.

While there was no attempt to restrict the programme to women (the composition of the Advisory Committee itself — 50 per cent of its members being men — indicated clearly that the ICSSR did not subscribe to the theory that research on women should be women's business only), there was a distinct feeling that unless the programme succeeded in activising and mobilising large numbers of women to fight for their rights, then one of its main objectives would be defeated. Prof. M.N. Srinivas added another dimension to this discussion by demanding that the needed correction in social science perceptions made it essential for more and more women social scientists to enter this arena and bring their perceptions into social science research.

The young generation of students and research scholars was viewed as a critical input, and Prof. Ganguli felt that apart from training an increasing band of young scholars to develop a new perspective on women, it was necessary to expose them to the lives and experiences of women leaders in the past — who had protested and fought for greater dignity and justice for women in society. 'The young students today particularly women students have no sense of their own history. We have to develop their consciosness of their own past, to give them a sense of priorities.'

As instruments to realise these objectives, the Committee identified the following priority areas for concentrating research during the first phase of the programme :

1. Changing occupational structure and employment patterns of women — emerging trends;
3. Nature, causes and consequences of excess of female over male migration in India;
3. Variations and changes in the patterns of family organisation and socialisation practices;
4. Evaluation of on-going programmes for women's development; and
5. The origin and nature of the women's movement in India.

Research was to be promoted through grants, fellowships, publication, documentation, seminars and workshops. In the matter of publications, the Council made a deliberate departure in stating that 'it would also like to encourage publications which are accessible and intelligible to non-professional readers'.[14]

What lay behind this combination of analytical, mobilising and policy-oriented objectives, and how did the anger and outrage which had affected members of the CSWI come to be shared by so many eminent social scientists who had not been associated with that enquiry?[15] The Chairman, Prof. Ganguli, had vivid memories of the women's movement during the freedom struggle and declared himself to be greatly disturbed by the grim and bleak findings of the CSWI's report.[16] Prof. Asok Mitra was one of the three 'angry men' that the CSWI came across during the course of its investigation.[17] Prof. M. N. Srinivas's response to the report of the CSWI was the selection of 'Changing Position of Indian Women' as his topic for the Thomas Huxley Memorial Lecture (1976) in which he made the blunt statement : 'all over the world the social sciences are male centred and male biased .... As most social science research has been done by men, we have only a view of the male half of the society and that only in those areas where studies have been carried out.' Summarising his findings on the political participation of women in India,[18] Prof. Iqbal Narain had pointedly drawn attention to the 'gap between symbolism and actuality'. Justice V. R. Krishna Iyer's strong leanings towards social justice was already well known. He too had responded very positively to the report of the CSWI and introduced the concept of 'gender justice' in many of his statements and judgements from 1975.

This shared concern of the members of the Advisory Committee emanated from different sources. For some, women's issues posed an intellectual problem which could lead to improving the methodology and relevance of the social sciences. For a few, it represented continued social injustice and the failure of policy that needed correction. For a very few, the concern was a personal involvement that had to be tempered by academic objectivity. The composition of the Committee prevented any ideological or disciplinary sectarianism. The political inclinations of the members can only be described as a broad spectrum of Indian brands of liberalism — with tinges of Gandhian and other shades of radicalism that could be accommodated because of the moderation that characterised most members' expression of their views.

On the women's issue itself, it is my belief that few members had seriously questioned their own attitudes to the implications of sex-equality before 1975. These men and women — all born two to four decades before independence — had absorbed, to some degree, the idealism of the freedom struggle, and the reformist enthusiasm of that period. The doctrine of women's equality had been in the air, particularly in educational institutions. Women members of the Advisory Committee, who had taken part in political demonstrations as students, recalled that they had instinctively included slogans about women's independence and rights with their demands for the nation's freedom. As professional women — the first generation beneficiaries of constitutional equality — they had also developed a complacency and seen the women's question as obsolete in independent India. The CSWI's enquiry was a revelation, and an intense personal experience, which shattered that complacency transformed their own consciousness and made them question their own lives, values, and their arrogance of knowledge. The heterogeneity of traditions governing the lives of women from different classes, the variety of roles performed by women and the fact that the same modernisation process which had helped middle-class women to come out of their confinement had adversely affected others, were all new experiences that exposed how little they had known about the position of women in Indian society or its direction of change

A definite result of the women's studies programme was the extension of this experience among other researchers, both men and women. The large majority of scholars who participated in the programme did not begin with any militant ideology of feminism, but developed a commitment through their research experience.

The operational methodology worked out by the Advisory Committee placed considerable responsibility on the ICSSR's programme unit, which consisted of two officers and two research assistants. The unit was expected to identify potential scholars and screen proposals, suggesting preliminary clarifications and even substantive extensions to the authors of the project proposals. It was assumed that the unit's experience and understanding of the focus demanded by the Advisory Committee gave it a definite advantage in discussing research proposals with potential scholars. After this preliminary screening, the proposals were evaluated by experts as required by the ICSSR rules. The staff tried to ensure that at least one of the consultants was from the Advisory Committee. Proposals were then considered by the Advisory Committee with the comments of the consultants. Very often Advisory Committee members suggested further additions to the areas of enquiry and made methodological suggestions to sharpen the analysis. In some cases, the programme unit directed these scholars to individual members of the Advisory Committee for detailed consultation at the stage of framing proposals. The Advisory Committee's recommendations to the ICSSR's Research Committee for financial assistance for such proposals were made only after all these steps had been completed.

In the case of the four annual Ph.D. fellowships awarded for women's studies, the ICSSR invited applications through advertisements and circulars to the universities. The preliminary screening of applications was done by small sub-committees in different disciplines with Advisory Committee members and one or two other experts. A short list of applications was then considered by the Advisory Committee which made the final selections.

Instead of the usual progress reports required by the ICSSR rules, project directors were requested to send interim reports which were placed before the Advisory Committee. It was quite usual for the members of the Advisory Committee to make new suggestions at this stage which were then fed back to the researchers. Some time this process resulted in slight extensions of the research projects.

In spite of this elaborate procedure, the completion record of the programme of Women's Studies as compared to other sponsored programmes of the ICSSR cannot be considered as poor. Up to September 1979, the programme approved fifty-five research projects. Of these, thirty-seven have been completed. Sixteen fellowships were awarded, of which two were for post-doctoral work, and fourteen for doctoral studies. The post-doctoral fellowships have been completed. Of the fourteen doctoral fellows, two dropped out after a few months, and five have completed their research. During the same period, eight monographs and two non-priced pamphlets were published, apart from the first volume of the series 'Women in a Changing Society' which was edited by the Unit, and published in collaboration with the SNDT Women's University.

In most of the sponsored programme committees of the ICSSR, the research projects are identified and taken up by members of the Committee. Members of Women's Studies Advisory Committee decided to play a catalytic role and did not take up projects themselves, except when they were specifically requested by the Council. Prof. Asok Mitra was already in-charge of the Re-analysis of Census Data Project initiated by the Council two years before the Women's Studies programme. As a result of his involvement in the Women's Studies programme, he undertook a substantial analysis of census data on women focusing on trends in the sex-ratio, literacy and employment of women, and shifts in occupational patterns.

Since the programme depended on the response of social scientists to the identified priority areas, the results have been uneven. The greatest response and the largest number of research projects were on changes in occupational patterns and the impact of development policies on different groups of women. There were only three studies on migration or migrant women, two on the women's movement and none on patterns of family organisation.

One reason for the predominance of studies on the impact of development was the request received from the Government of India to organise some research-based material for the proposed conference[19] of nonaligned nations on the Role of Women in Development. This request was received in 1977 and the Ministry of Social Welfare agreed to provide some additional funds for this purpose. Since the Conference focused on the impact of development policies on women, the Council had to commission a number of specific studies. Opportunity, however, was provided to universities and research institutes to identify projects of their own choice by circulating the agenda of the Conference and inviting them to send proposals.

In addition to circulating interim and completed reports, the programme unit also had to prepare an annual review of the programme for consideration by the Advisory Committee. The last such review was undertaken in September 1979, on the basis of which the Advisory Committee adopted a resolution recommending to the ICSSR the establishment of a separate autonomous institution for women's studies.[20]

III. *Impact on Policy*

In its review of the programme made in September 1979, the Advisory Committee felt that 'the success of the programme has been significant in the sphere of policy review and reorientation'. This view was based on the following factors :

1. Based on the results of the research carried out under the programme, a number of government agencies requested the Council and members of the Advisory Committee to provide them with advice on development policies;

2. The constitution of several working groups by the Planning Commission, the ministries of Social Welfare, Agriculture, Rural Reconstruction, Labour and Employment, and Industries to review earlier policies in the light of the problems identified by researchers;

3. A deliberate attempt undertaken by the Women's Bureau of the Ministry of Social Welfare, the Women's Cell in the Ministry of Labour and Employment, the Women's Directorate in the Ministry of Rural Reconstruction, and the Adult Education Programme unit of the Ministry of Education to promote discussions on the problems and suggest new strategies through seminars, conferences and meetings of various kinds in different parts of the country, involving representatives of government, voluntary agencies and the slowly expanding group of researchers who were evaluating the results of development on women; and

4. The reflection of this new consciousness within the government on recommendations made by official delegations at various international forums.

While there is little doubt that some questioning of earlier assumptions and strategies had started in a limited way in some circles of the government during 1975-76, the process of policy review and consideration of new strategies really became visible between the period 1977-79 when the government made a deliberate effort to associate researchers and voluntary organisations in these exercises. The context, and the opportunity, were provided by *(a)* the decision of the Janata government to advance the Sixth Five-Year Plan; *(b)* questions raised in Parliament by a small group of newly elected women MPs regarding implementation of the recommendations of the CSWI; *(c)* the entry of Prof. Raj Krishna into the Planning Commission as an expert on the problems of unemployment; and *(d)* the decision taken by the meeting of foreign ministers of nonaligned nations to hold a conference on the 'Role of Women in Development'.

At its second meeting held soon after the general elections in 1977, the Advisory Committee on Women's Studies took two decisions: *(a)* that the results of research which revealed extremely disturbing trends in women's status needed to be disseminated widely through a press conference to create a public demand for policy intervention; and *(b)* that the Committee should send a memorandum to the government of India suggesting certain immediate priorities for action. The Committee's recommendations amounted to some innovation in the ICSSR's normal procedures. While the Council had promoted and sponsored research on areas of national relevance and had also set up joint committees in collaboration with agencies like the ICAR, ICMR and CSIR to investigate areas of policy concern, the Council had not till then made any definite recommendations to the government of India in policy matters. Its efforts at the dissemination of research results had been also limited to publications and offer of publication grants to social scientists. In view of the strong recommendation of the Advisory Committee, the Council approved the suggested innovations, stating, however, that both the press conference and the memorandum should be in the name of the Advisory Committee. The Member-Secretary and the Chairman of the ICSSR could forward the memorandum to the government as advice being offered by an expert committee appointed by the Council.

The press conference was, therefore addressed by Prof. B. N. Ganguli, Prof. Asok Mitra and Prof. M. N. Srinivas, drawing the attention of the public to the disturbing situation indicated by demographic trends, e.g., the declining sex-ratio, the higher rate of female and particularly female infant mortality, and the declining economic participation of women. Prof. Ganguli focused attention on the declining rates in the political participation of women as revealed by election statistics and reminded the members that this indicated a regression in political norms since the time of the freedom struggle and the Gandhian vision of social equality. He also referred to the promises made by the Janata Party regarding women's rights in its manifesto, and called for media vigilance in keeping the government to its promises. Prof. Srinivas explained some of the social implications and bases of the political and demographic trends and observed that the catalytic role undertaken by the ICSSR Programme of Women's Studies could become more effective if the media collaborated in disseminating the research results and in encouraging more people to undertake investigations into the problems of women.

The Memorandum entitled 'Critical Issues on the Status of Women' identified employment, health and education as the priority areas for policy intervention and made fourteen recommendations for immediate consideration by the government. Before finalising the Memorandum some members of the Advisory Committee, including the Chairman, held informal discussions with Prof. Raj Krishna. The document was forwarded to the Prime Minister, the ministers for Education, Social Welfare, Agriculture, Industry, Labour and Employment and Health, the Planning Commission, the ICMR and ICAR by the Chairman and the Member-Secretary of the ICSSR in August 1977. Smt. Padma Ramachandran, Joint Secretary in charge of the Women's Bureau in the Ministry of Social Welfare (who was also a member of the Advisory Committee on Women's Studies) distributed the document to the Conference of Ministers and Secretaries of Social Welfare organised by her Ministry and the Planning Group set up by the Ministry of Social Welfare to prepare for the Sixth Five-Year Plan.

Before the end of the year, three more working groups were appointed by the government :

1. The *Working Group on Employment of Women*, constituted by the Planning Commission under the Chairmanship of Prof. Asok Mitra, included a number of researchers and representatives of the ministries of Labour and Employment, Agriculture, Industry, Social Welfare and the Planning Commission;

2. *The Working Group on Development of Village Level Organisation of Rural Women* was appointed by the Ministry of Agriculture and Rural Development under the Chairmanship of Smt. Padma Ramachandran to review the existing programme of Mahila Mandals promoted under the Community Development Programme and to suggest ways of making them more meaningful and effective;

3. *The Working Group on Adult Education Programme for Women* was appointed by the Ministry of Education under the Chairmanship of Smt. Chitra Naik (Member, Advisory Committee on Women's Studies) to recommend specific measures to bring the National Adult Education Programme being designed for the Sixth Five-Year Plan within the reach of women who formed more than two-thirds of the target population.

A few months later, the Ministry of Industries also appointed a *Working Group on Self Employment for Women.*

The Review Committee of the ICAR — which reviewed the functioning of the agricultural universities — appointed two working groups to examine the problem of extension of rural technology to women and the role of home science colleges in agricultural universities in rural women's development. All these groups included researchers who had undertaken studies on the impact of development on women under the ICSSR programme. Most of them included a few common members from the Advisory committee on Women's Studies. Practically all of them reported by 1978.

During the exercises undertaken by these working groups, there was a definite indication of an increasing sensitivity and awareness on the part of government representatives to the problems under discussion and some evidence of their support for the strategies being recommended by the working groups. Prof. Raj Krishna discussed the report of the Employment Working Group with the Members in 1978. He frankly observed that there was some resistance to the group's recommendations among his colleagues, but that he would do his best to see that women received some attention in the five-year plan. The results of that promise may be seen in the final plan document that emanated from the Janata government at the end of 1979.

From 1978, the Ministry of Social Welfare began an attempt to create some favourable opinion for measures to remedy women's situation. A grant was given to the Gandhi Peace Foundation to organise a conference of women legislators to acquaint them with the critical problems of women and the ICSSR Unit was requested to assist the Gandhi Peace Foundation in preparing both documentary and display material for this purpose. During 1978-79, the Ministry promoted state level and national level conferences on women and development and requested the assistance of researchers as well as women's organisations at these conferences to assist state governments to prepare adequate and well-informed material for consideration by the conferences. The National Conference which took place in May 1979 reflected the higher information base in the agenda papers and in the participation of social scientists in the Conference. The National Conference on Problems of Women Labour convened by the Ministry of Labour and Employment also indicated a similar situation. In each of these conferences, recommendations with regard to the new strategies suggested by the various working groups were sought on the basis of substantial discussions.

It may be noted that the state level and the national level conferences were suggested by Smt. Renuka Barkataki, Minister for Social Welfare, who had by this time become seriously involved in the attempt to remedy the government's previous neglect of women. She felt that there was no 'political will' for this purpose, particularly in the state governments. It was, therefore, necessary to 'generate political will' through dissemination, discussion and arousing consciousness. She repeatedly expressed her appreciation of the work undertaken by the ICSSR in promoting research in this area and sought research support in her attempts to generate political will. She justified these conferences to her own colleagues in the government as necessary preparation for the forthcoming UN conferences which would review the achievements in the first half of the women's decade.

As a member of the twenty-three nation Preparatory Committee for the UN's Mid-decade Conference (Copenhagen, July 1980), India played a major role — an identification of the women's issue as a major problem in *economic* as well as *social* development.[21] It was also at India's insistence that employment, health and education was accepted as a sub-theme for the Mid-decade Review Conference. Dr. Lucile Mair, Secretary-General of the Conference, observed repeatedly that it was the introduction of the sub-theme that enabled the Conference planners to project problems of Third World women far more into their review documents and the draft Programme of Action than had been possible at the Mexico Conference in 1975.

It is not generally known that the recommendation of the UN Commission on the Status of Women in 1978 regarding this sub-theme was also the result of an intervention made by the Indian delegate, Prof. Aloo J. Dastur (Member, ICSSR Committee on Women's Studies). Prof. Dastur attended this meeting a few months after the ICSSR Committee submitted its memorandum to the government which identified employment, health and education as the priority areas for government action. She felt that without such an effort to concretise discussions, the World Conference would be overwhelmed by the views of the more articulate women leaders of developed countries and would ignore the urgent problems of Third World women.

Many of the strategies included in the draft Programme of Action (prepared by the Conference Secretariat and approved by the Preparatory Committee) were suggested by the official Indian delegation. They were based, to a great extent, on the recommendations of the various working groups and conferences referred to earlier in this section. These included : (a) the strategy of establishing cells within various sectoral development agencies (e.g., for agricultural and industrial development, labour and employment, health, education and welfare) at different levels of national governments as well as in international agencies; (b) earmarking of a share of the sectoral allocations for investment in women's development to eliminate the problem of women's invisibility in most economic development programmes (instead of having separate agencies and programmes for women); and (c) promoting rural women's employment and development through their own collective organisations.

These strategies had first been recommended by the working groups on employment, village level organisations, and adult education programmes. They were suggested to the Nonaligned Conference by the Indian delegation (Baghdad, April 1979), and were endorsed by the Conference. They were also suggested to the ESCAP Regional Preparatory Conference for the mid-decade review (New Delhi, November 1979) and accepted by all delegations.[22] I understand that the idea of holding regional preparatory conferences had also been advocated by Mrs. Barkataki at the first meeting of the UN's Preparatory Committee for Copenhagen.

The Conference of the Nonaligned and Other Developing Nations on the Role of Women in Development also took place as a result of an Indian proposal. I have referred to the resolution of the Nonaligned Summit in 1976 on the integration of women in development in Section I. A meeting of the Coordinating Bureau of Nonaligned Nations was to take place in New Delhi in March 1977 to translate the Summit decisions into action programmes. While preparing the agenda of the Conference, the Ministry of External Affairs requested the Women's Bureau in the Ministry of Social Welfare to prepare an action-oriented paper on this item and suggested that the Women's Bureau should consult the ICSSR.[23] The Ministry was rather hesitant, but J. P. Naik felt that the Nonaligned Conference was an important forum where this question needed to be raised. He persuaded Smt. Padma Ramachandran to accept the assistance of the ICSSR Programme Unit in preparing a paper. The paper suggested *(a)* the need to organise a research and information system within the nonaligned countries on the inter-relationship between women and development; and *(b)* the organisation of a conference with research-based material to reconsider development strategies, so as to ensure women's participation in all aspects of development. The paper attempted to spell out some of the inter-relationships between patterns of development and the situation of women that were beginning to be recognised in other Third World countries.[24]

The question of including this item in the agenda became an administrative and political controversy in the peculiar political situation in India in March 1977. The Ministry of Social Welfare — the appropriate agency for approving this item — had reservations on the matter, but allowed its inclusion before the general elections. After the elections, however, the Ministry made a formal request for the withdrawal of the item. It is understood that the withdrawal was prevented by senior officials in the Ministry of External Affairs, who felt that this would undermine India's prestige among nonaligned nations, who might interpret this as a direct result of the defeat of Mrs. Gandhi in the general elections.[25]

The Foreign Minister's Conference considered this item under its economic agenda,[26] and accepted the proposal *in toto*. While drafting their proceedings, the Chairman of the Economic Commission insisted that the recommendations made in the paper be reproduced in detail so that the issue should not suffer from mystification as had been its fate in most international gatherings.[27]

There is little doubt that the Government of India earned considerable kudos among nonaligned countries for having provided leadership in this matter, in spite of the official delegation being rather unprepared to defend or speak on the item. At the preparatory meeting for the Baghdad Conference, several delegations and a senior officer of the Foreign Ministry of Iraq stated that they were looking forward to guidance from India on this matter as most other countries had done very little homework on the women's issue. At the final Conference it was evident that most governments had given very low priority to the Conference and made little preparation. India, on the other hand, had a mass of documents with substantial data and very frank evaluations of its own achievements in women's development in the economic, social, political and legal spheres. The Indian delegation had little difficulty in obtaining support for the recommendations that it put forward.

It should, however, be noted that in this instance too the ideas presented by the Indian delegation did not exactly reflect the considered views of the government. The Indian paper had pointed out that conferences on women were often treated by governments as unimportant matters to which it was not necessary to send responsible members of government. Most governments sent non-officials from women's organisations, or important women from public life irrespective of whether they had any connection with development policies or not. The paper had, therefore, suggested that participants at the conference should be selected from four categories : (a) development planners; (b) development administrators responsible for major development sectors; (c) researchers; and (d) women's organisations. As this recommendation had been endorsed by the foreign ministers, the Government of Iraq requested all participating governments to send at least four delegates. The Indian delegation, however, did not include these categories in spite of the suggestion made by the Women's Bureau.[28]

As compared to this, the delegation for ESCAP Regional Preparatory Conference (November 1979) was much larger, and better briefed. It included all the officers in-charge of women's cells in various ministries as well as a fair number of non-officials. At this conference also, the Indian delegation had very little difficulty in obtaining acceptance of its recommendations — including a clearer definition of the three goals of the decade : equality, development and peace — which have since been incorporated in the Copenhagen Programme of Action.

These indications of success — in direct collaboration with policy analysis and review, and incorporation of strategies based on research results — explain the optimistic assessment of the Programme's policy impact made by the Advisory Committee in September 1979.

There were many negative trends also. The number of persons within the government who supported or had become sensitive to the issues was extremely limited. The government continued its reluctance to make a clear policy statement in regard to women's development even though it was suggested by many expert groups. The development ministries and the Planning Commission refused to agree to the policy of earmarking sectoral allocations. Women's issues featured only marginally in major sectoral plans.

The Sixth Five-Year Plan, released in December 1979, contained definite admissions of failure to remove discrimination, disparities, and injustice in both social and economic life. It also incorporated (within the chapters on Employment and Manpower, and Rural Development) a significant statement that population policy objectives could not be achieved without bringing about major changes in the status of women. The plan marked a definite departure from earlier five-year plans where women had been mentioned only in the chapters on education, health and social welfare. In suggesting the need for administrative innovation and collection of sex-wise distribution data on development assistance, the Plan acknowledged previous neglect, the need for better information flow and new mechanisms to ensure women receiving their 'due share' of the government's attention and support, in order to achieve equal opportunity for growth and distributive justice 'to which this nation is committed'. Support for organisations of rural women was extended on the same principle as organisations of the rural poor — to improve their bargaining power and access to development assistance. It was, however, fairly clear that few persons within the government shared Prof. Raj Krishna's views or eloquence in these matters. The analysis reflected research results, but the prescriptions did not match the diagnosis.

Since this document no longer represents the government's plans for the sixth quinquennium, one may consider it futile to analyse its contents. But as a stepping stone to what has finally been accepted in the Sixth Five-Year Plan (1980-85) it represents an interesting and important landmark.

When the new draft, entitled 'Framework for the Sixth Five-Year Plan', was released in August 1980, it contained exactly six references to women and did not reflect any of the ideas which had emanated from various expert groups — official and non-official — between 1975 and 1980. Nor did it reflect the strategies advocated by Indian delegations to international conferences.

A group of national women's organisations took umbrage at this exclusion, and organised a symposium in September 1980 to which they invited Dr. M. S. Swaminathan and senior officers from various concerned ministries. The Women's Bureau in the Ministry of Social Welfare collaborated fully in organising the symposium, as it wanted that greater attention be paid to women in the Plan. The symposium resulted in a series of recommendations which were submitted to the Government of India by seven national women's organisations[29] as a Memorandum ('Indian Women in the Eighties: The Development Imperatives'). Women MPs were requested to press for these recommendations. This resulted in a series of meetings of some representatives of the Planning Commission, women's organisations, women researchers, and women officers.

The final outcome of this process is Chapter XXVII of the Sixth Five-Year Plan on Women and Development, which again incorporates a substantial part of the analysis of the situation of women. Some of the specific measures — e.g., child care facilities as an essential support service for all working women, including those in the informal sector, the use of rural women's organisations for promotion of economic activities along with basic educational and health services and the need to expand women's employment opportunities as an essential step to their 'economic independence' — represent significant advances in clarification of policy. A marked improvement in the previous policy of land redistribution is the statement : 'In cases of transferred assets such as agricultural or homestead land, government shall endeavour to provide joint title to husband and wife.' A recommendation to this effect had been made by a National Committee constituted by the Ministry of Agriculture in 1979-80 to undertake a Country Review and Analysis of the Role and Participation of Women in Agriculture and Rural Development. The research work for this committee and the draft report was prepared by the ICSSR Programme Unit at the request of the National Committee. The recommendation was again renewed by the national women's organisations in their memorandum.

An important strategy recommended by the Working Group on Employment of Women was reservation for women in all training programmes. There had been a definite demand for job reservation put forward by certain groups, including some members of the bureaucracy. The Working Group, however, felt that reservation in training was a better method to improve women's access to employment in general, whereas job reservation could be effective only in the public sector. The Janata Plan had emphasised the need to expand women's training and educational opportunities but had baulked at reservation. While the present plan does not contain any general acceptance of this principle, in TRYSEM,[30] the major training programme for rural areas, a 33.33 per cent reservation for women has been incorporated. State governments have also been asked to incorporate women's projects within the Integrated Rural Development Programme.[31]

On the issue of earmarking funds and a special component approach within sectoral plans, however, the present Plan's refusal is identical with that of the 1979 document. In addition, there are some negative remarks about the multiplication of administrative cells within various ministries and agencies which portend a regression from policies accepted earlier.

Researchers had sought to identify some instruments for making women and their needs *visible* at various levels of the government machinery as a minimum precondition for adapting governmental structures to women's needs. Without such mechanisms, there is no way to expand the area of awareness within the bureaucracy and programmes for women's development are likely to remain pious wishes like so many other gestures of the government. They will also remain totally dependent on a few sensitive individuals without resulting in any change in bureaucratic attitudes at different levels.

There are reports of moves to shift programmes for rural women's economic and social progress from the Ministry of Rural Reconstruction to the Ministry of Social Welfare. For five years, the ICSSR programme struggled to persuade policy-makers that women are entitled to development and not merely welfare. This represented both a principle as well as a pragmatic lesson drawn from past experience — of the low priority attached to social welfare within the framework of the govenrnment, of the absence of any administrative infrastructure for social welfare at the grass roots level, and of the lack of influence that social welfare agencies had on the big nation-builders (i.e., the economic ministries which command major resources and power). As long as women continue to be seen as targets only of welfare, the links between their situation and the pattern and process of development will continue to be overlooked.

IV. *Impact on Public Consciousness*

For a scientific assessment of the programme's impact in arousing public consciousness and in reviving the social debate on the women's question, one would need considerable research. All that I can offer here are some stray bits of evidence of a change of climate on the women's issue.

The International Women's Year was the occasion for a large number of meetings, rallies, and pageantry — sponsored either by official agencies or by women's organisations all over the country. With the exception of a few, most of these meetings displayed very little awareness of the complex and multiple problems. By 1978-79, however, there was a distinct difference in the nature of the issues being discussed at various meetings by or about women. The state and national level meetings, referred to earlier, demonstrated the effort on people's part to look at some serious problems that challenged women's lives — in urban and rural areas, among the poor and the middle class. There was a demand for more data on issues like women's health, education, employment, and political position. The declining sex-ratio emerged from being a subject of concern only to demographers and began to engage a wide range of social commentators. Two volumes of statistics brought out by the Ministry of Social Welfare went out of stock rapidly, and media representatives — national and international — recognised women's situation as a field for some public interest.

Sponsored efforts to mobilise members of the Youth Congress to take anti-dowry pledges during the emergency gave way to a completely unexpected and spontaneous explosion of women's anger against dowry murders. It found considerable support from the national and international media and created an embarrassing situation for the government. A human rights organisation in the United States threatened to complain to the UN Human Rights Commission about the Government of India's failure to protect women's 'right to life'.

Dowry being essentially a middle-class problem, the response from middle-class women to this movement was explainable. The agitation which developed in a number of places over the Mathura rape case was far more inexplicable and definitely indicated a change in women's attitudes.[32] From 1979, 'crimes against women' emerged as a new public issue attracting the attention of various groups and the media.

Some people try to underplay these demonstrations of public anger on the ground that they are the result of a few individuals seeking publicity for themselves or wanting to make political use of such incidents. The fact remains that crimes against women have resurfaced in public attention after a long gap, are being reported far more by the media and have attracted considerable response from the public. They have also led to the birth of a number of new women's organisations which try to assist, support or mobilise oppressed women from different classes to struggle for their rights. This has forced some of the older women's organisations — which had abandoned their militancy after the constitutional and legal reforms in the post-independence period — to rethink their roles. Organisations like the All India Women's Conference and the YWCA, which held strong views against an agitational approach, appear to be under some pressure to lend support to organised protests against such crimes.

The third sector where there appears to be some change in awareness is among organised trade unions. The CSWI had noted with regret the failure on the part of trade unions to adequately represent working women's problems or to involve women more actively in their decision-making bodies.[33] A number of trade unions have now formed women's committees within their own organisations and a National Conference on Women Labour convened by the Ministry of Labour in 1979 revealed a far higher level of information and understanding of issues among the trade union representatives as compared to their presentations to the CSWI only five years earlier. I do not have data on the actual expansion of women membership, but I am told by friends within the trade union movement about the increasing participation of women workers in trade union activity.

One women's trade union which has attained international celebrity is SEWA of Ahmedabad. Its unique character — as a union of the poorest self-employed women workers in the informal sector, and as an organisation which provides credit, training, health, educational and other development services to its members — has provided a model for women's development strategies, not only in India but in other countries also. The ICSSR programme's small report on SEWA,[34] according to a UN officer, 'went round the world' to all agencies searching for meaningful strategies to mobilise and assist poor working women in slums. Similar organisations have sprung up in Bombay and Madras. The protests from women's organisations and trade unions against SEWA's recent expulsion from the Textile Labour Association and the National Labour Organisation provide some index of the growing reputation of this type of organisation.

Women have been involved in student organisations and student movements for a very long time, but student bodies, by and large, had not taken up women-specific issues for discussion in earlier years. There appears to be a beginning of a trend in this direction in some student organisations. The evidence of this new brand of activism was visible during the recently held National Conference on Women's Studies. The organisers of the Conference had initially anticipated that the response would not exceed 150-200 participants. There were, in fact, over 400 participants including a large number of activists — young and middle-aged — from trade unions, student groups, voluntary organisations as well as women's organisations. The large number of papers submitted to the Conference and the information supplied by participants on their areas of research or action also indicated that interest in women's problems had become considerably more widespread than five years earlier. Discussions in the working groups on issues like work, development, health, education, media, organisations and institutions, science and technology, art and literature, and law also indicated a higher level of information and understanding than in the past. Students groups have organised protests against dowry, rape, eve-teasing and beauty contests, particularly in educational institutions.

As I said earlier, it is difficult to say that the ICSSR's programme provided the main or even a major stimulus to all this new consciousness. Much of the results of the studies promoted by the ICSSR still remain unpublished. The programme unit in the Council, however, had taken pains to give access to papers, and even incomplete research results available with them, to persons who came seeking such information. The summary of the report of the CSWI has undoubtedly been read by more people than the original report, a government publication which was not publicised to any great extent. The Ministry of Social Welfare's distribution policy is primarily aimed at state governments and other central government agencies. The members of the Committee have often discovered to their regret that this document was better known in international agencies concerned with women and women's studies institutions in different countries than among the academic community in India.

A second document published by the Advisory Committee on Women's Studies in 1977, entitled *Critical Issues on the Status of Women : Suggested Priorities for Action*, however, reached a larger audience through the Council's efforts to have it translated and published in different Indian languages by local agencies. The media reaction to this document was positive.

Reviewing the Programme's impact on public consciousness, the Advisory Committee observed in September 1979 :

> The Council's success in this field though significant has to be assessed as severely limited. It should, however, be noted that the published studies of the Council under this programme have attracted comments and even editorials in some leading newspapers in India. A remarkable effort was made by the *Hindu*, Madras, to publish a special supplement on the position of women by organising a round-table discussion of specialists including two members of the Advisory Committee on Women's Studies. The Council has received acknowledgements of the value of this supplement in creating awareness about women's problems from several readers of the *Hindu*.

One could perhaps say that the main contribution of the ICSSR's programme in awakening public consciousness on women's problems has been through its efforts at dissemination, the emphasis on the need for the use of scientific and empirical data, questioning of earlier assumptions regarding women's problems, and in persistently seeking to focus attention on the problems of poor women both in urban and rural areas. The Council, particularly the members of the programme unit, often had to face criticisms from social scientists for their neglect of the problems of middle-class women. The Advisory Committee's stand on this question was very clear. Good research proposals on any social issue would always receive consideration under the ICSSR's general programme of research grants and fellowships. The Programme of Women's Studies had undertaken to play a catalytic role in drawing the attention of social scientists to hitherto neglected areas and could not deviate from this policy during the early phase of the programme.

V.   *Impact on Social Sciences and the Academic Community*

While reviewing the results of previous research on women and comparing them to the reality revealed by the Committee's own investigations, the CSWI was forced to raise certain basic questions :

1. Why had the process of understanding women's contribution to society — social, economic, and political — been shrouded in such mystery ?

2. Why were women's concerns generally seen by planners and social scientists as welfare rather than development or as peripheral rather than central to the development process ? Why had the vision of equality, including the Gandhian vision, dimmed ? How had the perception of women by the national leadership changed — from viewing them as equal partners in nation-building to targets of somewhat patronising policies of welfare ?

3. Why had the demographic indicators of the decline in women's status and the adverse impact of development on them been ignored or pushed aside by both planners and social analysts ? Why had there been such a failure on the part of social research to study women's problems and needs, and to search for causal connections between what was happening to different groups of women and trends in economic development, social change and population dynamics ?

4. Do the empirical dimensions selected by social scientists to analyse women's roles and status actually represent operational indicators of women's status ? Are they applicable to all groups of women ?

5. What were the historical and ideological dimensions of women's roles and status in Indian society, and why had the debate on the women's question initiated during the freedom struggle faded out of the public arena ?

In spite of the difficulties in obtaining reliable data, particularly on the unorganised sectors of the economy and on women of the poor classes, the Committee's interdisciplinary approach identified inter-relationships between the disturbing demographic trends (the declining sex-ratio, increasing male-female gap in life expectancy, higher mortality, declining work participation, and increasing migration of women) and other unassessed social phenomena (escalation of the dowry system, increasing commercial use and traffic in women and development of derogatory social attitudes) as evidence of a process of the devaluation of women and 'regression from some of the norms developed during the freedom movement'.

Social science research concerns have always responded to shifting priorities and perceptions of social isues. Studies on women are no exception of this rule. Earlier researches, done primarily by social historians, ideologists and anthropologists, were heavily influenced by the ideologies and concerns of the social reform movement. Most social reformers concentrated on problems of the elite, particularly high caste women, and social research displayed the same contradictions that characterised the social reform movement. On the one hand was the implicit belief that obscurantist customs and social practices represented obstacles to India's resurgence and progress and gave her a bad name in the eyes of the western world. On the other hand, cultural nationalism and religious communalism tended to glamorise the image of a pristine Indian culture of the distant past which had ensured far better status for women. Customs like child marriage, purda, the oppression of widows, and the denial of educational and property rights to women, they argued, were the results of cultural degeneration, not intrinsic attributes of Indian culture. Opposition to this idea came only from a few radical thinkers,[35] who believed that the oppression of women was an *instrument* for maintaining a social order based on inequalities of class, caste, race and sex.

The democratic ideology of the freedom struggle introduced the concept of equality and removal of legal, educational and social disabilites of women; but the implications of these principles were not reflected in the work of social scientists. A trend survey of research on women up to 1974[36] revealed that until the seventies, the focus of research was primarily on women's role within the family, kinship and community; education took a second position. Legal studies focused on scriptural and statutory family laws which affected mainly the upper strata of society, especially the urban educated class. Serious research on customary laws which governed the lives of the majority of women did not begin till the seventies though anthropologists have accumulated information on this aspect from a much earlier period. In the economic sphere, research was totally concentrated on women entering the modern sector where their proportion remained utterly marginal. It is amazing that agrarian studies, which developed rapidly after independence, ignored the major role played by women in agriculture.

The CSWI offered some hypotheses as explanations for these

biases and failures. Persistence of the urban middle-class bias in the perception of social problems, over-concentration on economic at the cost of social development, the collapse of the women's movement and the abandonment of the Gandhian approach to development were offered as possible explanations. Some members of the Committee felt that the national consensus to keep the women's question out of the sphere of political controversy, projecting it mainly as a social issue of long-term changes in attitudes through education and development, contributed to this neglect. There is little doubt that this consensus emerged from the perception that sources of women's oppression were all to be found within traditional attitudes and cultural institutions rather than in the socio-economic and political structures of society.

A new emphasis emerged with the panic about the population crisis in the sixties. The volume of research on family planning and population problems argued that the spread of women's education alone would aid population control and improve women's status. These studies made little attempt to relate fertility behaviour to other major determinants of women's status like employment, family income, class and caste positions.

A marked feature of the social sciences' perception of women's issues was the attitude adopted by most economists. The large majority of them believed that women's participation in economic activity was determined by cultural attitudes and was thus beyond the concerns of economists. This was rationalised by the unsatisfactory nature of data, and the implicit acceptance of the theory that women's participation in the economy was a long-term objective, which will come about through expansion of education, urbanisation and modernisation.

Sociologists who occasionally forayed into studying 'working women' concentrated 100 per cent on demonstrating their 'role conflict'.[37] This preoccupation with the role conflict theory demonstrates the elite bias of such researchers and the inordinate influence of theories of social analysis borrowed from the west.

The beginnings of a recognition that women also work outside the organised sector emerged with the efforts to assess unemployment in the early seventies. It was the Dantwala Committee of Experts on Unemployment Estimates which emphasised the need to disaggregate labour force data 'taking into account such characteristics as religion, *sex*, age, rural and urban residence, status or class of workers and educational attainments'. Increasing preoccupation with poverty and inequality among scientists in the seventies has contributed most to the new interest in women's studies.

The ICSSR Programmes's overriding concern to improve the quality of intervention in favour of some target groups in order to arrest the high mortality and declining sex-ratio problems, has resulted in a concentration of research in the sphere of economic participation, particularly of women in low-income groups. While these have helped the search for new policy instruments, other vital areas that could help develop new theoretical instruments for understanding women's roles and position in society have been sadly neglected. While most studies perceive a linkage of women's status/roles with social stratification and unequal power relations, virtually no work has been done on the determinants of women's status as perceived by women and others at different levels of society.

In collaboration with the Tata Institute of Social Sciences and the ICSSR, the Centre of Women's Development Studies organised a seminar in 1981 on Women's Life Cycle and Identity. The objective of the seminar was to stimulate research interest in the world of women's consciousness, self-perceptions and internalisation of values. The seminar revealed that there are marked differences between women's perception of their roles and the established social sciences' perceptions of them. The seminar also emphasised the need for a new type of family studies to demonstrate the inter-linkage between variations in family structure, sex roles, values and the socialisation process, leading to identity formations.

Another uninvestigated area which raises serious questions regarding the biases of social scientists is the role of women in social movements. Evidence has been found of large-scale parti-cipation of women in all types of peoples' struggle — like peasant, working class, religious and social movements — both in the distant past as well as in the contemporary period. While there is con-siderable research going on on these movements, it is remarkable that most such studies, even when done by persons within living memory of them or with active experience of participating in them, seldom mention the women. Even women's response to the Gandhian movement, which is recognised, has not been investigated seriously by any scholar. Reviewing the status of women's studies in 1978 we[38] had noted that unlike the western countries, interest in research on women in India in the seventies came more from demographers,

economists, and sociologists, and far less from historians, political
scientists, and **analysts** of literature. We have to recognise that
without an adequate understanding and evidence of the historical
dimensions of women's situation it would be difficult to develop
any new theoretical perspectives.

Another major reason for the inadequate impact of the Programme
on social sciences and the academic community is the lack of
response on the part of teaching and research institutions in terms of
incorporating women's issues within their regular curricula. In its
final review of the Programme in September 1979, the Advisory
Committee recorded its sense of disappointment at the poor
participation of the university system in the Programme, its failure
to include the results of new research in the educational system,
and its consequent inability to provide adequate guidance to
students who

> do not benefit from whatever new developments have taken
> place both in India and in other countries of the developing
> world. Reviews of literature often continue to reflect theories
> about women's development evolved by western scholars in earlier
> periods, which have been demonstrated as invalid in the context
> of developing countries by contemporary research.

The Committee felt that some of the hypotheses and debatable
propositions thrown up by a few of the studies sponsored under the
Programme needed further testing and discussion — 'to conceptualise
major issues in a meaningful theoretical frame rather than continue
analysis with uncritical use of existing tools and concepts which
have in the past contributed to non-understanding and to over-
looking women's roles and problems'.

Delays in the publication of research results and failure to develop
adequate documentation and research information services because
of paucity of resources and personnel on the part of the ICSSR
were undoubtedly constraints, but the refusal of the university
system and major science research establishments in the country to
make use of the Programme cannot be explained away by the
ICSSR's failings. A Committee appointed by the UGC in 1975 to
consider the recommendations of the CSWI had recommended the
need to initiate research on the problems identified by the report
within universities and to feed their results back into the curricula

of the social sciences. Neither the UGC nor the universities, with very few exceptions, made any serious attempt to promote women's studies during the period. The fact was brought home in a very effective manner during the National Conference on Women's Studies at Bombay in April 1981. Reviews of the curricula of different humanities and social science disciplines of nearly 100 universities undertaken by Conference participants revealed that the omission of women's studies and/or issues affecting women from syllabi continues to be a powerful tool to reinforce and perpetuate biases against them in all these disciplines.[39] The inclusion of women's studies as a special scheme for UGC assistance outside the Sixth Plan allocations perhaps represents some rethinking on the UGC's part.[40]

There were several common members on the two Advisory Committees appointed by the UGC and the ICSSR.[41] While the UGC did not take up the constructive suggestions made by its Committee, the ICSSR took up the challenge in spite of some resistance from members of its Research Committee to the second objective of the Programme, i.e., that of re-examining social science methodology. There is little doubt that the difference lay in the convictions and personality of the key decision-maker, the Member-Secretary of the ICSSR.

There has been some impact of the projection of demographic data as disturbing indicators of women's status. Most official documents and a fair number of research studies now recognise the necessity of mentioning and attempting to explain phenomena like the declining sex-ratio or the declining economic participation of women. The press conferences given by the Registrar General after the 1981 Census repeatedly drew attention to the slight improvement in the sex-ratio (from 930 to 935 per 1000 men) and to the lack of evidence that higher female infant mortality is caused by neglect! The Thirty-second Round of the National Sample Survey made an effort to obtain better data on women's work,[42] which led a social scientist working in the Planning Commission to raise the question — Why the free collection of goods and services which occupied millions of women's time should not be included within the GDP? In some important seminars on problems of measuring employment and unemployment, room has been found for one or two papers presenting issues in measuring women's work. But all these remain peripheral efforts by a handful of committed social scientists. Some of the major academic associations have occasionally included a panel on women in their annual conferences, and a few journals, like the *Economic and Political Weekly*, now welcome articles by women studies specialists. But research proposals developed by Ph. D. candidates or even senior social scientists still display the bias that the subject of women must be the concern of researchers working only on women, and not of general studies on people.

The ICSSR Programme had never accepted this thesis. The National Conference on Women's Studies reinforced this stand in stating forcefully that women cannot be viewed as detached from society and its problems. *Nor can social analysis which omits women from its scope be considered as adequate.* On the other hand, such analysis can often be distorted, misleading, and false.

The hypotheses evolved by the CSWI for the neglect of women in social science research and planning have received some substantiation and extension from scholars who undertook studies under the Programme and others. The dominance of the middle-class perception and values about women's roles and problems, according to these scholars, results not only in ignorance of but even a refusal to see the plurality of women's experience. Social scientists have tended to perceive women as a category in social analysis and not as a category within different sections of the population. Even Marxist analysis, which introduced a class framework in understanding social problems, had failed to perceive the differences between women of different classes.

The neglect of the household and the unorganised sector in social analysis has been responsible both for the absence of information and misinformation about about women's economic position. Prof. Ashok Mitra has argued that the mystification of intra-household work and distribution has been used as an instrument to 'keep women in subjugation politically, economically, and socially'.[43]

The role, status, problems, and general situation of women continue to be viewed overwhelmingly as only culture-specific, without relating the problem to economic and political trends and institutions. This is in spite of the massive evidence being piled up of global trends, particularly in other developing countries which are parallel, if not identical, and their inter-linkages with the international economic order and unequal power relations within and between nations.

The latter has given rise to a theory among radical feminists in the west that capitalism promotes an ideology for increasing 'house-wification' of women. The beginnings of this theory can be found in Gunnar and Alva Myrdal's theory that the concept 'woman's place is in the home' is the product of the industrial revolution as it is meaningless in the context of agrarian societies. It appears to me that the radical feminists' theory suffers from the same limitation as that of the Myrdals' — in that it excludes the existence of a pre-capitalist dominant model in satisfied societies. European feudalism gave birth to the image of the protected, sheltered, and idle woman of the feudal classes, while the majority of women were actually engaged in all types of economic activity. The Indian counterpart was the high caste woman and her image as being confined to household duties was a much older one, giving birth to one of the most marked features of the sanskritisation process — the withdrawal by upwardly mobile families, or communities of women, from visible economic activity outside the home, as a symbol of the families' improved status.[44]

The most critical contribution of capitalism to social science theories in this sphere is the devaluation, and exclusion, of the whole sector of household production and reproduction as non-economic. The exclusion is continued in Marxist theory — which separates sharply 'social' from 'domestic' production. Feminists are questioning this exclusion by both schools. In the context of predominantly agrarian and forest-based economies, with large subsistence sectors, and the impossibility of separating the use and exchange values of goods and services, this questioning becomes still more relevant. Women perceive all their work — inside or outside the home — as involving *labour*, and undertaken for their own, and their families' survival. Problems of measurement notwithstanding, the exclusion of women's household work (including items like collection of water, fuel, food, and processing of goods which may thereafter enter the market as exchange items, or services under the 'reproduction' category — which have a market counterpart) from the valuation process, raises serious questions regarding the analytical objectivity and validity of the social sciences.[45] A removal of these biases thus involves requestioning the basic assumptions of these theories.

It is difficult to avoid the conclusion that the relatively lower values and invisibility given to women's work and roles, both within and outside the home, is tied up with the ideological issues surrounding women's subordination in society which is much more pronounced among those who do social science research — whether they be men or women. Awareness of this ideological intrusion could be the first step for a fairer and more realistic analysis of women's issues by social scientists.

Notes

N.B. An abridged version of this paper was published in Samya Shakti, Vol. 1, No. 1, July 1983.

1. The first leaders of the women's liberation movement in the USA were graduates of the civil rights and anti-war movements. Many European feminists have similar backgrounds in protests against nuclear armaments, etc.

2. For details, see *Towards Equality : Report of the Committee on the Status of Women in India,* Government of India, 1975; and Kamaladevi Chattopadhyay in Devaki Jain, *Indian Women,* Government of India, 1975.

3. The Committee's terms of reference were very wide — social, legal, administrative, educational, health (with special emphasis on family planning), and employment status of housewives, mothers and workers. The Committee added demographic and political status as major indicators of women's situation.

4. Prof. Lotika Sarkar, Professor of Law, Delhi University.

5. The Committee was reconstituted in September 1973, when Dr. Vina Mazumdar, formerly a Member, became Member-Secretary replacing Smt. Shakuntala Masani.

6. Seventy-eight studies, which included over twenty empirical ones.

7. *Towards Equality, op. cit,* p. *xii.*

8. This was a very large body appointed to advise on activities planned for the International Women's Year under the Chairmanship of the Prime Minister which came to an end with the International Women's Year and should not be confused with the National Committee established in 1976.

9. It may be mentioned that no meeting of the National Committee announced in September 1976 took place during the emergency and for a year after that. The first meeting of the Committee, reconstituted by the Janata Government, was held in April 1978.

10. Adopted at the UN World Conference for the International Women's Year : 'Equality, Development Peace' (Mexico, June 1975), endorsed by the UN General Assembly later that year.

11. He made attempts to develop a women's programme in the Vivekananda College for Women as he was the Chairman of its Governing Body. He also encouraged the Gandhi Smarak Nidhi to develop a plan for using the Agha Khan Palace in Pune for a women's institute. His last effort in this direction was in assisting the establishment of the Centre for Women's Development Studies in 1980.

12. During 1976 he began negotiations with the Netherlands Government for an Indo-Dutch collaboration programme of research in Alternatives in Development in which women's studies was to be included — along with industrialisation and primary health care.

13. The initial Committee had fifteen members, representing the disciplines of economics, sociology, political science, population studies, and law, and included the officer-in-charge of the Women's Bureau in the Department of Social Welfare. On the death of Prof. B.N. Ganguli, the first Chairman, in 1978, Prof. Asok Mitra was appointed as Chairman. The principle of involving officers responsible for policies for women within the government was extended in 1978 by including a new officer from the Ministry of Rural Reconstruction.

14. Programme of Women's Studies, ICSSR.

15. Of the fifteen members of the Advisory Committee, only three had served on the Committee on the Status of Women. Four had been called in to advise the Committee on areas of their special concern.

16. It is interesting to note that two of Prof. Ganguli's books — written during this last phase of his life — were on 'rebel women' : *(a)* Rosa Luxemburg (in Bengali) and *(b)* Emma Goldman (published after his death by the Centre for the Study of Developing Societies).

17. During his attempts to draw the attention of policy-makers and demographers to the disturbing trend of declining sex ratio for years, Prof. Mitra had used statements, like 'Indian society is treating its women as dispensable assets'.

18. Studies conducted for the CSWI.

19. For the background of this proposal and the role played by the ICSSR Programme, see Section III of this essay.

20. The resolution and the forwarding letter from the Chairman of the Advisory Committee to the Chairman of the ICSSR are given in the Appendix.

21. Prior to 1980, this question was only considered by the Third Committee (which dealt with problems of social development), the Commission on the Status of Women, an offshoot of the Human Rights Commission, and the Branch for the Advancement of Women which existed within the Centre for Social Development and Humanitarian Affairs. Since Copenhagen, the UN has accepted the principle of including women's issues within its various agencies and activities. Small cells for introducing and monitoring women's inclusion now exist in most specialised agencies and divisions of the UN. The Branch for the Advancement of Women, which had little executive functions and powers earlier, now coordinates inter-agency collaboration and participation in activities relating to the Decade.

22. Amongst the small body of persons involved in planning these conferences, this group of strategies is referred to as 'the Indian perspective' for achieving women's equality and development.

23. It may be noted that until 1977 the ICSSR's programme was perhaps the only one in a developing country where a national agency created and funded by the government had sponsored a research programme on women.

24. While the programme unit was conversant mainly with the results of research in India, participation in a few international conferences had acquainted the staff with some of the findings in Africa, Latin America, and other Asian countries. The two major conferences of this type in which my participation

was entirely the result of J.P. Naik's decision, were the Wellesley Conference on Women and Development (1976) and the Study Seminar on Role of Rural Women in Development, organised by the Institute of Development Studies at Sussex in January 1977, in which Devaki Jain and I functioned as Co-Directors with Prof. T. Scarlett Epstein. Though invited to these conferences, as an officer of the ICSSR I was not permitted to accept travel support from the organisers and could go only because the Council deputed me for this purpose.

25. Perhaps another reason behind the Ministry's sensitivity was the protest from women's groups in India and abroad to Shri Morarji Desai's critical remarks against women prime ministers in general.

26. As commented on by a UN woman official at that time, this itself was a major victory, since the UN system had persistently refused to include women's issues under economic matters till that time.

27. This was reported to me by a member of the Secretariat.

28. The suggestion that the delegation should be led by Mrs. Barkataki and include a Member of the Planning Commission, preferably Prof. Raj Krishna, was over-ruled. The delegation finally consisted of two women Ministers of Social Welfare from two states (who were apparently quite unaware of the problems), the officer-in-charge of the Women's Bureau and myself as the researcher. I understand that my inclusion was a last minute decision, reluctantly conceded by the Minister.

29. The All India Women's Conference, the National Federation of Indian Women, the YWCA, the Indian Federation of University Women's Associations, the All India Coordination Committee of Women Workers, the Janawadi Mahila Samiti and the Centre for Women's Development Studies.

30. Training of Rural Youth for Self-Employment.

31. The Secretary, Agriculture, UP, recently observed that the climate for women's programmes had never been as bright as now. This does not however seem to have resulted in the designing of any appropriate or meaningful programmes at the state level.

32. The agitation was in response to an open letter to the Chief Justice of India by four law teachers, one of whom, Prof. Lotika Sarkar, was a Member of the ICSSR Advisory Committee on Women's Studies. She had also been a Member of the CSWI. This group of law teachers have continued their efforts to bring about meaningful changes in the criminal and civil laws that affect women's position in society and have produced a definite impact on individual members of the legal profession and judiciary including the members of the Law Commission. Their detailed analysis helped a large number of persons to understand legal technicalities. The contributions made by this group had some impact on the decision of the government to amend certain laws for the protection of women.

33. The Report would have contained far stronger remarks but for the intervention of the late Maniben Kara, a veteran trade unionist on the Committee.

34. *Women in a Developing Economy, I — From Dissociation to Rehabilitation : Report on an Experiment to Promote Self-employment in an Urban Area*, New Delhi, ICSSR and Allied Publishers, 1976.

35. Jyotiba Phule, Gopal Hari Deshmukh, and Iswar Chandra Vidya Sagar. See Vina Mazumdar 'Social Reform Movement in India : From Ranade to Nehru' in *Indian Women : From Purda to Modernity*, Delhi, Vikas, 1976.

36. Kalpana Das Gupta, *Women on the Indian Scene : An Annotated Bibliography*, Delhi, Abhinav, 1976.

37. The CSWI identified forty-five such studies done in the period after independence. All of them focused on women, who were new entrants to the labour force i.e., teachers, doctors, nurses, clerks, etc.

38. Vina Mazumdar and Kumud Sharma, 'Women's Studies : New Perceptions and the Challenges,' *Economic and Political Weekly*, Vol. 14, No. 3, 20 January 1979.

39. *Report of the National Conference on Women's Studies, April 1981*, SNDT Women's University, Bombay, 1982.

40. The present Chairman of the UGC is known for her support for women's studies. She was the Chairman of the Organising Committee of the National Conference on Women's Studies, and Member of a Unesco Expert Group on Promoting Teaching and Research on Women in 1980.

41. Prof. M. N. Srinivas, Dr. Leela Dube, and Dr. Vina Mazumdar.

42. I understand that this was done mainly on Prof. Raj Krishna's insistence.

43. Ashok Mitra, *Status of Women in India : Shifts in Occupational Patterns, 1961-71*, Delhi, Abhinav, 1980.

44. M. N. Srinivas, *Changing Position of Indian Women*, Delhi, Oxford University Press, 1978.

45. I am told that the Chinese communes, in their initial stages, introduced work points for household work, but abandoned the practice later as being *too expensive !*

APPENDIX

Professor, Centre for Regional Development
Jawaharlal Nehru University

Phone : Off. 651812, Res. 375624
3 Kautilya Marg (First Floor)
New Delhi 110 021

17th September 1979

Dear Professor Kothari,

I like to recall how deeply weighed down I felt by a sense of responsibility, when, on the sad demise of Professor B. N. Ganguli, you and the Council asked me to accept the Chairmanship of the Advisory Committee on Women's Studies. I however feel only too happy to report how this task was rendered most enjoyable, exciting and worthwhile by the enthusiasm and cooperation of my eminent colleagues on the Committee.

It is unnecessary for me to recapitulate the genesis of this Committee and its subsequent career under the wise and imaginative guidance of the late Professor B. N. Ganguli and the members of the Committee or to commend the zest, dedication and anticipation with which the tiny division of Women's Studies over-fulfilled each appointed task. All this would not have been possible without the unfailing and continuing encouragement of the Chairman and Council of the ICSSR. An account of the Committee's activities since 1974-75 is however being appended to refresh the memories of the members of the Council.

From its very beginning this programme of the ICSSR laid stress on sponsored research arising out of the implications of the National Committee's Report in 1975 on the Status of Women. This was avowedly an extension of the Council's main approach on response research. With the blessings of the Chairman, ICSSR, this Committee, departing significantly from the practice obtaining in other Divisions of the ICSSR, decided to extend the scope and field of its activities and enter the field of policy and planning by identifying critical gaps in our national development. This decision was underlined by the publication of two ICSSR documents : *(a)* Critical Issues on the Status of Women : Employment, Health, Education : Suggested Priorities for Action; and *(b)* Programme of Women's Studies.

Since 1977 neither the Council nor the Advisory Committee has looked back. In quick succession the Council and the Advisory Committee blessed our active participation in the Working Groups of the Planning Commission and concerned ministries of the Government of India in shaping policy for the Sixth Five-Year Plan so far as it pertained to the priority areas outlined by our Committee. Simultaneously, the ICSSR encouraged the officers and members of the Committee to assume a very active international role. Officers and members of the Committee have had their part in preparing background documents, substantially contributing to and guiding deliberations with the help of research findings and perceptions, shaping resolutions and participating in follow-up action in international and national forums. In accomplishing all this, the Committee constantly drew its strength and sustenance from the large nationwide research network that it has over the years succeeded in establishing, by drawing into its fold veteran and fresh research scholars from diverse disciplines, some of which had persistently neglected this vital area of concern as being almost unworthy of serious study or investigation.

This Committee may claim to have generated new data and knowledge, new awareness of research areas and research needs, and in the process attracted veterans from other disciplines, groomed young and aspiring researchers in the new research areas and introduced them to a series of international and national research forums and debates, to which they might not have otherwise been exposed or inducted. The papers accompanying this letter will bear testimony to these assertions.

The Committee now feels that matters have reached a stage where the Division of Women's Studies has outgrown its habiliments and should now be invested with wider and newer opportunities. For one thing, the Committee feels that the principle of sponsored research (incidentally, it does not do to assume all too facilely that a scholar always 'knows' a problem entirely on his own) has been fundamentally sound inasmuch as it has *(a)* thrown this area open to veterans in other disciplines, who have hitherto felt hesitant to enter; *(b)* attracted new talent from a multiplicity of disciplines anxious to extend and enrich the bounds of their own; *(c)* rapidly built up a body of data and knowledge by insisting on time bound programmes and publication of their findings; *(d)* stimulated new methodologies and approaches by compelling researchers to work on small budgets; and *(e)* initiated a spirit of cooperation among researchers by reconciling them to the team approach and to the concept of incremental and even 'tentative' additions to knowledge. For another, the Committee feels that a point has been reached when newer types of training and awareness are required in the design and methodology of research, calling for a reappraisal of existing tools, techniques and approaches. Thirdly, the Committee feels that assistance must be rendered to the base operative areas of national programmes in order to train and orient an expanding body of grass-roots executives and operatives to enable them in turn to become effective partners in further research and evaluation. Finally, the Committee feels that a successor institution to the ICSSR Division should now be established, endowed with sufficient mandate and viability, to enable it to operate with a due sense of its destiny with research and teaching institutions, along with the various ministries of the Government of India and the constituent States.

These considerations have been weighing with the Committee for some time. In its eighth meeting held on 15 September last, the Committee finally took up this matter at the instance of Mr. Justice V.R. Krishna Iyer and Professor M.N. Srinivas and took a unanimous resolution which I have the honour of enclosing. I am desired by the Committee to request you to place it before the Council. We trust that you and the Council will look at the proposal in the light of the considerations I have briefly set out in this letter and lend your good offices to initiate steps along with the Government of India to establish an autonomous institution for pursuing those aims which you and the Council have so jealously nurtured and promoted so far. And for this the Committee will remain deeply grateful.

I remain,

Yours truly.
[Sd/-]
A. MITRA

Professor Rajni Kothari
Chairman,
Indian Council of Social Science Research,
IIPA Hostel
Indraprastha Estate
New Delhi 110002

RESOLUTION

At the eighth meeting of the Advisory Committee on Women's Sutdies held on 15 September 1979, the following resolution, moved by Mr. Justice V.R. Krishna Iyer and seconded by Professor M.N. Srinivas, was warmly acclaimed and unanimously accepted by the Chairman and members of the Committee who desired that it be transmitted for due consideration to the ICSSR and the Government of India.

Resolution

1. **On surveying** in detail the genesis, progress, mode of past and current working, range and sum of total output, its impact on social science research in India and on public policy in the extraordinarily vital and seminal area of women's status in the context of social and economic development;
2. **After reflecting** on the plans, programmes and fields of activity to which this area of concern could reasonably aspire in the future;
3. **On appreciating** the constraints and impediments, were the programme to continue without change in its present form, that could come in the way of determining and developing the scope, priorities and execution of its future tasks and programmes;
4. **Realising** that a structural and institutional change has become necessary and desirable at this juncture;
5. **Taking note** of the fact that the Government of India in the Ministry of Social Welfare has already under consideration a proposal to this effect;
6. **The Committee resolves to recommend,** for the consideration of the ICSSR and of the Government of India in the Ministry of Social Welfare, that a separate autonomous institution for women's studies be established with the active participation of and close links with the ICSSR and other concerned Ministries of the Government of India.
7. **Further resolved** that this resolution be forwarded to the ICSSR for its active consideration with the further request to the Council that it be transmitted to the Government of India in the Ministry of Social Welfare.

Authenticated

Asok Mitra
Chairman,
Advisory Committee on Women's Studies,
ICSSR

IV

The Policy Field
in India
in Perspective

S. GUHAN

10 Towards a Policy for Analysis

It has been felt that while India is rich in both policy and analytical expertise, it is rather poor in policy analysis.* Reasons for this situation have been attributed to the demand and to the supply aspects of the equation.[1] The Government, it has been argued, is not sufficiently interested in promoting or encouraging policy analysis; it does not part with data, act upon the results of analysis, or encourage the wider dissemination of research findings. The complaints from the other side are that the academic community is ignorant or disinterested in the working of the government, is shy of attacking practical problems, and tends to take refuge, in Myron Weiner's phrase, under a 'radical orthodoxy' that wishes to take no part in reforming the existing system because it sees no hope except in its total change.

With all governments, the capacity for introspection and the desire for self-improvement are limited; but it seems to be even more so with governments, both central and state, in India. Given also our levels of literacy, linguistic fragmentation, kind of legislatures, weak media and so on, the scope for reasoned policy dialogues is rather limited. In such a situation, the policy analyst is left with little sponsorship or audience. All that he can do is to plough his little furrow hoping that some day it will get seeded and fertilised. Yet it need not be a lonely furrow if policy analysts could occasionally come together to consider what policy analysis could most usefully attempt in the long run.

* I am grateful to C. T. Kurien for his comments on an earlier draft of this paper.

The first thing that strikes any student of public policy in India is the large mass of policies that exist in an articulated form. There could be more than one reason for this. Prof. Wilfrid Harrison, contributing to the *Dictionary of Social Sciences,* points out that the term 'policy' seems to be peculiar to the English language.[2] Early leadership in India was clearly influenced by the British (and the American) tradition which believes that policies should be deliberately adopted and publicly articulated, apart from being heirs to more ancient traditions that codified the *smriti* (what was remembered) and the *sruti* (what was heard) in the *Vedas* and *Dharmasastras.* They seem to have felt an inner need, indeed a compulsion, to make and articulate policy. But, perhaps, this Mandarin impulse was not the only, nor even the most important reason.

The more important reason, I believe, was that when India became independent, it faced pretty much an ideological vacuum. The 'social contract' in India had not been defined either as part of a historical process (as in the older western societies and in Japan) or as a result of revolutionary change (as in the Soviet Union). During the course of the freedom movement, as is well known, conflicts between different economic and social interests were sought to be sublimated in the struggle against the One Big Enemy, the colonial power.[3] When, with the withdrawal of that power, a situation arose in which genuine and basic conflicts could not be ignored, the need for orderly nation-building demanded that a consensual framework be established. In these circumstances, a synthetic ideology drawing from various sources, and reflecting a balance of interests, had to be forged. It had to represent the aspirations of a new country emerging into freedom in the latter half of the twentieth century. At the same time, the ideology had to be 'workable' in terms of a large, diverse, democratic and federal polity in which a variety of economic, social and political interests had to be recognised and accommodated. The degree and kind of articulation that basic economic and social policies have received in India are traceable to the need thus felt for putting consensus ahead of conflict, reversing their natural order in history.

It is in this historical context that we should take stock of the main sources of initial policy and their further evolution. Starting with the Constitution of India, twenty-five policy statements can be located between Articles 38 and 51 in Part IV on the Directive

Principles of State Policy. Most of them are quite specific in their content and cover a wide variety of items. The list is a rather mixed bag. Some of its contents — the banning of cow slaughter and the prohibition of liquor, for example — merely reflect a proper sense of respect for our founding fathers. Some are high aspirations of which, given the nature of our economy and society, there is no reasonable hope of fulfilment in any foreseeable future. These aspirations are regarding areas like unemployment insurance, compulsory education up to the age of 14, the right to work and for an adequate means of livelihood, of even equal pay for equal work between men and women. Many others, notably the preservation of wildlife and of historical monuments, however lend themselves to implementation.

Proceeding from the Constitution, we have had seven five-year plan documents each of which contains a *tour d' horizon* of social and economic policies that are proposed for pursuit in the relevant plan period. These documents also discuss the state of performance in regard to established policies. By and large, however, one cannot look to the plan documents for the generation of new policies or towards a radical alteration of the *status quo*, although in some cases, as in the Janata government's draft five-year plan (1978-83), it is possible to discern noticeable shifts in emphases and an unusual honesty in introspection. Given their basically documentational character, the plans have provided steady grist to many academic mills in India. A whole body of policy analysis in the country is addressed to policy continuities, contradictions, slippages and graduation in the language of the plans apart, of course, to issues relating to promises *vis-a-vis* performance.

Another genre of policy literature in India consists of a whole series of specific policy statements. These cover a wide range of topics — for example, foreign policy, various aspects of industrial policy, science and technology, foreign investments, export policy, food, agriculture, energy, environment, transport, education, health, family planning, basic needs, poverty, and employment. Some policy statements, like the Industrial Policy Resolutions of 1948 and 1956, have acquired a great deal of historical sanctity. Some might have been articulated during the course of a statement in Parliament or in a White Paper or in a Government Resolution on a Committee Report. The point however is that, on a large number of topics, it is possible to locate one or more documents on the basis of which it can be said with reasonable assurance that 'this' and not 'that' is the public policy in India on a particular topic.

Legislation is another signal source of policy literature. Normally, legislation follows and operationalises policy announcements. In doing so, it might refine, dilute or elaborate policy. In certain other cases, it is law that has given the first intimation of policy as happened in the nationalisation of major commercial banks in 1969. Somewhat similar is the case with a whole set of operational policies such as the annual budgets, seasonal monetary policies, quinquennial fiscal devolutions from the centre to the states, and procurement prices set on the recommendations of the Agricultural Prices Commission. In these instances, action and policy coincide.

Enough has been said to make the point that India offers rich clinical material for the policy analyst to practise his trade and skills. But this may not be an unmixed blessing. In the first place, there is a danger that is inherent in the very fact that a great mass of policy texts exists in India. As has happened widely with plan documents, texts can be taken too seriously and textual analysis can be carried on with little reference to the contextual facts. To guard against this danger, it might be useful to review what we know by now as a result of both analysis and state conduct. One or other of the following features, I suggest, characterise the bulk of social and economic policy in India.

1. Quite a few statements of policy remain aspirational. They are not intended to be implemented at all. They can be identified by a reading of Part IV of the Constitution. (These are sleeping dogs that will not be woken up).
2. Some major policies, land reform being the classic example, are ritualistic. They are kept alive by a periodic reiteration of the intent to implement and the difficulties that continually face implementation. (These are dogs that bark but do not bite).
3. The third category consists of policies that are sabotaged through executive action or inaction. A major example is the curbing of the concentration of economic power : The Monopolies Act exists but will not be made use of. (To conclude the canine analogy, some dogs are tranquilised by the master to let his paramour in by the back door).

In policy, as in crime, it is *mens rea* or the intention that is crucial.

Intention can be judged in a straightforward manner by looking at implementation, its mode and extent. It can also be judged by observing the extent to which contradictions are accommodated in Indian policy by dexterous tight-rope walking. We may recall in this connection that in the examination of policy in India, the most common criticisms made by analysts commenting on different sets of policies are :

1. A weak nexus between policy and instruments;
2. the large degree to which administrative discretion has been retained and used to dilute or defeat policy objectives ;
3. the use of a single or a small set of instruments to promote a large number of objectives, not all of which may be capable of consistent pursuit ; and
4. internal intra-policy inconsistencies and inter-face inconsistencies in allied policies.

On a technical plane, critics of policy have dealt with such inconsistencies as faults or fissures in policy formation. But, I would suggest, that the Freudian insight that traces lapses to intention may be highly relevant in understanding policy contradiction. 'The model of reference could be Freud's treatment of lapses or errors as symptoms of conflicts; that is, as results of the mutual interference of two different intentions, the intention interfered with and the interfering tendency.'[4]

The existence of such implicit, explicit, or empirical inconsistencies in policy indicate in large measure the intention to interfere with 'intention'. Such second-order intentions surface when in practice the contradiction between sets of dual objectives gets resolved in one of two ways. Either both are stalemated or one triumphs at the cost of the other. In either situation, there is revelation of hoax and hypocrisy. Industrial policies based on the concept of mixed economy offer many illustrations of how it is possible to say one thing and do another (promotion of big business under the name of backward area development or export promotion, for example). It is, of course, what is done and not what is said that matters. And, the analyst need not waste his time taking too seriously what is said when the government itself does not do so.

One may then consider how far we can get by looking at what is done in relation to what is said. *Prima facie*, there is much scope for policy evaluation in terms of the programmes into which they are decomposed, the design of these programmes, the fulfilment of quantified targets, and so on. As a corollary to such analysis, prescriptions could also result in terms of improvements to ongoing programmes and/or the development of alternatives. A great deal of policy research, policy-oriented research, or plain programme evaluation has taken this form. Undoubtedly, useful results have been generated. There is, therefore, a great temptation to strengthen this genre of programmatic policy research through more funding, course development, training, internships interdisciplinary co-operation, development of analytical skills and methods, networking with like-minded institutions in India and abroad, and so on.

Without in any way questioning the value of such policy research in principle, I feel that it is necessary to be alive to its limitations and even to some of its dangers in our context. To start with, one set of difficulties seem to consist of the following :

1. The entry into policy through the programme route may leave untouched a considerable amount of policy that has not been translated into programmes (e.g., aspirational policies) or does not lend itself to translation in the form of specific programmes (e.g., prohibition of dowry or the enforcement of minimum wages for agricultural labour and such other policies which demand wider social or political action).

2. Many policies (such as Harijan uplift) have to depend for their realisation on the adequacy, coordination and integrated pursuit of several programmes that cut across various sectors of activity. Programme-based policy research will need to be very comprehensive, quantitatively and qualitatively, to capture policy in these cases.

3. Paradoxically, a high degree of programme success can coexist with a poor degree of policy realisation. Much depends upon how the programme has been plugged into policy in its adequacy, design and implementation. Thus, targeted beneficiaries might get covered in IRDP programmes but no durable increases in incomes or employment might result. An irrigation project might have been successfully executed, but its utilisation be poor.

These and other such difficulties may seem to be solvable given due care and caution in analysis. However, a more serious danger lurks in the pursuit of programme-oriented policy analysis. This is that the conventional type of this form of analysis might distract attention from essential features of policy. Inasmuch as the main tradition of 'policy science' has originated in the United States, it may not be inappropriate to quote two perceptive (British) commentators on the American situation in this connection. Prof. Keith Hope incisively points out:

> The typical American word for an unsatisfactory social state is 'problem', something, that is, which can be solved and thereby disposed of : and the typical word for ameliorative social action is 'program', something, that is, which has a preordained beginning, middle and end.[5]

Elaborating on this, Prof. L.J. Sharpe adds :

> This characteristic of American politics means that the Federal Government has to conduct periodic bursts of activity, 'carried out on a stretcher' .... Instead of being a product of a continuous doctrinal battle within the political system about the speed and direction of the secular trend to greater equality within society (which is very roughly what seems to happen in other western democracies), social amelioration has often to come from on high, from the executive branch in large doses dressed up as emergency measures to combat a temporary national crisis. Such was the lot of the New Deal legislation, the social legislation of the Second World War period, and the 'War on Poverty' initiated by Presidents Kennedy and Johnson.[6]

This is the context in which it is not surprising that much of policy research in the United States is programme-analytical and programme-related. The US being an efficient exporter of research philosophy and techniques, it is not unnatural also that such research should find a receptive clientele in other climates. Moreover, this philosophy acquires a certain germaneness in the Indian context where also the main plank of social policy has been to generate or rejuvenate programmes, with 'a preordained beginning, middle and end' to deal with issues like poverty, unemployment, provision of basic needs, balanced regional development, welfare of backward classes, health for all, and adult literacy. Policy being cast in this mould, analysis also seems to get channelled accordingly. The danger to be underlined is that, in this process, the 'continuous doctrinal battle within the political system about greater equality within society' may well be left out.

I may appear to be moving towards a nihilistic conclusion that policy research based either on what is said or on what is done is not likely to be very fruitful in the Indian context. This is not my intention. The thesis which I would like to advance is rather that it does not matter whether we start with analysing articulated policy or policy performance but, in either case, we need to go beyond both what is said and what is done to the 'continuous doctrinal struggle' that lies behind them. This is the motivation with which we should continually examine state policy following Marx's prescription 'to look at the State, for the State is the official resume of society, the table of contents of man's practical conflicts.'[7] The examination of state policy in this sense will involve expanding and deepening policy research to include not only what is said but not done, but also *(a)* what is done but not said ; *(b)* what is said and unsaid at the same time ; and *(c)* things that are neither said nor done. And why this is so, i.e., to the roots of these syndromes in the political economy of the country and in the policy process in which many powerful interests and lobbies constantly interact at various levels. The surface of policy has to be pierced to lay bare the underlying structure of conflict and to evaluate to what extent policies are a facade.

If this is so we also have to live with the position that in India today much of policy analysis has to be in the nature of exposure and exposition rather than evaluation leading to blueprints. It will have to be addressed largely to, and from the point of view of, the beneficiaries, non-beneficiaries and victims of policy than to its makers and custodians. It will also mean that policy analysis can not be expected to be 'balanced' or 'neutral' as is implied by the term 'policy science'. Policy analysis, like policy itself, is not art or science but politics. As such, it is legitimate for it to be openly partisan. 'Only if conflict arises', says a Tamil proverb, 'will justice follow.' In his limited way, the policy analyst can also promote justice but only by helping to promote conflict through a systematic identification of its sources and courses. Who gains and who loses has to be the central question in examining the makings and workings of policy, for in our context major games are mostly zero-sum.

Notes

1. See, for instance, Myron Weiner, 'Social Science Research and Public Policy in India,' *Economic and Political Weekly*, 15 and 22 September 1979.
2. Gould and Kolb (eds.), *A Dictionary of the Social Sciences*, London, Tavistock Publications, 1984.
3. It was Rajaji who said 'In seeking the votes of the electorate, Congress has taken care to eliminate all issues at the ensuing elections other than the constitutional-political issue between the Government and the Congress'. Quoted in C. J. Baker, *The Politics of South India 1920-1937*, New Delhi, Vikas, 1976.
4. Victor M. Perez-Diaz, *State, Bureaucracy and Civil Society*, London, Macmillan, 1978, p. 86. His reference is to S. Freud, *A General Introduction to Psychoanalysis*, edited by Riviere, New York, 1973, p. 65.
5. Keith Hope, 'Indicators of the State of Society' in Martin Bulmer (ed.), *Social Policy Research*, London, Macmillan, 1978.
6. L. J. Sharpe, 'The Social Scientist and Policy-making in Britain and America : A Comparison' in Martin Bulmer (ed.), *ibid.*
7. I owe the quotation to Arun Shourie 'From an Athetoid State to an Absolutist One,' *Indian Express*, 16 August 1981.

S. R. GANESH • SAMUEL PAUL

11 Autonomous Research Institutions and the Public Policy Process

Introduction

A couple of decades ago, individual scholars from the academic world were the dominant policy advisors to the Government of India. They were invited to offer advice on specific problems in their individual capacities. Typically, these scholars were professors or other eminent experts attached to universities or other important national institutions. It was common practice to invite them to be members of committees and task forces. Some of them were also called upon to informally advise political leaders and ministers on policy issues. The Research Programmes Committee (RPC) of the Planning Commission was, perhaps, one of the first institutional devices used by the Government of India to encourage policy relevant research on a broader and more systematic basis. Scholars were invited to undertake investigations of specific projects, evaluate their impact and research a variety of problems which had important policy implications. Their findings have generally been disseminated and utilised by different agencies within the government. A number of these studies have also been published.

The Indian Council of Social Science Research (ICSSR) grew out of this early experience and has evolved a fairly large programme of policy relevant research over the past few years. The establishment of a new set of social science research institutions in different parts of the country in the late sixties and early seventies is an important development in India. Only a few of them were set up in New Delhi. Most of them were located in the different state capitals and had formal or informal support from the respective state governments.

Against this backdrop, we have chosen to focus on one category of research institutions, namely, the autonomous research institution with special reference to a sub-set of institutions which have been in existence for about a decade and have engaged in policy-relevant and policy-oriented work. In doing this we have sought to touch upon aspects which could provide pointers for future work. The institutions whose experiences we draw upon are as follows :

Centre for Policy Research (CPR), New Delhi;
National Institute of Public Finance and Policy (NIPFP), New Delhi;
Sardar Patel Institute of Economic and Social Research (SPIESR), Ahmedabad;
Centre for Development Studies (CDS), Trivandrum;
Institute for Social and Economic Change (ISEC), Bangalore; and
Madras Institute of Development Studies (MIDS), Madras.

Except for NIPFP all the other institutions receive ICSSR support. The NIPFP receives support from the Ministry of Finance. The state-based institutions, the last three in the list above, receive support from their respective state governments. In this context, we would like to take stock of the following aspects :

1. The objectives of these institutions — whether policy research and impact was an explicit concern;
2. Nature and sources of work and political linkages;
3. Use of the institutions by the government and their modes of influence;
4. Some recent experiences in dissemination of research; and
5. Methodologies.

Lastly, we draw some lessons for work by these institutions in the public policy area. We hope that these would stimulate debate and discussion as a prelude to informed action.

Objectives of the Institution

Is policy analysis an explicit concern of autonomous research institutions? Except for the Centre for Policy Research and the National Institute of Public Finance and Policy, there is no explicit statement of policy research in the objectives of the other four institutions. However, policy-relevant research pertaining to regional development problems, training programmes, conferences, and publications are all part of the programmes of these institutions. This implies (as in the case of ISEC) assisting the state and central governments through special studies. Building data banks also appears to be an explicit concern. Consultancy and operational work are the explicit concerns of the CPR and the NIPFP. Thus, policy-relevant work appears to be a concern of all these institutions.

Another major influence is institutional leadership. In all the six institutions, the initial leaders have shaped the course of work in the 1970s. Second generation leadership in MIDS, ISEC, SPIESR and CDS is in the process of recharting the direction of work of the institutions.

> The role of the Institute like ours is to make a decisive, though possibly modest, contribution in this creative but difficult area (of breaking the isolation of the science and scientists from the social reality that surrounds them). Our work, therefore, will have to have a qualitative difference, some aspects of which may be touched upon.
>
> In the first instance, it must be noted that the difference consists of not merely in moving into applied research from what is frequently referred to as pure research . . . .
>
> The difference is not between 'policy oriented' research and 'fundamental' research either, for although policy issues will certainly come within the purview of the kind of research postulated, what is required is more and not less fundamental research.[1]

The document goes on to argue that social scientists must listen to a much wider cross-section of society to choose the social issues on which factual evidence, clarity of thought and precision in analysis are required. It moves a step further in stating:

Where concrete social problems are taken up for study the purpose must also be to see that a socially satisfactory solution is found through bringing about necessary changes. Hence, if the aim of social science research so far was to understand society, it must now become to change society.[2]

At the CDS the accent is on relevant economic and social problems and not methodological contributions, although the latter are not ruled out. This does not mean that members work only on problems of immediate interest. One of the current projects looks at the evolution of education in Kerala going back over three centuries. This involves an understanding of the nature of Kerala's development by looking at the historical and cultural forces which have operated in that part of the country, and not merely at conventional economic analysis. However, the research is not directed administratively or otherwise by the leadership. This is also true, by and large, of the ISEC.

Somewhat in contrast to MIDS and CDS, the other four institutions are much more concerned with immediate problems. Part of the reason for this lies in the linkages that these institutions have with the government. The strengths of these linkages have varied over time, but the linkages have always remained.

When the linkages are strong, there is an interest in work on immediate problems of interest to the government. When barriers exist, the institutions tend to take up problems for study on their own. The distinction is one of the relative emphasis and not exclusive focus. However, both kinds of work are policy-relevant although work which is not directly related to providing immediate policy would have a more rigorous analysis. Thus, there is a shift towards creating a sound basis for public policy-making. Kurien's work on *Economic Change in Rural Tamil Nadu : 1950-1975* (Madras Institute of Development Studies, December 1980) is a move in this direction. A current study on the agriculture and the food system in the state undertaken by the MIDS on its own initiative is yet another example. Sources which generate pressure for work are an important part of the scope and focus of the work.

Nature and Sources of Work and Political Linkages

The range of policy-relevant research undertaken by the different institutions is impressive. To illustrate, NIPFP has specialised in taxation and public expenditure analysis, rationalisation of fiscal systems in the states and improvement of tax administration. CDS has worked on agrarian structure and change in Kerala, the economics of irrigation with special reference to the potential of ground water resources as against major irrigation, policy issues in industrial development, population, and the economics of fisheries and livestock. SPIESR has done considerable work on state level resource allocation problems, taxation, and policy options in relation to large and complex projects. MIDS has undertaken evaluative studies of selected development programmes in Tamil Nadu and the agrarian and rural structure and changes taking place in selected districts of the state.

Government, both state and central, international agencies and faculty interests are three sources of pressure for different types of work. While some state governments have tended to draw heavily on the institutions consistently over time, the experience has been one of close linkages in the early stages to benign indifference later in some of the institutions. Thus, when the Chief Minister in power in a state was a close friend of the first Director of one of the institutions, there were close links with the state government. In the case of NIPFP, state governments, e.g., Bihar, Assam, UP, Gujarat and Tamil Nadu, have come forward with requests for work involving changes, primarily in systems. The Centre has not been as active a source of work as the states. In the case of the CPR, the central government is a major source of work.

International agencies have been a source of projects for some institutions. Such work has primarily come through the stature of the individual faculty and its earlier associations with international agencies. However, it cannot be said that this is a major source of work. But, whether the initiative is institutional or individual, international agencies may be sought as a source of funding. It is important to note that the research institutions are *consciously* keeping their faculty size small, and their work within the budgets available through the ICSSR and the state governments. MIDS for example, has a faculty of eight academicians and expects to add four to six more people by the end of the Sixth Plan period. It expects to stabilise with a 15-core faculty thereafter. Hence, in the case of MIDS, where individual initiative is an important determinant of research work, adequacy of funds is not a concern. On the other hand, ISEC responds more to the project requests of different agencies, both governmental and international. In general, *contract research* of any kind is not taken up unless it fits in with the institutional mission. The proportion of contract research varies from institution to institution.

Use of Institutions by the Government and Modes of Influence

The state and the central governments use the institutions in a variety of ways :

1. Background studies on various issues around policies, programmes and projects.
2. Association of faculty members with committees, commissions and task forces. Chairing as well as membership of such groups has brought in demands for research studies and position papers.
3. Associating individual faculty members as advisors and consultants to the Planning Commission at the state and central levels as well as to various ministries and departments.
4. Informal discussions by both political leaders and administrators with faculty members.
5. Participation by political leaders and administrators in seminars organised by the institutions.
6. Cooption into government agencies; for example, the Planning Commission at the centre and chairmanship of state committees and boards.

Governmental use of these institutions is much more for advice and preparation of background studies and papers rather than for systematic research and analysis in relation to specific projects, programmes or policy issues. While the institutions have some feeling of being 'useful' the larger feeling is one of lack of systematic and continuous impact on policy-makers through institutional efforts. Another predominant feeling is one of inability to make any headway in respect of policies where the political stakes are high. There is also a feeling that with increasing centralisation in the political arena, the ability of state level institutions to influence local policy-makers has also decreased, thus limiting the role that policy research plays in public policy-making.

Some Recent Experiences in Dissemination of Research

Institutions like CDS, MIDS and ISEC have moved in the direction of creating a climate of opinion among the public rather than focusing on the government as the sole actor in the policy arena. MIDS, for example, considers its mission to be one of creating an awareness among the larger community on important problems. It considers social policy as a much broader concept than government decision-making and would like to challenge the governmental line *wherever appropriate*. The *modus operandi* may be set out as below :

Take up a problem
↓
Analyse
↓
Make it known to a wider section
of society than the government
↓
Influence and educate public opinion
for more worthwhile outcomes

There is a fair degree of consensus among the institutions, that, at best, their work could indicate the limitations of governmental actions. Both CDS and MIDS have brought out reports in Malayalam and Tamil in order to reach the common man. In the same vein, faculty members at ISEC felt that improved contribution from an institute like theirs could come from *creating a climate of opinion in the larger community and bringing about an awareness of issues*. The NIPFP, by the nature of its work, has moved towards educating bureaucrats and politicians about the social and economic consequences of policies, e.g., through its training programmes for Assistant Income Tax Commissioners.

As a result of the experiences of the last decade, there is a feeling that in the next decade if the institutions do quality work, their impact will be more discernible. There is the realisation on the other hand, that such institutions may only be minor factors in the entire process of public policy-making. However, there appears to be a distinct upward trend in terms of the use of research. Similarly, there is a growing awareness in government circles of the need for advice on specific types of socio-economic problems. This is also because the role of the state has shifted away from law and order to socio-economic and social-welfare programmes. This has thrown into sharp relief data gaps for understanding complex development issues.

Methodologies

The creation of a data base emerges as one of the major needs of development policies. In many ways this has shaped the use of methodologies. Bench-mark surveys and data collection from the field, both quantitative and qualitative, are quite common. Standard economic methodologies — such as, cost-benefit analysis, demand modelling and other econometric tools, survey research techniques and programming models — are commonly used. Complex models are the exception rather than the rule. The consumption sub-model of the Sixth Five-Year Plan developed by SPIESR is an example of an area in which the institution has made a contribution. Institutions like the NIPFP believe in the use of methodologies with intermediate sophistication appropriate to the level of under-standing of the policy-makers, data availability and the problem. There is also a realisation that such institutions are in a better position than university departments to undertake analysis leading to policy.

There is also a fair consensus that methodology is significant. This is because where work has been done on a sound footing, public opinion and pressure begin to build up over time. Users are also getting better equipped to evaluate advice.

Economic ministries, the Planning Commission, the state planning boards and special commissions not only draw upon a wide range of expertise, but have also developed in-built analytical capabilities which put policy advice to very searching scrutiny. This necessitates increasing methodological soundness. Methodological sophistication *per se* is not an end for these research institutions, although such contributions are not ruled out.

Thus, the role of these institutions in the public policy process may be characterised as

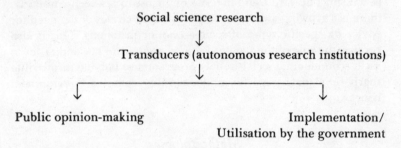

Social science research

↓

Transducers (autonomous research institutions)

↓

Public opinion-making   Implementation/
                                         Utilisation by the government

Some Lessons

In taking stock one can draw a set of conclusions, a set of trends for research institutions and some areas that emerge as common concerns for improving the impact of autonomous research institutions.

1. A pool of resources is now available in each institution which can be tapped by interested government/public agencies. The dominance of individual experts has yielded place to institutional groups and their joint responses to policy problems.
2. The proximity of the new institutions to policy-makers in the states and the relatively stronger focus of the institutions on research have facilitated communication between researchers and users. Institutional dissemination of findings seems to make a more visible impact than individual and *ad hoc* publication of research.
3. Joint thinking and participation in research at the institutional level have helped the centres to map out their research strategies more systematically. Rather than merely responding to *ad hoc* requests for policy advice, some of the new institutions have been able to initiate work in important policy-relevant areas.

Some trends for the roles and contributions of autonomous research institutions in the public policy process are evident :

1. State governments, which seldom looked for external policy advice, have become more open to research inputs as a result of linkages with the new institutions. It is also possible that the policy inputs needed by the numerous projects and programmes initiated by the government, often with external donor support, have made it necessary for them to turn to these institutions. Thus, there is an upward trend for utilisation of research by government agencies.

2. While there is a realisation that research is only one of the inputs to the policy process, there is an increasing concern to make social science research more relevant to policy concerns by addressing critical problems at the state and central levels. Further, there is an increasing concern to influence public opinion through quality research which would call for sounder and more sophisticated methodologies over time.

3. There is an awareness that interdisciplinary work is useful although there is no consensus on whether such capabilities should be built within the institutions or whether they should be drawn from outside. Further, though interdisciplinary (as distinct from multidisciplinary) work has not gained much momentum, the focus on 'problem-oriented' group research rather than individual academic research has led the new institutions to seek inputs from the relevant disciplines. In this process, the barriers between disciplines have been lowered.

Thus, the common concerns for improving the impact of the autonomous research institutions are :

1. Development of interdisciplinary competence in social science research. Problem orientation and group research are two moves in this direction.

2. Influencing the policy process through training activities is another area which has received little attention in these institutions. The few educational programmes (primarily Ph.Ds) do not aim to supply policy analysts to the government. The recruitment policies and personnel practices of governments are important reasons why training in policy analysis has not received much support.

3. Linkage of autonomous research institutions with institutions which train administrators so that research is disseminated

appropriately and there is a greater chance of its impact on yet another area. The implicit assumption behind this is that senior administrators are the key influences in policy-making. If a link is forged between them and the social science researcher, there is a greater chance of sponsored policy-oriented research and a greater chance of its utilisation. A related area of concern is the capabilities of these training institutions to assimilate and disseminate such research.

In our view, the above seem to be areas which should engage the attention of the research institutions and govern their future roles and contributions in the area of public policy-making. Our review suggests that the autonomous research institutions have now come to conceive of their roles as broader than merely doing research in response to the needs of officials. There is thus a movement in the right direction and also a sense of hope.

Notes

1. MIDS — Review and Perspective, Madras, 1978, p. 9.
2. *Ibid.*, p. 10.

RAM MOHAN RAO

12 Some Recent Committees and Commissions — A Review

Introduction

The complex nature of modern government, including our own in India, is reflected not only in the continuous addition of new activities and proliferation of new departments and ministries, but also in the *modus operandi* of getting things done, of framing and implementing public policies. More specifically, in the parliamentary form of government a large number of people — be they members of legislatures or the executive — participate at different stages of the policy formulation and implementation process. Apart from the legislators and bureaucrats who are continuously associated with this process, from time to time the government also requisitions outside advisers and entrusts them with the responsibility of providing *counsel* on specific matters of public interest. Many a time, the government also seeks the advice of experts on specific issues by making them members of commissions and committees.

For instance, commissions and committees have been appointed, since independence, not only by the government of India,[1] but also by several state governments. Discerning analysts, naturally, put forth the following questions :

1. What kind of role do the commissions and committees play in the policy process ?

2. What kind of experts become members of these bodies?
3. To what extent are the recommendations of these committees accepted and implemented by the government?
4. And to what extent do students and researchers of public systems concentrate their attention on studying the impact of the work of the committees and commissions?

Responses to these questions could be negative, or at best nebulous. For instance, a quick look at the literature in public administration reveals that, barring one or two exceptions,[2] there has hardly been any full-length exposition on the work of commissions and committees in general.

How about the periodical literature? The daily newspapers do come out with symbolic, and cryptic, comments in editorials and leading articles as and when the report of a committee or commission is submitted and its findings publicised. The intensity of the media debate fades away as the newspapers, in their search for sensationalism, move over to other, more newsworthy, items. Thus, it is very rarely that a scholarly, and critical, review of the work of a committee or commission is undertaken by the newspapers at large. Apart from the newspapers, how about the other kinds of publications, such as the weeklies, and other periodicals? While the general-purpose periodicals happen to be not very different from the newspapers in their coverage of the work of commissions and committees, we have discovered that there is an occasional exception to this common trend. The *Economic and Political Weekly* published from Bombay, has displayed, over the past couple of decades, a continuous interest in issues affecting public policy. Thus, we are curious as to where we could discern any trends or patterns in the abiding interest of this particular periodical in the public policy process, particularly in terms of its comments on the work of important commissions and committees. This paper makes an attempt to recapitulate some of these trends and patterns, over a particular period of time — between 1974 and 1981.

This review paper consists of three parts. The first part discusses the generic nature, the role and purposes of committees and commissions. Part two contains brief summaries of views expressed by the *Economic and Political Weekly* on some important committees and commissions. Part three contains a summary and attempts to see whether any trends or patterns are discernible in the views expressed by a particular periodical, as also the variety of issues tackled by committees and commissions. Table 1 contains a classification of committees and commissions for the period 1947 to 1969. Table 2 contains a similar, but partial, classification for the more recent period 1974 to 1981.

Committees and Commissions

In the previous section we have cursorily touched upon the role of commissions and committees in the ever-increasing complexity of governmental systems. For, 'modern governments all over the world have come to rely on committees and commissions'.[3] Moreover, 'such governments make an extensive use of the instrument of public inquiries which ultimately help in lessening managerial tensions as well as quietening allegations of misrule.'[4]

What is the difference between a commission and a committee and how does one distinguish one from the other? '[A] commission is a governmental agency created to perform a particular function, such as special investigation or governmental regulations of business'.[5] Further, a commission is appointed mainly when it is thought that a matter involves some financial questions. There are other aspects as well for which a commission is appointed, e.g., in matters pertaining to the welfare of the state and its citizens and for improving the efficiency of administration. The status of a 'committee' is also the same as that of a commission. But it does not have as wide powers as enjoyed by a commission and would have to limit itself in relation to specific work assigned to it under the terms of reference.[6] In this context, it would be interesting to refer to the practice in vogue in Great Britain, where Royal Commissions are appointed from time to time to deliberate on matters of specific interest. According to Prof. Redlich :

A Royal Commission has many advantages over a Parliamentary Committee; it can, while a parliamentary committee cannot, prolong its work beyond the limits of a session, if necessary even for years; and it is possible to appoint scientific experts as members, so as to secure a complete impartial treatment of the subject; the consequence is that commissions have, largely, superseded parliamentary committees when elaborate enquiries have to be made.[7]

In India the constitution, composition and working of commissions and committees is governed by the Commissions of Enquiry Act, 1952.

Commissions can be classified as being of two varieties : *ad hoc* and permanent. *Ad hoc* commissions have a specific purpose and tenure, and once the purpose is served they cease to exist. On the other hand, we have permanent commissions which come into being either in accordance with the provisions of the Constitution or under some Act of Parliament. Examples of the former are the Public Service Commission and the Election Commission. Examples of the latter are the Law Commission, the University Grants Commission, the Planning Commission and the Tariff Commission. The Finance Commission, though appointed under a provision of the Constitution, belongs to a distinct category; it is appointed every five years and it ceases to exist after it completes its business.

We can broadly distinguish two categories even among committees. Some of the committees of Parliament (e.g., Public Accounts, Estimates and Public Undertakings) exist on a permanent basis and are called standing committees. These are appointed by the Speaker of the Lok Sabha or Chairman of the Rajya Sabha, in accordance with the 'Rules of Procedure' of the House. Apart from these standing committees, Parliament may also appoint, from time to time, special committees. The purpose of all these committees is to facilitate the business of the House since Parliament, with its busy schedule, is unable to fully look into all matters of importance by itself.

Apart from parliamentary committees, the various administrative ministries of the government also appoint committees on an *ad hoc* basis for a specific purpose. The government may also constitute advisory committees, attached to a particular ministry, on a semi-permanent basis.

The primary function of an advisory committee is to advise the administration on how to frame public policy and/or how to implement it. From this stand-point, advisory committees are classified into two types. Some are associated with the policy-making stages, though, to be sure, the ultimate responsibility for taking the decision rests with the Government. The Export Advisory Council, and the Import Advisory Council advise the government on general policies regarding exports and import respectively. The second category of committees consists of those bodies which, while functioning within the framework of the general policy, advise on how to administer or implement that policy. The National Railway Users Consultative Council and the Customs Advisory Council illustrate this type.[8]

From the variety of committees in existence, would it be possible to generalise about the kinds and categories into which they can be arranged? K. C. Wheare classifies committees into the following six categories :

1. Committees to advise;
2. Committees to do inquiries;
3. Committees to negotiate;
4. Committees to legislate;
5. Committees to administer; and
6. Committees to scrutinise and control.[9]

Virendra Kumar, on the other hand, provides the following classification of committees and commissions which is more germane to the Indian situation :

1. Investigative committees;
2. Committees on relationship between employer-employees;
3. Committees enquiring into administrative deficiencies at central, state and local levels;
4. Commissions appointed by the President of India (under provisions of the Constitution);
5. Committees appointed by Parliament; and
6. Committees appointed by ministries and departments.[10]

There is wide latitude available to commissions and committees to frame procedures relating to their work. For instance, when a commission or committee is large (like the Administrative Reforms Commission) and its work becomes voluminous and complex, it is divided into many study groups or sub-committees. These study groups or sub-committees submit their reports on the specific issues as laid down in their terms of reference. Finally, the main committee or commission takes cognizance of their recommendations and, after scrutiny, incorporates them in the main or final recommendations.[11]

Some Committees and Commissions

Table 1 contains a classification of committees and commissions by sectors and purpose for the years 1947 through 1969. To provide a perspective on the recent past, this part concentrates on the period 1974 to 1981, with the help of the comments from the *Economic and Political Weekly*. In this part it is intended to give a brief sampler of the kind of work being entrusted to committees and commissions, as also the kind of views expressed by the media on the work and recommendations of these bodies.

In the first section, we look at the work of the Hathi Committee on the Drugs and Pharmaceutical Industry appointed by the Ministry of Petroleum and Chemicals, Government of India. In the section following that we briefly touch upon a variety of views expressed on the findings of the Shah Commission appointed by the Janata government in 1977. The third section of this part contains a review of reactions to the Report of the Study Group on Wages, Incomes and Prices headed by Boothalingam.

The Jaisukhlal Hathi Committee

Early in 1973, there was considerable commotion on the role of the foreign manufacturing firms in the drug industry and the government's policies towards them. These issues considerably agitated Members of Parliament and to assuage their feelings the government appointed a Committee, headed by Jaisukhlal Hathi to look into the drug industry. The following were its terms of reference :

1. To inquire into the progress made;
2. To ensure leadership of the public sector;
3. To suggest ways for the rapid growth of the Indian sector and regional dispersal of the industry;
4. To regulate the flow of technology;
5. To ensure quality control; and
6. To look into prices, etc.

The Committee submitted its report in April 1975.[12] It suggested three main measures to streamline the drug industry. First, a list was drawn up by the panel cataloguing what in its opinion should be regarded as essential drugs and household remedies. These

TABLE 1

Committees and Commissions by Sectors and Purpose, 1947 Through 1969

Sector	Purpose		Total
	Advise	Enquire/ Inquire	
Education	56	3	59
Health	19	2	21
Science and Technology	9	—	9
Railways	10	31	41
Food, Agriculture and Animal Husbandry	52	11	63
Irrigation, Power and Water Management	30	3	33
Industry and Mining	30	1	31
Language and Press	5	1	6
Law and Order	—	2	2
General Administration	70	3	73
Commerce and Trade	23	4	27
Energy	1	—	1
Economy, Finance, Banking, and Insurance	24	9	33
Miscellaneous	177	3	180
States and Local Government	12	9	21
Total			600

Source: Virendra Kumar, *Committees and Commissions: 1947-73* (9 Vols.), Delhi, D. K. Publishing House (for Volume 1) and Delhi, Concept Publishing Company (for Volumes 2 to 9), 1975, 1976, 1977, 1978 and 1979.

drugs, the Committee said, should be manufactured freely and impediments to their manufacture removed. The other two recommendations of the panel were :

1. (a) Drugs be distributed through the postal department, Indian Oil Company depots, kerosene depots;
   (b) The downgrading of pharmacists' academic training; and
2. Progressive replacement of brand names of drugs by generic names.

The *Economic and Political Weekly* carried four articles between 1975 and 1978 which reacted to the Hathi Committee's recommendations.

Chatterjee[13] reacts adversely to the suggestion that pharmacist's qualification be downgraded, in case the drugs are to be sold through general purpose outlets. While generally favouring the switch-over from brand names to generic names, he points out the practical problems involved in operationalising the switch-over.

The Hathi Committee made a recommendation that the 'new type of multi-ingredient preparations should not be allowed to be marketed hereafter unless they are mentioned in the National Formulary or Pharamacopoeia and approved by the Drug Controller of India'. Chatterjee's reaction to this specific recommendation is :

> ... the evolution of competent formulation emerges generally out of research carried out in the laboratories of reputed manufacturing houses. Whether our government will eventually have laboratories of comparable competence is a matter of conjecture. Meanwhile, this type of research must go on in the laboratories of manufacturing houses. The incentive angle should be kept alive.[14]

While generally agreeing with the tenor of the recommendations of the Hathi Committee, DJSK[15] concentrates on the methodological lacunae. The work of the Committee, for instance, began with four sets of questionnaires sent to the pharmaceutical units in the organised sector, to the manufacturer's associations, and government departments. Yet nowhere in the bulky report, DJSK states, have the data from these questionnaires been tabulated, analysed, or discussed.

One of the tasks of the Hathi Committee was to suggest effective control measures in the drug industry. The Committee's chapter on quality control extends over 110 pages, containing chiefly the recommendations of earlier committees. DJSK states :

> If the reports of the earlier committees on quality control could not be implemented, or were not adequate to improve matters, the Hathi Committee's report is unlikely to be any more effective. Further, the report itself does not spell out any measures to bring order into the chaos of medical system (5000 formulations, brand names and high profiteering). Indeed, as long as present commercial practices yield unduly high profits, large-scale production of socially useful drugs is impossible.[16]

Commenting editorially on the government's decisions on the Hathi Committee Report, the *Economic and Political Weekly*[17] was very unambiguous in its reactions :

The government's long-awaited decisions on the pharmaceutical industry are an impressive example of the proverbial mouse emerging from a mountain of labour. In his statement in the Lok Sabha on March 29, the Minister for Petroleum, Chemicals and Fertilizers enumerated at length the series of meetings with representatives of pharmaceutical industry, interministerial consultations and deliberations of Cabinet Committees, spread over a period of almost three years following the submission of the Hathi Committee's report in April 1975, which have ostensibly led to the decisions announced this week. For all that, the impact of these decisions in terms of expanding the production of the most vitally needed medicines at prices which bear a more realistic relationship to the majority of the population at present and the closely related objective of regulating the operations of the multinational drug companies in the country will be minimal or even actually negative.

The editorial also very sharply points out the lukewarm treatment given to the most critical of the Hathi Committee recommendations :

On the two points most important to them, the government has given in to the multinational companies. First, the government has thrown overboard the Hathi Committee's recommendation that the proporaon of foreign equity in the Indian subsidiaries of the multinational companies should be reduced to 40 per cent immediately and progressively to 26 per cent. Second, the government has agreed to regularise capacity installed by pharmaceutical companies, including the subsidiaries of multi-nationals, in excess of the licenced limits .... Government policy should, therefore, be aimed at drastically curbing the production of non-essential drugs and expanding manifold the production of the relatively small number of essential drugs which meet the health requirements of the bulk of the population. These drugs have been repeatedly identified, including by the Hathi Committee.

In a special article on the new drug policy,[18] an author, who wishes to remain anonymous, takes a comprehensive and critical look at the policies of the government with regard to the drug industry in the aftermath of the Hathi Committee's recommendations. The author examines the new drug policy from the standpoint of the extent to which it is likely to promote and achieve the objectives outlined in the statement the Union Minister of Petroleum and Chemicals made to Parliament in March 1978. Briefly, these objectives are :

1. That the country should be self-reliant in technology;
2. That there should be self-sufficiency of drugs; and
3. That the quality drugs should be available in abundance at reasonable prices.

The author also examines separately the measures proposed in the new drug policy to expand production, especially of bulk drugs, measures relating to drugs and, finally, those pertaining to other matters such as research, quality control, brand names, etc.

The Shah Commission Reports

The Shah Commission — headed by Justice J.C. Shah and appointed by the Janata government in 1977 to look into the various facets of the Emergency regime of the previous Congress government — submitted a number of interim reports to the central government as and when its proceedings warranted such a step. The year 1978 reverberated with different findings of the Shah Commission. In keeping with the gravity and the startling nature of the revelations contained in these reports, there was extensive debate in the media about different aspects of the emergency regime. The *Economic and Political Weekly* too continuously reflected the importance of the Shah Commission's findings through editorial comment, brief reports and the publication of excerpts from the interim reports. The following pages give a very brief sampler of the kind of debate the Shah Commission triggered off in the nation.

In an editorial, the *Economic and Political Weekly*[19] states :

The first interim report of the Shah Commission was submitted to government on March 13; the second interim was submitted on April 27; and both the reports were presented to Parliament on May 16. The findings of the two reports contain few surprises. The carefully prepared 'case summaries' had admirably summed up facts generally, though only fragmentarily, known, and had themselves constituted a most convincing indictment of Emergency in action. What the Shah Commission had done is to subject the facts mentioned in case summaries to further judicial analysis in the light of evidence offered in support — and in refutation, too — of them.

In a similar vein, further reports appearing in the *Economic and Political Weekly* on the work of the Shah Commission highlight very specifically particular findings of this body. For instance, the report of 3 June highlights the misuse of the media during the Emergency by the ruling party.[20] Similarly, the comment in the next issue of this periodical highlights the abuse of power by the family members of the powers that be.[21] The comment which was carried in the 24 June issue concentrates on the wanton destruction of the poor people's dwellings in Delhi during the Emergency.[22] The comment which appeared on 1 July pinpoints the callousness and the excessive brutality unleashed by the police forces during the emergency, bringing much agony and hardship to the hapless and helpless victims.[23] The 16 September issue of this periodical comments on the third interim report of the Shah Commission which, among other things, focuses on the illegal detention of relatives of political prisoners, the conditions in jails and so on.[24] The final chapters of the third interim report also provide summaries of the working of the Shah Commission itself, and the Commission's general observations and conclusions.[25] The 30 September issue of the journal further commenting on the third and final report of the Shah Commission provides glimpses of the manner in which the Emergency era ran its course in various states of our Union.[26] Chapters 18 to 22 of the third interim report highlight the situation in the States — dismissals, premature retirements and supersession of public servants; arrests and detentions; conditions in prisons; implementation of the family planning programme; and demolitions. *The Economic and Political Weekly* of 11 November 1978 provides an extensive commentary on the overall summary of the Shah Commission's findings.[27] The Final Report also indicts in unambiguous terms, persons who played an authoritarian and anti-people role during the emergency.

The Boothalingam Committee Report

The Study Group on Wages, Incomes and Prices, under the Chairmanship of Mr. Boothalingam, submitted its report to the government in May 1978. This report triggered off quite a controversy and sharp comments from different quarters.

Commenting editorially on this report the *Economic and Political Weekly*[28] states :

> The Study Group on Wages, Incomes and Prices, an official summary of whose report was released this week, was put on the defensive, right at the outset by the widely-shared suspicion that the government's purpose in appointing it was to create a climate of opinion in favour of restraint in wages, especially of the relatively better paid sections of the working class in the public and private sectors ... In fact, it may be said the Group has made no definite recommendations on this or on almost any other subject. Instead, it has sought to shift the responsibility to some half-a-dozen or so commissions, committees and other bodies whose constitution it has proposed.

BM, in the *Economic and Political Weekly* of 3 June 1978,[29] commenting on the Boothalingam Report states : 'Judging from the upshot of the appointment of the Boothalingam Committee on Wages, Incomes and Prices policy, it can actually aggravate matters. The Committee's report has met with total rejection from all the organised sections concerned with it — the trade unions as well as the employer's organisations.'

While reviewing the Boothalingam Committee's report, Papola[30] makes the following significant comments :

> The appointment of the Study Group was not well-advised, as this task is continuously being handled by several policy making organs of the Government, especially the Planning Commission. If the idea was to frame a policy on wages and salaries *vis-a-vis* other incomes and prices, the Government again had before it a large body of well-considered recommendations made in the past by several committees and commissions. The Boothalingam Study Group could not be expected to achieve anything substantially

more fruitful in view of the limited time and co-operation that it had at its disposal. The Group, therefore, ended up by repeating some of the past recommendations in a disjointed manner and justifying the continuation of the *status quo*. We hardly have a refreshing and integrated framework, therefore, on wage policy, much less, of course, on incomes policy. Its utility is likely to be further reduced when the Government finds it difficult to accept such recommendations as it has been bold enough to make — which require a break from the past.

Substantive Issues

Tables 1 and 2 reveal the wide-ranging areas and subjects which the commissions and committees had deliberated upon, over a long

TABLE 2

Committees and Commissions by Sectors and Purpose, 1974 Through 1981
(as per the *Economic and Political Weekly*)

Sector	Purpose		Total
	Advise	Inquire/ Enquire	
Education	2	—	2
Health	1	—	1
Science and Technology	—	—	—
Railways	—	—	—
Food, Agriculture and Animal Husbandry	—	—	—
Irrigation, Power and Water Management	—	—	—
Industry and Mining	—	—	—
Language and Press	—	—	—
Law and Order	1	—	1
General Administration	2	—	2
Commerce and Trade	1	—	1
Energy	—	—	—
Economy, Finance, Banking, and Insurance	6	3	9
Miscellaneous	4	—	4
States and Local Government	—	—	—
Total			20

Source : Various Issues of the *Economic and Political Weekly*.

period of time. As far as the kinds and variety are concerned, the commissions and committees fall into one or the other categories which were enumerated in the first part above. As far as the range of the subjects being investigated is concerned, they vary very widely — from matters pertaining to a particular ministry (e.g., drug and pharmaceutical industry) to more general policy issues (e.g., wages, incomes and prices policy) to more substantive matters (e.g., administrative reforms). Similarly, a judicial inquiry might follow in the aftermath of an unforeseen event (e.g., an airplane crash or a railway accident) or pursuant to charges of abuse of official power against a high dignitary (e.g., ministers at the centre or in the states). At the same time, in the aftermath of an extra-ordinary situation (such as the political change after the 1977 general elections) a general purpose omnibus inquiry commission (e.g., the Shah Commission) could be constituted to examine a number of issues underpinning significant actions of high dignitaries.

In this part, we make an attempt to discern any patterns or trends in the way committees and commissions are constituted, the way they go about their business and the kind of analyses which precede the voluminous reports that they prepare. What kind of questions do these agencies seek to answer ? What kind of information processing occurs as a prelude to the suggestions and recommendations which they invariably make ? What kind of impact does the work of these agencies have on the public policy-making process ? We seek to grope for answers to some of these questions in the next few pages. The first section concentrates on methodological issues while the next focuses on the substantive trends and patterns, if any, which we can discern from the repertoire of details available with us.

Methodological Issues

The composition of a committee assumes critical importance where the matter to be deliberated upon happens to be centred around a controversy cutting across the concerns of different interest groups. The composition of a committee should be such that it represents different interest groups, facilitating an appreciation of problems and issues from a wider perspective, as also arriving at a broad-based consensus with regard to solutions to such problems. For example, the Committee on the Integration of Co-operative Credit Institutions appointed by the Reserve Bank of India under the Chairmanship of R. K. Hazari illustrates the problems inherent in giving representation to different interest groups : 'The Committee consisted of 15 members, with all except two representing the Reserve Bank of India or Government or government-owned organisations, and, thus, grossly under-representing the other interests.'[31] This could be one of the important reasons why the recommendations of these committees tend to be vague.

Apart from the need for representative membership, a far more limiting and inhibiting methodological issue pertains to the delimitation of the scope of a committee's work. While the terms of reference are supposed to take care of this problem, unfortunately much confusion prevails in this area. Nebulousness about the scope of a committee's work gives rise to issues like the definition of the very problem. For instance, the report of the Krishna Iyer Committee on Legal Assistance suffers from 'three major lacunae : (a) failure to perceive and define problems; (b) disdain for facts; and (c) evasionary rhetoric'.[32] Similarly, in 1977 the government constituted a single committee to look into both company law as well as the monopolies and restrictive trade practices (Committee on Company Law and MRTP Act). This is an instance of leaving the scope of a committee's work, though undefined, quite wide indeed ! But 'the objectives, scope and machinery for implementation of the Companies Act and the MRTP Act are very dissimilar. It is difficult to understand, therefore, why the government should have entrusted the task of reviewing both these acts to the same committee.'[33]

Even when a committee is endowed with the right type of membership, as also clarity in its broad terms of reference, it can come up with formidable methodological dilemmas. For example, one of the problems frequently faced by these agencies happens to be the kind of weightage that should be given to the work done by earlier committees. Recapitulation of the past can sometimes overwhelm the main thrust of the report. For example, the Report of the Committee on Drugs and Pharmaceuticals, headed by Jaisukhlal Hathi, devotes nearly 110 pages to recapitulating the recommendations of previous committees on just one issue — the problem of quality control in the drug industry. One writer, commenting on this practice, irreverently states : 'If the reports of the earlier committees on quality control could not be implemented, or were not adequate to improve matters, the Hathi Committee's report is unlikely to be any more effective.'[34]

Yet another methodological issue — a very important one — pertains to the collection of primary information by a committee. The collection of such information and its processing acquire critical importance, particularly if the recommendations of the committee tend to be controversial. Interestingly, even when a committee collects a lot of information, the same may not have been utilised optimally even for formulating the most important recommendations. For example, the Hathi Committee on Drugs and Pharmaceuticals Industry had collected voluminous data through questionnaires from manufacturing units and government department. 'Yet nowhere in the bulky report, have the data from these questionnaires been tabulated, analysed or discussed.'[35] Thus, inadequate processing of available or freshly-gathered information, though many a time for very genuine reasons, deprives the committee of freshness in its approach as also its recommendations.

The committees do come up with many useful recommendations and sometimes propose the constitution of new organisations and agencies for the operationalisation of such suggestions. Many a time a committee may not bother to spell out, in sufficient detail, the role and functions of such organisations. For example, the Hathi Committee recommended the setting up of the National Drug Authority without clearly spelling out what it should do.[36]

Sometimes, even after protracted and prolonged deliberations, a committee may not emerge with any concrete suggestions. For example, the Boothalingam Study Group on Wages, Incomes and Prices has not come out with any definite recommendations on any aspect of the very complex problem. 'Instead, it has sought to shift the responsibility to some half-a-dozen or so commissions, committees and other bodies whose constitution it has proposed.'[37]

Thus, as far as the broad methodological issues are concerned, the following appear to have a bearing on the way a committee or a commission functions and whether it comes out with worthwhile insights: the composition and scope of the committee; the methods used for collection and processing views and information; the way it defines the problems; and the way it formulates and frames its recommendations. Confusion about any of these methodological issues not only delays the work of the committee, but also results in the final output turning out to be less than satisfactory in its usefulness and impact.

Trends and Patterns

Can one discern any trends and patterns from the foregoing analysis and narrative? It is difficult to come out with any significant generalisations about the work of commissions and committees which is quite variegated in terms of the range of subjects covered, the reasons and rationale for their establishment and the variety of outputs they come out with. It is also not easy to make statements about the impact these bodies have on the policy process, since this happens to be one of the rather under-explored areas in public administration. Hence, what we attempt to do in this section is only a very sketchy narrative, primarily based on the information culled from the *Economic and Political Weekly*.

A committee's work seems to attract the greatest attention only when the subject matter dealt with happens to be of critical importance to a wide cross-section of the population. For example, the Hathi Committee's report and the work of the Boothalingam Study Group triggered off quite a bit of interesting — and even polemical — debate since the subjects they dealt with were of great importance — namely, the drug industry and a policy for wages, incomes and prices. Similarly, the work of the Shah Commission evoked a good deal of debate throughout its existence, primarily because of the momentous nature of the problem it was dealing with — the abuse of authority by the government in an extraordinary situation, namely the Emergency. Even the work of successive finance commissions evoke quite a lot of debate and controversy since the subject matter of these bodies pertain to the distribution of fiscal resources among the states and the centre. Even committees which break new ground and evoke new norms in any field also trigger off a great deal of controversial debate, for example, the Tandon Committee on Bank Credit. The work of bodies such as the Administrative Reforms Commission, which was supposed to look into the whole administrative system, evoked a lot of debate since the various reports it prepared provided an unique opportunity to view issues in a wider perspective. Thus, the kind of response the committees and commissions evoke is very much linked to the nature of subjects they deal with and the kind of recommendations and suggestions they make.

What kind of impact do these committees and commissions have on the public policy process? The recommendations made by these bodies are not mandatory. It is the prerogative of the government to accept or reject the suggestions, either in whole or in part. Nevertheless, the government more often that not endeavours to implement as many of the suggestions made by a committee as are feasible for it to implement. But this process is not fully revealed to the outsiders. The different ministries from time to time take stock of the situation with regard to the suggestions of past commissions and committees. But a systematic account of such processes is not available with us. One exception to this trend happens to be the work of the parliamentary committees, such as the Public Accounts Committee, the Estimates Committee and the Committee on Public Undertakings. The parliamentary committees not only prepare continuously reports on problems but also draw up review reports at regular intervals which establish the extent to which the government has accepted the earlier recommendations, and the way they have been implemented. Such a continuous monitoring system provides us with helpful clues about the extent to which a committee's work has an impact on the policy process. But with regard to the work of the committees appointed by different administrative ministries, there is hardly any systematic monitoring system. The only way out in such circumstances is the vigilance of Members of Parliament who from time to time can demand information about the fate of the recommendations of committees. Similarly, the press also can play a very helpful role by keeping the debate alive. We have noticed how even serious periodicals like the *Economic and Political Weekly* play a significant role in discussing very incisively the issues arising from the work of committees and commissions.

In the ultimate analysis committees and commissions play an associative or adjunct role in the process of administration. They are not a substitute for the continuous challenges of day-to-day administration, of policy formulation and implementation. As we have pointed out earlier, these bodies are set up to sort out knotty issues which may not be amenable to any clear-cut solution through the normal process. But the overall impact of the work of commissions and committees is very dependent on the receptivity of the administration to new ideas and its sincerity to translate suggestions into policies. At the same time, the task of ensuring that such synchronisation does indeed take place rests largely on the political leadership. In a parliamentary system like ours even the legislators, the press and the public at large can play a vigilant role in ensuring that meaningful suggestions are indeed transformed into implementable policies.

Notes

1. See Virendra Kumar, *Committees and Commissions in India, 1947-73*, 9 Vols. (Delhi, D. K. Publishing House, 1974-79), for a brief summary of the reports of commissions and committees appointed by the Government of India since independence and up to 1969. Kumar's work is still continuing but, at a rough guess, the central government alone appointed over 600 commissions and committees up to 1969.
2. See S. R. Maheshwari, *The Evolution of Indian Administration* (Agra, Laxmi Narain Agarwal, 1970), for an exposition of the evolution of Indian administration since the time of the East India Company till 1967, through an analysis of commissions and committees. Also see, by the same author, *Government Through Consultation : Advisory Committees in Government* (New Delhi, Indian Institute of Public Administration, 1972), for an analysis of the work of advisory committees; and *The Administrative Reforms Commission* (Agra, Laxmi Narain Agarwal, 1972), for an analysis and critical appraisal of the various sub-committees of the Administrative Reforms Commission.
3. Virendra Kumar, *Committees and Commissions in India, 1947-73, op. cit.*, Vol. 1, pp. *xii-xxxiii.*
4. *Ibid.*
5. *Ibid.*
6. *Ibid.*
7. Quoted in *ibid.*
8. S. R. Maheshwari, *Government Through Consultation. op. cit.*, p. 15.
9. K. C. Wheare, *Government by Committee* (Oxford, Clarendon Press, 1955).
10. Virendra Kumar, *op. cit.*, Vol. 1, p. *xxix.*
11. *Ibid.*
12. 'Report of the Committee on Drugs and Pharmaceuticals Industry,' New Delhi, Ministry of Petroleum and Chemicals, April 1975 (mimeo).
13. K. C. Chatterjee, 'Distribution of Essential Drugs and Common Household Remedies,' *Economic and Political Weekly* (henceforth, *EPW*), Vol. 10, No. 14, 5 April 1975, pp. 588-89.
14. *Ibid.*
15. D. J. S. K., 'Much Chaff in Hathi Report,' *EPW*, Vol. 10, No. 24, 14 June 1975.
16. *Ibid.*
17. 'Mouse that Roared,' *EPW*, Vol. 13, No. 13, 1 April 1978, pp. 561-62.
18. 'New Drug Policy,' *EPW*, Vol. 13, No. 21, 27 May 1978, pp. 875-79.
19. 'After the Indictment,' *EPW*, Vol. 13, No. 20, 20 May 1978, pp. 825-26
20. 'Shah Commission's Findings : Misuse of Mass Media,' *EPW*, Vol. 13, No. 22, 3 June 1978. p. 898.
21. 'Shah Commission's Findings : The Family Connection,' *EPW*, Vol. 13, No. 23, 10 June 1978, p. 941.

22. 'Shah Commission's Findings : The Wrecking of Delhi,' *EPW*, Vol. 13, No. 25, 24 June 1978, p. 1019.
23. 'Shah Commission's Findings : Kill and Don't Tell,'' *EPW*, Vol. 13, No. 26, 1 July 1978, p. 1052.
24. 'Shah Commission's Final Report : Masters and Servants,' *EPW*, Vol. 13, No. 37, 16 September 1978, p. 1583.
25. *Ibid.*
26. 'Shah Commission's Final Report : Reports from States,' *EPW*, Vol. 13, No. 39, 30 September 1978, p. 1660.
27. 'Shah Commission's Final Report : Roll Call of Dishonour,' *EPW*, Vol. 13, No. 45, 11 November 1978, p. 1838.
28. 'Dangerous Doctrine,' *EPW*, Vol. 13, No. 21, 27 May 1978, pp. 857-58.
29. B. M., 'Evasion on Wages Policy,' *EPW*, Vol. 13, No. 22, 3 June 1978.
30. T. S. Papola, 'Facts and Fictions on Incomes Policy,' *EPW*, Vol. 13, No. 38, 23 September 1978, p. 1625.
31. K. K. Taimni, 'Unconvincing Case,' *EPW*, Vol. 12, Nos. 1 and 2, 6 January 1977, pp. 15-16.
32. Upendra Baxi, 'Legal Assistance to the Poor : A Critique of the Expert Committee Report,' *EPW*, Vol. 10, No. 27, 5 July 1975, pp. 1005-13.
33. A. N. Oza, 'Committee on Company Law and MRTP Act : Exercise in Futility,' *EPW*, Vol. 12, No. 32, 6 July 1977, pp. 1268-71.
34. D. J. S. K., 'Much Chaff in Hathi Report,' *EPW*, Vol. 10, No. 24, 14 June 1975.
35. *Ibid.*
36. *Ibid.*
37. 'Dangerous Doctrine,' *EPW*, Vol. 13, No. 21, 27 May 1978, p. 857.

V

The International
Experience

BERNARD DONOUGHUE

13 The Present State of Public Policy Analysis in Britain

Awareness of the concepts and approaches used in policy science has increased strikingly in Britain in the past decade. A growing number of people are professionally engaged either in simply analysing and describing how the governmental policy-making process functions, or in trying to make prescriptions for better, actual, policy decision-making in government. The British central government machine itself has been amended in certain ways to allow a more systematic input of policy analysis.

I will attempt to briefly describe these main developments in order to provide a thumb-nail sketch of the present state of play. It is as well to hint from the beginning, however, that my general conclusion is that in reality the advance in public policy analysis in Britain is much less than appears on the surface.

Policy analysis is conducted or practised in five main locations in Britain :

—— Policy advice units within the government;
—— Royal commissions and committees;
—— Policy research institutes;
—— Departments of universities and polytechnics;
—— Research departments of political parties, trade unions and employees' associations.

I will say something about each in turn. Throughout it should also be borne in mind that one is often referring to different animals : to the analysis of policy options, to the use of policy analysis in policy formulation, to the instruments of policy analysis, to the institutions of policy decision-making, to policy implementation and to the theoretical analysis of any one, and the relationship between any number of these.

Policy Advice Units within the British Government

Departmental Policy Units

Policy analysis and planning units exist in most departments of the British government, though they are a relatively recent development, having been recommended by the Fulton Commission on Government in the late 1960s. Some, as in the Departments of Health and Housing, have a good reputation. The conclusions of their analysis are certainly fed into the regular decision-making machinery of the department, and occasionally their work is published. However, these departmental units are not central to the policy-making process of the government in Whitehall. Their members do not usually participate in the key governmental committees and they rarely have access to ministers. British civil servants who serve in these units usually see them as merely an interesting temporary experience, a pause from the main bureaucratic power-play in government. The reasons for this low priority are not easy to demonstrate but they certainly lie in the culture of the British Civil Service, which is 'generalist' and 'political' in approach, viewing scientific analysis and specialisation with a mixture of scepticism and disdain. It was mainly because of this scepticism — shared by ministers — that the system of Programme Analysis Reviews, which was introduced by Prime Minister Heath in 1971 (whereby departments would monitor, analyse and revise policy programmes) was allowed quickly to wither away and was buried without ceremony or regret in 1978.

The attitude of the British government to policy analysis is clear to anybody who works in Whitehall or observes it closely and with perception. There is no clearly defined profession of policy analysis in the regular British Civil Service and the few cases of planning units within departments are not usually at the heart of the policy-making process.

Policy Advice to the Prime Minister and Cabinet :
The CPRS and the Number Ten Policy Unit

While the regular British bureaucracy has ignored systematic policy analysis — and perhaps because it did — there was in the 1970s a dramatic infusion of outside policy analysis geared to the needs of the Prime Minister and the Cabinet. It began with the setting up of the Central Policy Review Staff (the Think Tank) by Prime Minister Heath in 1971. Soon after, in 1974, Prime Minister Wilson established the Policy Unit at 10 Downing Street (again following the recommendation of the Fulton Commission).

Since the War, British prime ministers — operating a political system in which they must personally and simultaneously be leader of the cabinet, of the majority party in Parliament, and of the mass party in the country — have suffered from serious 'overloading'. A whole range of factors have been identified, or have alleged, to contribute to this. The insoluble complexity of current economic and social problems, increased international interdependence and the consequential obligations on heads of government, the greater and more sophisticated pressure from organised pressure groups are a few worth mentioning. Prime ministers are now required to initiate and guide policies whose grasp requires a staggering range of personal qualities — a capacity for in-depth and specialist knowledge, yet coupled with an ability to simplify and synthesise; a capacity for risk analysis; a capacity to disaggregate the component parts of a problem, to identify policy options, and to select the best practical policy solutions. No single politician, or cabinet of politicians, can be expected to have these qualities. The regular bureaucracy has some of them but is often culturally antipathetic to systematic policy analysis — especially if it might point to radical policy solutions.

Therefore, recent British prime ministers have, with varying degrees of enthusiasm and success, made use of the innovations of Prime Ministers Heath and Wilson. The Central Policy Review Staff (CPRS), which is located in the Cabinet Office, has usually been composed of around twenty staff, some regular civil servants, some outsiders. Its role is to analyse current major policy problems, or those which threaten to be before Cabinet, and to recommend solutions. Its director sits in Cabinet and its policy papers go to all members of the Cabinet. Although its work has inevitably been of mixed quality, the CPRS has generally been highly valued by ministers. When Robert Levine of the University of Washington conducted his recent review of 'Programme Evaluation and Policy Analysis in Western Nations' he was above all impressed by the CPRS. He concluded that only in Britain among the larger nations does analytical information, properly processed for decision-making, enter the highest levels of policy-making regularly and effectively.

However, his tribute may sadly and rapidly have become a requiem. For Prime Minister Thatcher has made only narrow use of the CPRS since 1979, concentrating it mainly on industrial policy. Surprisingly, she has just appointed a new director, taken from a merchant bank, with little previous experience in policy analysis. It is too early to write off the CPRS, since its value has previously been demonstrated to governments of both parties. But it is certainly entering a difficult period in terms of morale and reputation.

The Policy Unit established in Downing Street in 1974 (headed for five years by the present writer) employed between six and ten policy specialists, the majority having a background in various branches of economics. It worked directly with the Prime Minister. It was 'political' in the sense that its members broadly supported the approach of its Prime Minister. It contained no regular civil servants and its membership terminated employment on the resignation of its Prime Minister. Its director sat on all Cabinet Committees chaired by the Prime Minister. So it was different from the CPRS in a number of ways, but the two institutions worked closely together (in my time at least), providing a substantial core of specialist policy analysis within the central capability of government. Backed personally by the Prime Minister, they could together wield substantial power. A good deal of academic literature has concluded that the Policy Unit, at least under the Labour governments (1974-79), exercised considerable influence on policy formulation.

Mrs. Thatcher retained a Policy Unit in Downing Street composed of her own appointees after 1979. But it was much attenuated in size and, at the present moment, its future is in doubt (at least until the return of another Labour or Social Democratic government).

We may conclude therefore that whereas the 1970s saw considerable progress in the use of systematic policy analysis within the British government, at least at the Prime Minister and Cabinet levels,there has recently been some slippage. It is perhaps inevitable that the extent of utilisation of policy analysis will always depend greatly on the temperament amd wishes of the top politicians — at least while the bureaucracy lacks enthusiasm.

Royal Commissions and Advisory Committees

Royal Commissions set up with terms of reference to analyse a particular problem area have long been the traditional way for British governments to recruit independent policy analysis. Some commission reports have undoubtedly been immensely useful and professional, based on serious quantitative research and analysis of the substantive problem. But Royal Commissions are certainly not a *consistent* input of scientific policy analysis into government. It is only the occasional chance of events and ministerial interest which leads to a commission being established — and often this is done to delay rather than to advance policy action. Membership is crucial to effectiveness and the civil service has a major influence on membership selection, thus ensuring that unconventional people and uncomfortable thinking are minimised. The reports of Royal Commissions are often ignored for years, sometimes for ever. Their existence is not a good excuse for not introducing serious policy analysis into all levels of British government, and certainly not a substitute for it. The same observations apply to advisory committees, whether parliamentary or departmental.

Policy Research Institutions

Given the inadequacy of policy analysis within British government, it might be expected that a whole range of policy research organisations would be energetically filling the intellectual gap. Indeed there are roughly a hundred such organisations, mostly very small, but there are half a dozen with some international reputation : the Policy Studies Institute, the National Institute of Economic and Social Research, the Royal Institute of International Affairs (Chatham

House), the Institute of Strategic Studies, and the Royal Institute of Public Administration. But regrettably they are not, singly or collectively, a major force in the public policy debate in Britain. These 'Big Five' employ no more than a hundred research staff between them and spend less than $ 7 million a year (about a quarter funded by government). They are curiously muted in their approach. Their emphasis is on basic research and in general their style is to try to emulate universities rather than to intimidate governments. They have shown little sense of 'policy marketing,' seeming shy to target on live policy issues and reluctant to define policy options. I do not wish to be over-harsh in my criticism of the British Research Institutes; certainly the ISS is consistently effective in the defence debate and RIPA has shown fresh signs of life under its new leadership. But as a whole they have not been very active in pressing a policy agenda on politicians or government departments; certainly they are not as active as their North American equivalents. After all, Britain has recently experienced major crises in many policy areas. It has suffered its biggest economic recession and its highest unemployment for half a century. It has large numbers of young and middle-aged people with no prospect of getting jobs. One quarter of its manufacturing industry has disappeared in five years. It has become a major oil-producing nation — dependent on a finite resource. It has become a multi-racial society within one generation. Its education and its health services are patently under strain. Its management and its trade union principles and practices clearly do not achieve their sectional, let alone any national, interests. And, at the same time, its systems of government, national and local, do not cope with and respond effectively to the demands put upon them. Yet in this welter of crises, the policy research institutions have had too little to say. When I was in the Prime Minister's office during three administrations, in the middle of a succession of battles, hungry for high quality analysis and policy options, I was hardly made aware of the existence or output of these institutes. I sent for their publications (they rarely sent them to me) and found them merely interesting rather than urgently relevant. Almost the only time I recall the institutes exhibiting any great energy was when they mobilised collectively to prevent the establishment of a British Brookings Institute, which promised to provide the kind of high quality policy analysis which they were sadly failing to do.

Policy Analysis in British Higher Education :
Universities and Polytechnics

The section must inevitably be brief and fail to do justice to the rapid escalation of policy research in this large and varied educational sector. However, as a broad generalisation it must be said that though British academics increasingly occupy the ground of public policy analysis, they have not so far cultivated the land very profitably. This may be because, deep down, most British academics do not actually believe that there really is a discipline of policy analysis. They see it as a currently fashionable label for the old disciplines of political science, political institutions, public administration, and the newer economics of choice.

However, an increasing number of academics certainly are using the label not least because, in the competitive climate now prevailing, it may attract students or give access to foundation grants and research funds. Classes on public policy are now offered at several universities, including Strathclyde, Birmingham, Bristol, Kent, Manchester and the London School of Economics, as also at various polytechnics. But closer examination shows that this activity is still only modest. No institution in Britain pursues policy analysis on the scale of Wildavsky at Berkeley, California. There are few complete courses and no full degree in policy analysis. No graduate is able to call himself a professional policy analyst and if he did the British Civil Service would not recognise him and recruit him as such.

Most of the British university courses are more strictly 'policy studies' — that is descriptive — rather than training for, and research in, prescriptive policy analysis. The main exception is Strathclyde University in Scotland which offers a part-time Masters Course in Public Policy, mainly to people already working in local government (which in Britain shows more awareness of the value of policy analysis, than the central administration has so far). Apart from Professors Rose and Gunn at Strathclyde, it is striking how little British academics have contributed to the literature on public policy analysis. Professor Anthony King of Essex University, himself a traditional institutionalist, has contributed some welcome clarification and common sense. A few other individuals have carried out useful case studies of policy areas, particularly in the field of Social Policy (Richard Titmuss' *The Gift Relationship* is still probably the best of these). Often, older studies of interest groups, the bureaucracy, or the welfare state are rehashed with a beginning and an ending using the language and concepts of policy analysis, and served up as the new policy science. An examination of the reading lists for British university courses in this area shows the overwhelming dominance of North American literature. At the LSE, for example, there are two courses on public policy and policy analysis and the reading lists are almost totally North American : Dahl, Lindblom, Simeon, Truman, Buchan, Tolloch, Heclo, Wildavksy, Cameron, Wilensky, Lowi, Garo, Schulze, Beer, Allison, Downs, Sorenson, Newstadt.

The only British based authors on the list are King and Rose (both actually North Americans in origin), Rudolf Klein, Peter Dunleovy, and Peter Self (a professor of public administration who runs the course). Most striking of all is how little the British have so far contributed to the theoretical side of the subject.

The inevitable conclusion is that British universities are still unconvinced that there is a distinct discipline of public policy analysis. The have made gestures towards it but, in general, behind the new label, lie the old faces and the traditional approaches. Little attempt has been made to recruit into the universities people who have practised policy analysis in government. With one or two exceptions, little attempt is made to train policy analysts for the government. It would be churlish to deny that some progress has been made. A different prime minister may generate renewed interest in systematic policy analysis within government. A new generation may in time infiltrate the minds of our academics. But for the present the prospect is less encouraging than it may at first seem to be.

Policy Research Departments of Political Parties, Trade Unions and Employees' Associations

A distinctive feature of current British politics is the existence of highly programmatic political parties. Whichever party enters government after winning a general election does so with a detailed programme of policy commitments. These policies have usually been formulated in the research departments and policy committees of the party. They may also have been incorporated into party policy. They also have been inserted into the policy formulation process from outside — from the trade unions, which work closely with the Labour Party, or the employees' associations which are allied to the Conservative Party. Policies are brought together into a broad party programme and then condensed into a party manifesto in time for the election, when exposure to questioning by the electorate may produce further refinements. One implication is that the research staff of the political parties have a role in policy formulation in Britain. Also, party ideology provides a formative influence, sometimes a strait-jacket, on the evolution of policy. Yet another implication is that policy analysts and policy-makers within the government do not begin with a blank sheet on which to write and construct new policies. The broad shape and parameters of many policies would have already been formed. However, although the party research departments provide a further location and outlet for policy analysis, often with a good prospect of having access to power and influence, it does not necessarily follow that these advance the reputation of the nascent profession of policy analysis. Low standards and political slogans often dominate these party research departments.

Conclusion

Policy analysis has expanded in Britain as academics have responded to the desire to be more 'relevant' and as governments themselves have felt the need to be more systematic in assessing alternative programmes, especially in an era of 'demand overload' when there are increasing doubts whether democratic governments can cope at all. There has also been some experimentation in introducing policy analysis units into governments. These have had some (temporary?) success at the level of the head of government and also in some areas of local government, but not in the mainstream of Britain's central bureaucracy.

The bulk of our indigenous policy research — whether in higher education or in independent research institutes — remains of the traditional, descriptive and case-study kinds. It can be classified according to its substantive policy areas — social policy, agriculture and others. Many of the academics involved are really conventional public administration or political institutions specialists dressed up in a new garb. They are frequently merely describing the institutional machinery and policy output of government and any prescriptive conclusions often involve tinkering with the government machinery to make it more efficient. I do not wish to dismiss this approach, especially if well done — after all, it is my own academic background. But it does seem a pity that so little of value has emerged in Britain on the way that the political process, or the distribution of organised power within it, or the socio-economic environment, or the prevailing ideology and dominant values of contemporary Britain, shape policy-making. Most striking is the paucity of theoretical insights into the science of policy science itself.

The future may be brighter. A new generation of politicians may generate greater demand for and respect for policy analysts in Britain. But one thing will remain certain in Britain as elsewhere — policy analysis can never be a substitute for the political process itself.

ROBERT E. KLITGAARD

14 The Emergence of Public Policy : Studies and Prospects for Comparative Work

I

As we discuss 'public policy studies' in India and other countries, one of our implicit aims would be to consider just what this term might mean, how we might fruitfully cooperate, and specifically what sorts of comparative research on policy issues some of us might undertake. The answers are not obvious. People who do public policy studies are a diverse lot. We have been trained in different disciplines, we work at different kinds of institutions, and we study subjects ranging from agriculture to health to international negotiations. We come from many regions and countries. What do or could we have in common?

I want to approach this question in three ways. First, I will briefly describe the emergence of 'public policy studies' in the United States. Second, I will describe some selected instances of similar endeavours in the developing countries. Finally, and quite schematically, I will suggest lessons from other subjects where comparative research has been around for several decades. What can be learned from such diverse fields as comparative politics, comparative education, comparative economics, and comparative public administration? What are the implications of these lessons for comparative work in public policy?

II

One of the signal developments in higher education in the United States during the last decade was the rise of training and research programmes in public policy. The idea of 'policy studies' was not new. One might trace it back twenty-five years to the call by Lasswell and others for an active orientation of the social sciences, psychology, and other disciplines to the solution of public problems, and for the development of 'the policy sciences'. But I trace the actual emergence of *professional* programmes in this area to the failure of two wars in America during the 1960s — the war in Vietnam and the war on poverty.

The sixties were a time of unprecedented involvement of academicians in government policy-making. The McNamara 'whiz kids' with their techniques of systems analysis; the new military strategists; the optimistic involvement of economists, sociologists, and educators in programmes designed to combat poverty; and even the great participation of professors in overseas development activities — all were instances of an expanded influence of social scientists in policy-making circles.

By the late sixties, however, a degree of disillusionment had set in. The best and the brightest had failed said many critics. Even those who defended the war in Vietnam on moral grounds, calling it a noble defence of democracy carried out for altruistic motives, criticised the failure of good ideas to be properly implemented. The war on poverty's many components in manpower training, urban renewal, and education had disappointing results — perhaps not because the underlying theories behind the reforms were invalid, said supporters, but because good ideas were not well-managed and implemented. To many of the academics involved in the policy formulation process of the 1960s, an important gap had been overlooked : between politicians and bureaucrats on the one hand, and the techniques and promise of the applied social sciences on the other.

The failure was on both sides of that gap. The politicians and bureaucrats were intimately familiar with the ways of government, and they understood how organisations worked and did not work. But they did not fathom the fine points of modelling. They were ignorant of economic theory. The subtleties of statistical manipulation, which had become so necessary for programme evaluation, remained mysteries to them. And, indeed, they might need further training in the art of management.

. But there were also shortcomings on the other side. The economists and other social scientists who were heavily involved in policy formulation understood little of the political process in Washington or the state governments. They had too much confidence in the effortless and distortion-free translation of good ideas into smoothly functioning programmes.

What was needed, some people said, was nothing short of a new profession. A new sort of government official must be created who would combine the analytical skills of the hard social sciences with the political sense and managerial talents of the best of the seasoned government officials. The watchwords were 'policy analysis' and 'public management'. And to ensure that this blend did not lead to the formulation of a heartless technocracy, the new professionals should also receive training in ethics and social justice.

New training programmes emerged — at Harvard, Duke, Berkeley, Michigan, and elsewhere. They contained common elements. They were concerned with substantive policy issues, as well as with processes of policy formation and implementation. They relied heavily on economics and quantitative tools of planning and evaluation. According to Ernest A. Englebert, graduate curricula were usually built around a core consisting of

> (a) quantitative methodology including mathematical programming and modelling and descriptive and inferential statistics; (b) the political and institutional environment of policy formation and implementation; (c) economic theory and analysis with emphasis on public-private sector relationship in the allocation of resources; (d) behavioral and non-behavioral decision-making and implementation strategies and processes; and (e) program management, control, and evaluation. In addition, public analysis programs appear to be giving increasing attention to ethics and values.[1]

One new school described its focus in a typical fashion : 'A profession is now developing in which people are trained to examine alternative approaches to public policy programs, to evaluate the effects of policies, and to facilitate the implementation of programs.'[2]

Despite these common features, these new efforts contain differences of great magnitude, and they are important in considering public policy studies in India and other countries. I find it helpful to use a linguistic analogy. A person may become a distinguished linguist by studying the structure of various languages, their rules of operation and their patterns of change, and their quasi-mathematical structure. On the other hand, a student may learn to speak a language without understanding any of these linguistic features. (If you prefer an athletic analogy, consider learning to swim : you need not understand the physics of buoyancy or fluid dynamics.) At the same time, a superb theoretical linguist may be unable to speak a single language, and the expert on hydrodynamics may not know how to swim.

This distinction applies to public policy studies as well. Many of the new policy programmes that derive from public administration or from political science departments are like the 'linguistics' approach, in my opinion. They provide typologies for the policy formulation process. They categorise administrative systems. They study the utilisation of policy research. They comment on the role of policy analysts in government. And they criticise the limitations of various analytical approaches to public policy.

Unfortunately, people trained in this way may not be effective professionals. They may be able to *talk about* policy analysis or public management, but not be adept at *doing it.*

But other programmes of policy studies — the ones deriving from economics or business administration — emphasise the 'speaking language' side. They try to train students in the basic, practical techniques of statistics, economics and operations research — even at the cost of theoretical superficiality. They employ the case method to teach what might be called the 'craft knowledge' of public management, in contrast to more theoretical or typological approaches to management science. Indeed, some schools, like my own, have virtually jettisoned all of public administration and political science from the curriculum. In this second sort of programme, ethics will be taught not based on deep theoretical understanding but through the case method. Those who favour this second approach to public policy studies will say that it is designed to create professionals, not teachers or theorists.

Of course this distinction is a caricature. Probably no single department or school falls at either extreme, and it is probably healthy for any public policy enterprise to have courses and teachers from both camps. But a tension between 'academic' and 'professional' approaches to policy studies is probably endemic to the field, and we may expect it to occur in India and other countries.

III

Despite important differences among American policy studies programmes, most of these efforts in training and research have agreed on several matters : the curricular combination of analytical tools and management skills, a commitment to begin with problems rather than methods, and a concern for both the broad, ethical issues and the narrow, practical essentials of government.[3]

A similar movement is under way at universities and institutions in many places in the developing world. Consider a few examples :

1. The College of Public Administration of the University of the Philippines, implemented a new degree in Policy Studies and Program Administration in 1977 which combines statistics, analytic methods, political analysis, and some aspects of economics, as well as public administration. In 1979, the University President and Academic Vice-President led a two-day conference of deans on the subject of policy studies throughout the University and how academic resources might best be marshalled to deal with public policy issues.
2. At the University of Indonesia, the core curriculum of the Department of Economics goes beyond economics to include business administration, political analysis, analytic methods, accounting, and 'ideology'. The majority of senior faculty members are simultaneously officials in government, and they bring their policy concerns and experience to the classroom.
3. In Cuba, top policy-makers complained that a new sort of government official was needed — one who understood economics, business administration, and accounting, and had a grounding in Communist ideology. In 1976, Raul Castro personally inaugurated just such a programme.
4. In Pakistan, the University of Karachi's Applied Economics Research Centre initiated in 1977 a new post-Master's degree

programme combining analytic methods, statistics, 'institutions,' and a workshop in applied economics.

5. In Mexico, the Instituto Nacional de Administración Pública, granted a high priority by the Mexican government, is initiating a new professional programme in public management and policy analysis. So is the Centro de Investigación y Docencia Económica, also in Mexico City.

6. In Thailand, the National Institute of Development Administration (NIDA) has, since the middle 1960s, featured a core curriculum of public administration, economics, statistics, and business administration.

7. INCAE, the leading school of business administration in Central America, is adding a concentration in 'policy'. Not surprisingly, a prime focus will be crisis management and policy-making.

8. In Turkey, Bogadiçi University has a committee of professors of economics, business administration, and public administration designing new courses and research in public policy, with the help of OECD.

These efforts are of course quite varied. Some build from business administration; others are based on economics curricula; still others are located in faculties of public administration. And yet in talks with the key actors in many of these programmes, I have heard quite similar ideas of the *need* which these programmes are designed to meet. And this 'need' is not unrelated to the reasons described earlier why a 'new profession' was thought desirable in the United States. In various words, people talk of training future public leaders who would combine analytical skills, political and managerial know-how, and ethical sensitivity. That kind of policy research is needed which combines careful analysis with a concern for politics, management, and implementability.

Consider, for example, the remarks of Kuldeep Mathur of the Indian Institute of Public Administration :

When India became independent and soon launched its First Five-Year Plan for development there was widespread faith in what the national leadership intended to do. There was confidence in the ability of leaders to build consensus around nation building and consolidation activities and a fervent hope that freedom had brought an end to all troubles. Essentially, then, policies for development represented a vision, a dream, but were assured to be adequate representation of reality for they were projected by a group who had already shown their mettle during the independence struggle.

As the years passed and one five-year plan was replaced by another disillusionment started setting in. Goals were not so easy to achieve, policies were distorted at the ground-level and intended beneficiaries began to be recognized as losers in the developmental process. Not questioning the policies, focus of attention shifted to the process of administration and management of programmes. Most developmental shortfalls and failures were blamed on the lack of ability to implement programmes and policies . . . .

[In the 1970s], however, it was the emergence of the turbulent period that led to the questioning of the policies that had been followed since independence and the beginning of the Plan era. It was no more a question of implementation alone; the argument was that policies themselves were faulty . . . .

During the middle of 1970s it also began to be felt that the problems facing the country cannot be demarcated into the narrow confines of a single discipline. The feeling was that problems were multidisciplinary but solutions were being sought from a single disciplinary source.[4]

Despite many contrasts in the setting of public policy between India's huge democracy and Indonesia's long-standing military government, the needs for training and research are apparently similar. S.B. Joedono of the University of Indonesia puts it this way:

For these reasons it is likely that Government will continue to predominate. This means that for the next ten to twenty years, the most important choices for society will continue to be made by Government.

There is therefore a continuing need to educate people to intelligently and responsibly make and/or criticize Government policy-making.

What characteristics need to be developed?

What environment must be created and maintained?

Professor Sumitro Djojohadikusmo, one of Indonesia's politically most influential scholars, has summed these up as follows:

1. *A deep sense of social responsibility*
   People involved in government policy-making should have an intimate knowledge of the fundamental problems faced by the population and must be committed to furthering their aspirations and needs.

2. *A keen political perception*
   People involved in government policy-making must be able [to] choose from the concerns of everyday life those problems which are fundamental in the sense that their solution are prerequisites for the solution of a host of other problems through systematic interaction. This ability should be complemented by the ability to distinguish between personal preferences and what is objectively necessary given the problems faced by the people and by the ability to judge what is realizable in a certain time frame given the constellation of power within the time frame.

3. *Solid professional and technical expertise*
   In addition to substantive theoretical and factual knowledge in their respective fields of competence, people engaged in policy-making should be versed in planning techniques relating policy instruments to policy targets.

   To the extent that these skills are lacking, greater amount of effort should be made to develop these.

4. *A framework of effective power*
   For policies to be able to create or change social realities, power is necessary. However, this ability to make people do things they would not have done if left to their own preferences, should be rooted in a commitment to the public good and in a willingness to listen to what people themselves feel what the public good ought to be. Without the active support and participation of the people, power will never be lastingly effective.[5]

I have heard strikingly similar remarks from those involved in public policy programmes in Korea, Mexico, Chile, Turkey, the Philippines, Thailand, Taiwan, and the United States. I am not arguing that such sentiments are new, only that in many places around the world — in leftist regimes and rightist ones — the perceived need in the environment is similar and is being met, if only in a small way, with identifiably similar though idiosyncratic policy studies programmes.

These similarities are not the result of a conspiracy or even, it appears, a contagion. Unlike many of the educational reforms that swept through the developing world in the 1950s and 1960s, these are not the products of massive efforts by foreign aid agencies to build new institutions and introduce new curricula. Most of the new programmes are not closely acquainted with the American educational movement in public policy and management. Indeed, they are usually not aware of each other's efforts.

A final area of similarity may be noted : the problems faced by the new, interdisciplinary programmes in public policy. Thailand's NIDA has been at this business as long as anyone. Notice how familiar are the difficulties cited in interviews by top NIDA officials :

1. *Problems of integrating the different disciplines involved in public policy studies.* Despite a core curriculum in which each student must take common courses in the four faculties of public administration, business administration, economics, and statistics, neither students nor professors seem well integrated across the departments. There is a strong tendency to specialise, to return to one or another parent discipline.

2. *Problems of maintaining quality.* Typically, public administration faculty will be considered 'weaker' than faculty members in economics, with fields like statistics, accounting, and business somewhere in between. But another problem plagues policy studies programmes under whatever name : raiding from the public and the private sectors, which robs institutions of leading professors. (Sometimes the raiding involves part-time work, which nonetheless can drain talent from the academic mission.)

3. *Problems of integrating teaching, research, and executive training.* Too often, policy research does not find its way into the classroom. Surprisingly, teaching often remains sterile and theoretical, despite the numerous policy studies carried out by the faculty members.

4. *Problems of forming a research agenda.* Frequently faculty members respond individually to short-term government needs for intellectually unexciting surveys, feasibility studies, and evaluations. Seldom in policy studies programmes does one find a group of researchers working on a well-defined, medium-term policy research agenda.

One finds common features among the disparate programmes in public policy that are emerging in the developing world in terms of origins, basic direction, and operational difficulties. Given these similarities, it is natural to ask whether some forms of collaboration might not prove fruitful. In particular, does it not seem likely that the next step would be comparative research projects on topics and themes of mutual interest?

IV

Comparative studies of public policy in developing countries would not be something completely novel. Indeed, much of 'development economics' has had a focus on practical policy-making.[6] And in disciplines as diverse as political science, education, and public administration, comparative research has been widespread for at least twenty-five years. As we consider what sorts of comparative research in public policy we might pursue — to what ends, on what subjects, with what methods — might we discern lessons from the record of comparative studies in these other fields? In short, might we learn from a comparative study of comparative studies?

In an informal effort to find out, I have been reviewing articles and books that have tried to assess the progress made in comparative politics, comparative education, and comparative public administration. I have also interviewed experts in other comparative sub-fields, such as comparative religion and comparative economic systems. There are, I think, a surprising number of parallels across these diverse enterprises.

1. *Comparative studies as disciplinary sub-fields had similar origins.* Often the 'new' comparative studies emerged after World War II, led by outstanding emigré scholars whose backgrounds and new homes led naturally to comparative work. Foundations made important grants that catalysed the development of each comparative sub-field. Separate journals emerged.

2. *Methodologically, comparative studies have faced similar tensions.* Many scholars emphasised, in principle perhaps more than in practice, statistical techniques based on cross-sectional data. Especially in comparative politics, models were constructed with countries as data points, in an effort to discover underlying processes that were

the same except for 'random error'. Durkheim argued that all
social science was comparative; the new comparativists went further,
sometimes contending that only when their disciplines made
international comparisons would they truly lay claim to being
scientific. In every field, too, these claims were contradicted by
what might be called 'relativists'. In contrast to many comparativists,
specialists in particular cultures or geographical areas focused on
the 'separate realities' found around the world. They stressed the
irreducible, the *sui generis*, the idiosyncratic, and they criticised the
quest for general theories. Many of the best studies appearing
under the rubric of 'comparative research' involved work on a
particular problem in a particular country at a particular time —
with no 'comparisons' except implicitly. At their best, of course, both
comparativists and area specialists in each discipline recognised
the inevitable duality of similarity and difference.

3. *By the 1970s, comparative studies had encountered hard times.*
Funding from the foundations had abated, and able students were
harder to recruit to the comparative sub-fields. *More importantly,
the basic premise that comparative work would lead to new theoretical
insights had come to be increasingly questioned.* Consider these typical
complaints :

From this review it seems that the promising departures that
have given comparative politics such vitality over the last few
years may now be threatened by a basic problem of relating
theory to evidence that cuts across all approaches. In our necessary,
but also highly ambitious, desire to conceptualize and compare
total political systems, to classify patterns of history, and to relate
culture and personality to the structures of politics, we have been
driven either to extremely high orders of abstraction or to such
complex manipulations of data that the bonds between theory
and evidence are constantly being shattered.

Stated in another way, the problem of comparative politics
seems to be that we are no longer adhering to the textbook
canons of the scientific method, and yet we have not agreed upon
any new rules.[7]

Apart from [failures to contribute to] theory, the record of the
CAG [the Comparative Administration Group, which led work
on comparative public administration] does produce two

disappointments. The first is what I would term a failure to live up to the promise of discovering through comparative analysis methods and approaches that would be useful in developmental situations. By useful, I mean simply ideas that would economize on scarce resources by suggesting a new way to puruse an old problem ... or to alert statesmen to the unintended consequences of various choices ....

The second disappointment is related to the first; an inquiry that is progressively less empirical is likely not to say anything of value for those people who dwell in the world. The record shows that the CAG did not produce a body of empirical materials .... Moreover, as propositions were advanced about variables, no attempt was made to specify the limits and thresholds of, say, changing organizational form and levels of productivity. The 'how much' dimension was so slight as to give the impression that the gathering of empirical material was demeaning. There were theories, theories about theories, analyses of others' theories.[8]

In sum, comparative public administration is far less developed than would have been anticipated a decade ago. Most of the work forming the field's slim theoretical-conceptual core is now quite dated. Nor has the field produced much in the way of cumulative research literature .... If ever there were a field to which Jorgen Rasmussen's supplication 'O Lord, deliver us from further conceptualization and lead us not into new approaches' [which was made concerning comparative politics — REK] could be applied, this field must be comparative administration.[9]

[In comparative education] up to now such searching after generalizations has either led to statements so abstract that they lack practicality or to others which merely confirm an educational truism ....

The bubble was pricked when the money ran out. We who have survived these thirteen years are left deflated. We find ourselves not much farther along the road than when we started. What new theories have we evolved? What new educational practices have been adopted through our studies? The answer, if we are honest, must be : very few. Whereas the psychologists, the sociologists — even the philosophers — of education have had their hour or favour with educationists who operate in the real world, the comparative educationists have been left out in the cold. It is difficult to point to any single decision in education — at least in the Western world — which has resulted from the direct research of a comparative educationist. It is not difficult to cite names from other fields : Bruner, Coleman, Jencks — to name only Americans — have exercised a profound influence. Where do the comparative educationists stand?[10]

The division between scholars who prefer quantitative and those who are more comfortable with non-quantitative analyses runs deep, and this division characterizes comparative education as it does other specialities. Yet even adherents of the latter viewpoint often display little capability for reporting the main features of their own educational system or of one in which they are professional guests. Similarly, when confronted with proposals for academic rearrangements that would subvert existing criteria of excellence, individuals of a quantitative bent often cannot defend their positions with well-mobilized data. Methodological positions held 'in principle' turn out often not to be reflected in the craft skills utilized for daily work ...

We are compiling more field surveys, exploring more archives, and we are building longer series of data about all aspects of life in different types of society. But incisive and unequivocal conclusions remain elusive ....

The outlook for specialists in comparative education is not easy, apart from the dolorous outlook for all academics. Positions on faculties of education have declined disproportionately.[11]

These are not to be viewed as summary judgments of vast fields, but they do convey a sense of disillusionment about comparative work that, I have been surprised to find, seems to cut across disciplines.

4. *Comparative studies can nonetheless help 'main-line' research in a discipline or profession.* With a comparative approach one can often identify important but overlooked variables operating in one's own environment. Comparisons help avoid premature generalisations; they may engender both academic and practical sophistication. Thus anthropologist Clifford Geertz's appraisal of the influence of comparative research :

The sense of intellectual self-sufficiency, that peculiar conceptual and methodological arrogance which comes from dealing too long and too insistently with a pocket universe all one's own (the American business cycle, French party politics, class mobility in Sweden, the kinship system of some upcountry African tribe), and which is perhaps the most formidable enemy of a general science of society, has been seriously, and I think permanently, shaken. The closed society has been as thoroughly exploded for most of those who have studied the new nations as it has for most of those who live in them.[12]

5. *Comparative studies can be valuable when they look for successful practices to emulate or unsuccessful ones to avoid, rather than universal laws or models.* This lesson emerges particularly strongly in the field of comparative education. As Tricia Broadfoot notes with several examples :

Comparative studies can provide very valuable insights, particularly in respect to the likely results of various innovations. In a sense they can provide an experimental situation not possible in any one education system, in that they obviate the need for each society to try out for itself ideas which are untested but seem to have potential.[13]

Looking for successful performers in order to learn why they succeed — and eventually to copy them — is an old activity in education, development, and other fields. A major school of research in education in the 1920s and thirties involved the description and codification of 'best practice' in schools. One might interpret some uses of the case method of research in business along similar lines, although clearly there are other, pedagogical motives here and most cases do not focus on 'successes'.

But it is something of a departure in recent public policy research to look for unusually effective performers, rather than doing cross-sectional studies or evaluations across all of them. Can we find and study outstanding schools, unusually effective rural development projects, exceptional public health clinics, and the like?[14] And Samuel Paul's recent work on the strategic managerial dimensions of unusually effective public programmes — including six detailed cases — is path-breaking in its comparative focus on 'what works'.[15]

Perhaps this is an insight we should retain as we contemplate comparative research in public policy.

V

In a brilliant review article, Elliot J. Feldman warns, 'There is no "field" of comparative public policy'.[16] Perhaps this should not be a source of regret, even for those interested in doing comparative work in this area. If it is permitted to generalise from other comparative 'fields,' one might conclude that the endless debates over models and data — and, indeed, the objective of building a universally valid, comparative theory — are not worth emulating. To suppose that 'comparative public policy' might lead us to generalised models of the policy-making process, or to theories from which successful policy measures could be deduced, is likely to be a mistake. That sort of comparative research in public policy might best be left on the shelf.

What might we do instead? I have three suggestions. First, we might study cases of *success* — across different instances of the same policy mechanism (e.g., schools, police stations, and agricultural extension agents), across innovations, or across policies. Some of the 'comparisons' inevitably involved here may be intra-national, but others could be international. Professor Paul's recent work (cited above) in identifying how strategy, structure, and environment interact in successful national programmes exemplifies what I have in mind. From his cases, readers take away a detailed sense of what concepts like 'decentralisation' and 'integration' might mean in practice. And from his careful analysis, readers may derive useful middle-level generalisations about the ingredients of successful strategic management.

Second, we might focus some of our work on comparative studies of problems that might be called 'inter-sectoral' — issues that require us to integrate the various disciplines included in 'public policy studies' and to avoid sectoral blinders. Consider, for example, policy-related comparative studies of issues like corruption, elitism (e.g., personnel selection systems for the civil service and higher education), and policies to combat racial inequalities. All involve economics and 'analytics' as well as public management. All cut across the usual sectoral lines and have policy ramifications at the

local, provincial, and national levels of government. The objective
of such comparative research would not be a grandiose theory of
policy-making — although we might end up with some useful
models to clarify these particular issues. But a comparative approach
would help.[17] We might try to combine the disciplines of public
policy studies while reminding ourselves, through examples, of
what stays the same and what changes as we move from context
to context.[18]

What might be learned from such comparisons? I think of the
analogy of designers or artists. When they have a show or an
exhibition, they look carefully at each others' work. When asked
what they learn from doing so, those of my acquaintance do not say
they are trying to induce a general theory of design, nor that they
wish to copy what others have done. They say instead something
like, 'I get *ideas*'.

This remains vague. But something useful is conveyed, without a
theory or an attempt to emulate, from watching how others have
addressed their design problems and moved to solve them. I hear a
similar sort of lesson from policy-makers, such as Minister of
Planning Widjojo of Indonesia when he speaks in praise of the
usefulness of studying other countries' policies.[19]

Third, apart from comparative research in the academic sense,
new programmes of policy studies stand to gain from other sorts of
collaboration. Despite many differences among the many emerging
programmes, we have a lot in common. We might usefully share
teaching materials and techniques. We can learn from each others'
institutional successes and failures. We might exchange students
and faculty. And various programmes of policy studies can, through
closer interaction than has heretofore occurred, sustain each other
in the creation of a new professional field of training and research.

Notes

1. 'University Education for Public Policy Analysis,' *Public Administration Review*,
Vol. 37, No. 3, May/June 1977, pp. 230-31.
2. Stuart Nagel and Martin Neef, 'What Is and What Should Be in University
Policy Studies?' *Public Administration Review*, Vol. 37, No. 4, July/August 1977,
p. 387.

3. I might add that there is also a strong concern about the legitimacy — and unintended consequences — of 'policy analysis' itself. To be called 'technocratic' is still anathema, and teachers and students of public policy are sensitive to the charge. Lawyers like Lawrence Tribe and political scientists like Edward Banfield have published well-reasoned warnings about the 'new profession' — more generally, about the objectivity of its methods. At the Kennedy School and elsewhere, courses have emerged that question, in a healthy and constructive way, the tools and assumptions of policy analysis and public management.

4. 'Policy Analysis in India,' Background Paper for a Regional Conference on Public Policy Education and Research, Manila, 7-8 January 1980, pp. 1, 2, 3.

5. 'Policy Studies at the Faculty of Economics in the University of Indonesia : A Sketch,' Background Paper for a Regional Conference on Public Policy Education and Research, Manila, 7-8 January 1980, pp. 3-4.

6. I cannot resist opening a parenthesis on the subject of development economics. As a sub-field of economics, it has in the last decade rapidly lost any sense of the intellectual vigour it may have enjoyed in the 1960s, and its practical contributions are increasingly questioned by leading proponents (for example, in recent speeches by Nobel Laureate Theodore W. Schultz and Dudley Seers). In the next decade, economists will make new contributions of relevance to public policy in developing countries, but in my judgement the contributors will not be 'development economists' but those working in the economics of information and uncertainty, macro-economists, and those studying the economics of 'sectors' such as education, labour, transportation, and so forth. Regarding practical contributions, I concur with the late Harry G. Johnson's summary judgement made in reference to Amartya Sen's *Employment, Technology, and Development :*

    > It is indeed a rather wry reflection on the state of development economics — which mirrors that of economics in general — that professional reputations are made by sophisticated mathematical treatment of very simplistic *a priori* ideas of the kind surveyed in the text book, while real contributions are made through the detailed practical application of simple (but *not* simplistic) concepts of the kind masterfully deployed in the appendices.

    Sen's appendices deal with the measurement of employment, public schemes for export expansion, Indian agriculture, and tractorisation. (Johnson, 'Review Article : Disguised Unemployment in a General Theoretical Context,' *Economic Development and Cultural Change*, Vol. 26, No. 2, January 1978, p. 389.)

7. Lucien W. Pye, 'Advances and Frustrations in Comparative Politics,' in Fred W. Riggs (ed.), *International Studies : Present Status and Future Prospects*, Philadelphia, American Academy of Political and Social Sciences, 1971, p. 102.

8. Warren F. Ilchman, *Comparative Public Administration and 'Conventional Wisdom,'* Sage Professional Papers in Comparative Politics, Volume 2, Beverly Hills, Sage, 1971, pp. 44-45.

9. Lee Sigelman, 'In Search of Comparative Administration,' *Public Administration Review*, Vol. 36, No. 6, November/December 1976, p. 623. The other papers in this issue, also devoted to 'comparative and development administration,' are equally gloomy in their assessments. Relevant to Rasmussen's plea is Robert Ward's label for the debate over how to do comparisons : 'a constipated dialectic'.

10. W. D. Halls, 'Comparative Studies in Education, 1964-1977 : A Personal View,' *Comparative Education*, Vol. 13, No. 2, June 1977. Professor Halls was one of the founders of this journal.

11. C. Arnold Anderson, 'Comparative Education Over a Quarter Century : Maturity and Challenges,' *Comparative Education Review*, Vol. 21, No. 3, June/October 1977, pp. 406, 407, 414. Professor Anderson also makes a number of encouraging remarks about the growth of sophistication in the field.

12. 'Politics Past, Politics Present,' *European Journal of Sociology*, Vol. 8, No. 1, 1967, p. 1.

13. 'The Comparative Contribution — A Research Perspective,' *Comparative Education*, Vol. 13, No. 2, June 1977, p. 134.

14. Robert E. Klitgaard, 'Identifying Exceptional Performers,' *Policy Analysis*, Vol. 4, No. 4, Fall 1978.

15. Samuel Paul *Managing Development Programs. The Lessons of Success.* Boulder, Colorado, Westview Press, 1982.

16. 'Comparative Public Policy : Field or Method?' *Comparative Politics*, Vol. 11, No. 1, January 1978, p. 298. The author proposes 'that common cross-sectoral problems replace sectoral "policy areas" as the vehicle for analysis' (p. 301), much as I do. He also stresses that 'a theoretical perspective at the least of the systems chosen for study ... should guide the comparison,' which makes me uneasy.

17. I believe that most such comparisons will probably not draw great sustenance from the various sub-disciplines called 'development' (with prefixes like 'economic,' 'political,' or 'sociology of'). Moreover, such studies will lead many of us to see that many such policy issues have similarities across developed and developing countries. The actual solutions chosen will of of course vary, depending on a multitude of idiosyncratic features. But useful frameworks for analysing policy choices — useful 'ideas' — will often transcend the 'developed-developing' dichotomy.

18. Adherents of the scientific method may rebel at the last phrase, as it seems to beg the question of the appropriate theoretical framework. Without an agreed framework, how does one define 'what stays the same and what changes'? Here we enter into all the theoretical turmoil that has surrounded other areas of comparative research. But the aim here is not to use our comparisons as data points in a cross-sectional model, but to use comparisons (a) to help us merge the disciplines of 'public policy studies' and *(b)* to help us *discover*, rather than to test, which variables and 'hypotheses' seem most promising.

19. A similar point has emerged in discussions of historian George M. Fredrickson's *White Supremacy : A Comparative Study of American and South African History* (New York, Oxford University Press, 1981). Professor Richard Graham of the University of Texas criticises the book for a failure to derive a theory or draw general conclusions : 'I think that's a problem, because if you don't look for any kind of generalization, why are you doing comparative history? Professor Fredrickson describes the aims of his comparative work less ambitiously — and, in line with the arguments of this paper, more appropriately :

> I was not trying to develop a theory of race relations. I consciously avoided that. I wanted to do a comparative study that showed all the complexity and ambiguity in each society, that was faithful to the interest of the historian in the particular. The payoff, I hope, is that at the end of the book, you know more about two different kinds of contexts of race relations.

(*Chronicle of Higher Education*, Vol. 24, No. 10, 5 May 1982, p. 20.)

Notes on Contributors

Aqueil Ahmad heads the Centre for Science Policy and Management of Research at the Administrative Staff College, Hyderabad. He is currently a Visiting Scholar at the Centre for the Interdisciplinary Study of Science and Technology in the USA.

J. N. Barmeda is the Honorary Secretary and Treasurer of the Indian Society of Agricultural Economics, Bombay. He has had wide-ranging experience in banking and agricultural finance.

M. L. Dantwala is Professor Emeritus in the Department of Economics, Bombay University. He is also President of the Indian Society of Agricultural Economics and is on the Central Board of Directors of the Reserve Bank of India.

Bernard Donoughue is currently with the *Times*, London. He was formerly with the Central Policy Review Staff in the office of the British Prime Minister and has been advisor to Prime Ministers Wilson and Callaghan.

R. S. Ganapathy is on the faculty of the Public Systems Group at the Indian Institute of Management, Ahmedabad. He has previously worked with the Indian Academic Energy Commission.

S. R. Ganesh is Chief Executive of the Foundation for Organizational Research and Continuing Education, Bombay. He has been a faculty member of the Administrative Staff College, Hyderabad, and the Indian Institute of Management, Ahmedabad.

G. Giridhar is on the faculty of the Indian Institute of Management, Ahmedabad. His major area of interest is population planning and management.

S. Guhan is currently a Senior Fellow of the Madras Institute of Development Studies. He was previously a senior officer of the Indian Administrative Service.

Robert E. Klitgaard is on the faculty of the John F. Kennedy School of Government at Harvard University. He has worked with many universities in the developing world to help them develop programmes of study in policy analysis and management.

Rushikesh M. Maru is Chairman, Public Systems Group, Indian Institute of Management, Ahmedabad. He has been a consultant to numerous public organisations both in India and other developing countries.

Vina Mazumdar is the Director of the Centre for Women's Development Studies, New Delhi. She was previously with the Indian Council of Social Science Research where she played a pioneering role in developing the women's studies research programme of the ICSSR.

Samuel Paul is Senior Advisor on Public Sector Management at the World Bank, Washington, D. C. He has served as Professor and Director of the Indian Institute of Management, Ahmedabad.

Ram Mohan Rao has been involved in social science research for over a decade and has undertaken numerous teaching and consulting assignments. He has been a research scholar at the Indian Institute of Management, Ahmedabad.

T. V. Rao is on the faculty of the Organisational Behaviour Area and the Public Systems Group at the Indian Institute of Management. His main research interests are the management of educational systems and human resources management.

J. K. Satia is on the faculty of the Public Systems Group at the Indian Institute of Management, Ahmedabad. An industrial engineer by training, he has been involved over the past decade in the development of the field of health and population management.

T. C. Schelling is Professor and Chairman of the Public Administration Program at the John F. Kennedy School of Government, Harvard University. He is one of the pioneers of the public policy movement in the United States.

T. L. Shankar is with the Indian Administrative Service and is currently Director of the Institute for Public Enterprises, Hyderabad, as also Industries Commissioner in the Government of Andhra Pradesh.

Ashok Subramanian is on the faculty of the Indian Institute of Management, Ahmedabad. His main interests are the management of social development programmes and voluntary organisations.